Roscoe Pound

Roscoe Pound, Dean of Harvard Law School

Roscoe Pound
Philosopher of Law

David Wigdor

Contributions in American History, Number

GREENWOOD PRESS

Westport, Connecticut ● London, England

Library of Congress Cataloging in Publication Data

Wigdor, David.
 Roscoe Pound.

 (Contributions in American history, no. 33)
 Includes bibliographical references.
 1. Pound, Roscoe, 1870-1964.
KF373.P6W5   340'.092'4 [B]   72-852
ISBN 0-8371-6419-2

Library of Congress Catalog Card Number: 72-852
ISBN: 0-8371-6419-2

First published in 1974

Greenwood Press, a division of Williamhouse-Regency Inc.
51 Riverside Avenue, Westport, Connecticut 06880

Manufactured in the United States of America

To Sandy

Contents

Preface

Roscoe Pound was modern America's foremost legal scholar. His sociological jurisprudence blended legal concepts with pragmatism and social science into a new synthesis that replaced the sterile conception of law as a closed system of timeless doctrine. As the leader of the sociological movement in law, Pound is remembered largely for his contributions to legal philosophy, but he regarded all law as his province, and contemporaries respected him as one of the law's last great generalists. His practical experience was as wide as his intellectual interests, and he played every role that the common law system acknowledged. He was office-trained and school-trained; he was a trial lawyer in the rugged courthouse world of pioneer Nebraska and a master of the appellate brief; he was a judge, a teacher, a dean, an adviser to government, and a scholar whose name became a synonym for legal wisdom.

From the beginning, Pound's background fitted him for the role of pioneer, for the combined influence of his parents, the prairie, and a dynamic frontier university encouraged an experimental attitude toward life. His early training in botany introduced him to modern intellectual themes, and his studies under a leading American Darwinist gave him an appreciation for environmental influences that few contemporary lawyers possessed. Yet in spite of an impatience with the ordinary that his youth suggested, Pound's personality was a curious blend of boldness and caution. His desire for a conventional career, the demands of his parents, and an exciting year at the Harvard Law School led him to abandon science for a more practical profession.

The tension in his choice of a career was a prelude to conflicts in his intellectual development. His mature jurisprudence reflected competing tendencies in his personality, and themes of caution emerged to establish the limits of bold demands for change. Pound earned a reputation during the Progressive era as one of the most innovative American legal theorists, but his commitment to the common law fostered a fascination with organicism, traditionalism, and professionalism that restricted his intellectual range. His creativity, checked by internal contradictions, was spent upon particularities. The separate instrumental and organic elements of his thought, developed in isolation, created an unresolved dualism within his jurisprudence and made it impossible for him to develop the grand system that he pursued so assiduously. When militant legal theorists in the 1930s, conscious of the reform potential in Pound's jurisprudence, employed his ideas in ways that he found unacceptable, he could no longer live with the dualism in his thought and gradually deserted his progressive insights for a celebration of traditional common law values.

Most of the debts that I have incurred during the course of this study are suggested in the footnotes, but I am also privileged to acknowledge some personal obligations. Allen F. Davis and David P. Thelen have been constant sources of encouragement, and William P. Murphy lent his lawyer's learning to my interpretation of one of the law's great men. Arthur E. Sutherland, Austin Wakeman Scott, and James H. Chadbourn shared their memories of Pound with me. William R. Roalfe sent me copies of materials relating to Pound from the John Henry Wigmore Papers. Clarke Chambers provided copies of Pound's correspondence with Paul Kellogg. David Levy, editor of the Louis Brandeis Papers, checked the collection for me. I received generous assistance from librarians and archivists at the Library of Congress, the Nebraska State Historical Society, the University of Chicago Archives, the Wisconsin State Historical Society, the Omaha Public Library, and the University of Missouri Library, but I owe a special debt to Mrs. James H. Chadbourn, curator of manuscripts and archives at the Harvard Law School Library.

As a full partner in this project, my wife, Alexandra Kent Wigdor, deserves a line of her own.

Roscoe Pound

1

Nebraska Boyhood

Lincoln, Nebraska, the new capital of the most recent addition to the Union, was three years old on 27 October 1870, when Roscoe Pound was born. Although only a step removed from empty prairie, it was already a city of great hope and immense vitality. Pioneer Lincoln seemed determined to compensate for a short past by creating a feverishly active present. Purpose and determination were constant themes in contemporary accounts of the city. Cyrus Woodman, the peripatetic railroad promoter, wrote in 1869 that the "residents [of Lincoln] are looking forward to a great future." They were willing to endure enormous hardships for that future, for their burdens were lightened by the conviction that success was certain.[1]

The optimism that characterized the community was not unfounded, for the city did possess certain genuine advantages. The town site itself was an attractive one; its elevation was sufficient to guarantee thorough drainage but level enough to require little grading. It had abundant supplies of timber and water, contained inexhaustible rock quarries, and occupied the center of Nebraska's most populous region. Although the city was initially rather isolated, an aggressive citizens' committee, on which Pound's father played a leading role, quickly secured an essential ingre-

3

dient of Western urban development—railroad service. In 1870 the sounds of sledgehammers and Irish curses shattered the silence of the Nebraska prairie, and soon the roar of the Burlington became a familiar sound to the people of Lincoln.[2]

Lincoln expanded rapidly throughout Pound's youth. Letters home and railroad advertising encouraged immigration, as did free land and easy credit. Lincoln's tiny population of about thirty people in 1867 increased over eight-fold within three years; by 1880 the town claimed 13,000 citizens, and by 1890 it had become a metropolis of 55,154. Prosperity allowed the city to develop new urban services to meet the rapid growth of the 1870s and 1880s. A public water system was initiated in 1882, an event that Pound recalled vividly, and a comprehensive scheme of street plotting and paving began in 1888. Before the city, and Pound, had concluded a second decade, Lincoln had established an electric light plant, a fire department, a police force, a post office, a library, and a telephone system.[3]

Town-building was a creative and ·exciting experience, and the pioneer booster seemed to transcend a crass materialism. There was an infectious idealism about many of these early civic ventures that was part of the nineteenth century's peculiar charm. The first telegraph message that flashed into Nebraska was not a market report; it was a line of poetry—"Westward the course of empire takes its way."[4]

An example of this idealism was the early founding of a state university. On 23 September 1869, just two years after statehood, Nebraskans laid the cornerstone of University Hall. The site chosen was a few blocks from the state capitol, and thus the university was added to Lincoln's growing collection of state institutions. In 1871 the University of

Nebraska opened the doors of its single building, housing the college of literature, science, and arts and a faculty of seven, to an eager class of ninety students. The university quickly assumed an important place in the life of the community. The lectures, concerts, and plays that it offered did much to elevate the cultural level of the city and encouraged a polite and genteel social life centering on literary societies and discussion clubs.[5]

Statehood, the coming of the railroad, the opening of the university, the expansion of commercial activities, and the population explosion created an atmosphere of progress that dominated the new city, but many characteristics of an earlier era lingered to remind residents of the frontier. Urban growth did not immediately affect the animal population; citizens continued to capture deer, wolves, and other wild animals, which ranged freely through the streets during the 1880s.[6] Vestiges of unsuccessful ventures also served as reminders of the past. The earliest settlers had hoped that the salt lakes around Lincoln would yield incredible riches; the flavor in Eastern foods would mean money in Western pockets. The lakes did not prove sufficiently productive to sustain profitable commercial operations, but they did serve regional needs. Lincoln children in the 1870s often saw Indians coming to the basins west of the city to get salt for curing buffalo meat.[7]

The community and region in which Pound grew to maturity placed a premium on growth and development. This environment undoubtedly helped prepare him for a positive conception of social and institutional change and gave him confidence in man's ability to control his destiny. Furthermore, the frontier legacy and the fascination of the plains created an environment with an emphasis on diversity. The rich multiplicity of his Nebraska boyhood would pay dividends in later years. As he found diversity there, so he would find it in life and law and other things that mattered.

The influence of the region on his development was subtle. The influence of his parents was more direct and determinative. Both parents were highly educated and placed great value on learning. Both led full, active lives that provided a model for their city as well as their children. "Stephen B. Pound," wrote a contemporary, "with his wife, Laura Biddlecombe [sic] and the three children born to them, has left the greatest influence in a social and cultural way of any of these pre-Lincoln pioneers."[8]

Stephen B. Pound came to the area in 1866, the year before statehood, when the future capital was a frontier crossroads town called Lancaster. He was born in upstate New York in 1833 on lands that his Quaker ancestors had farmed for generations. After receiving his early education in the grade schools of Wayne County, he attended Walworth Academy, Macedon Academy, and graduated from Union College in Schenectady in 1859. Union College had become an important institution under the imaginative leadership of Eliphalet Nott, who introduced courses in science and modern literature to supplement the classics. Union graduates of the Nott regime included a President, six Cabinet members, thirteen United States senators, ninety-one members of the House, twelve governors, almost two hundred judges, and eighty-six college presidents.[9]

Stephen Pound began the study of law immediately after his graduation from Union and was admitted to the bar in 1863. He practiced law in Lyons, New York, with Judge Lyman H. Sherwood, but in 1866 he left the Empire State for the West. After brief residence in Platteville, Wisconsin, he moved to Nebraska, exploring Nebraska City and

Omaha before finally settling in Lincoln. Near the end of his life he remembered that he had been eager to stay in Omaha, but Omaha's many lawyers "left slim picking for the youth with little money who could not starve while sitting with his feet on the office desk waiting for prospective clients." He also fondly recalled that Lincoln "had an air of push and hope that was infectious."[10]

Although the law was his profession, Stephen Pound did not hang out his shingle immediately. It was not uncommon for a frontier lawyer to take odd jobs, teach school, or farm before establishing a practice.[11] Upon his arrival Pound took a job as deputy postmaster, then opened a general store in the front room of a small log cabin. Some months later, after passing the bar examination, he entered active practice.[12]

It was difficult for a newcomer to establish a practice, but, once established, a capable man could expect success to follow rather quickly. The sod-house frontier did not have a highly skilled bar. Many pioneer lawyers were illiterate. Standards for admission to the bar required that the candidate be twenty-one years of age, possess a sound moral character, and pass an examination administered by a judge. Since the judges were frequently ignorant of the law, the examination was often perfunctory. J. J. Ingalls, a New Englander with legal training, won a reputation in frontier Kansas soon after his arrival. "My success," he confessed to his father, "is not so much attributable to superior personal merit as to the want of ability among the practitioners generally. A more ignorant detestable set of addle-headed numbskulls and blackguards I have seldom met."[13]

With a clear field as well as unusual ability, Pound soon achieved eminence in the Nebraska legal profession. Although a recent arrival, he played a significant role in the negotiations that led to the selection of Lancaster as the capital. People began to take notice of the cultured storekeeper-turned-lawyer. Soon after his admission to the bar, the city of Seward retained him to conduct its suit against a contender, Milford, in one of the typical county-court struggles of the era. Pound conducted the case with brilliance and eloquence, and both client and counsel emerged triumphant.[14]

Personal success and public acclaim followed rapidly for Stephen Pound. He and his partner, Seth Robinson, Nebraska's first attorney general, were ornaments of the local bar. Pound was the first president of the Lancaster County Bar Association, and he became judge of the county probate court in 1869. But he did not remain a probate judge for long. He was elected to the judgeship of a district court on the Republican ticket, defeating his Democratic opponent by a substantial margin. He presided over the district court, a state trial court of general jurisdiction, for thirteen years, running unopposed in his last two elections. During his tenure as a judge, he served as a delegate to the Nebraska constitutional convention of 1875. There, as chairman of the committee on finance and revenue, Judge Pound authored the clause that barred the state from ex-propriating property without just compensation.[15] He had a profound respect for the rights of property, and his insistence that property must enjoy legal stability was a legacy that he passed on to his son.

In addition to the high value that he placed on the protection of property, Judge Pound also displayed a mistrust of legislatures and a commitment to the doctrine of laissez-faire. By the turn of the century, he was bemoaning the erosion of individual initiative. "Very much depends on the individual," he insisted, "and very little on the legislation." He condemned the idea that "in order to get on in the world and to develop the resources of our state it is necessary to form corporations, to consolidate, to combine." The judge was suspicious of the consolidation movement in all its myriad forms; to him it meant the end of individualism.[16]

Judge Pound presided over his court with dignity. He was a man of firm convictions and certain judgments; he did not tolerate fools lightly, nor did he hesitate to tell them so. He had a deep sense of responsibility and an intense respect for the bench. He had, even as a probate judge, refused to engage in practice, although it would not have been unusual to do so.[17] But he was not aloof or humorless. Once when it became apparent that a trial could not continue because one of the attorneys was drunk, Judge Pound rapped his gavel and brought the proceedings to an abrupt close. "Case postponed for one week," he announced. "The lawyer for the plaintiff is trying to practice before two bars at the same time. It can't be done."[18]

After he retired from the bench, Judge Pound resumed the practice of law. His former partner, Seth Robinson, had urged him to come to San Francisco, but he remained in Lincoln for the rest of his life. His judicial experience and his careful attention to clients' interests made him a popular and respected attorney. His reputation for integrity became almost legendary in Nebraska. "I was on a jury once in that early day," recalled Charles Wake shortly after Judge Pound's death, "and we failed to get a verdict because half of the jury declared, they would not convict a man whom Mr. Pound defended, as they knew *he* must have been convinced of the man's innocence, or he would not have taken his case."[19]

The law demanded much of his time, but he was not a slave to his profession. Judge Pound lived a full life. An avid baseball fan, he often startled spectators in the grandstand with rousing cheers. This interest in athletics persisted throughout his life; at the age of seventy-six he was still the complete fan, eagerly awaiting the results of the World Series, the Johnson-Ketchel fight for the heavyweight crown, and the weekly football games.[20] In January 1868, when he was busy launching his law practice, he wrote Laura Biddlecome that he had been elected president of a literary society. He was reading Bulwer's *Rise and Fall of Athens*, and he was trying to find a copy of Hallam's *History of the Middle Ages*. He also found time for local politics, and he informed Miss Biddlecome that the Nebraska Republicans would probably support Grant for the party's presidential nomination.[21]

Bulwer, Grant, and literary societies filled some of the idle hours, but it was still lonely in pioneer Lincoln. In January 1869 Stephen Pound journeyed back to Macedon, New York, where he married Laura Biddlecome, whom he had known for many years. She had been born in Phelps, New York, in 1841. Her Yankee farm family had roots that ran deep into New England history. Four of her ancestors followed Roger Williams to Rhode Island. Two others fought with distinction in the Revolutionary Army.[22]

Laura Biddlecome Pound attended public schools and Macedon Academy before entering Lombard College, a coeducational institution in Galesburg, Illinois, which offered a much broader curriculum than the female academies of New York. One of her uncles, a Universalist minister, lived in Galesburg and wrote exciting accounts of life at the college. Founded in 1851 as the Illinois Liberal Institute, it was a Universalist college, and its avowed purpose was to create a liberal alternative to the narrow sectarianism of neighboring Knox College. "The Universalists," writes Earnest Calkins, a local historian, "were the first liberal thinkers to modify the tight-laced puritan pattern of the town."[23]

One of the most interesting of Laura's teachers was John

Van Ness Standish, acting president and professor of mathematics and astronomy and, if the need arose, logic, philosophy, and classical languages. Standish, a wealthy man, returned from his numerous trips abroad with treasures to grace his lavish home and stories to amuse his students. Carl Sandburg remembered students referring to the Standishes as "Culture Vultures." Standish also had a passion for horticulture, and he organized a local society. Perhaps it was here that Laura first developed an interest in botany.[24]

She must also have developed an interest in public affairs, for Lombard College was a hotbed of abolitionism. On 7 October 1858, when Lincoln and Douglas staged their fifth debate, the Lombard students gave Lincoln an elaborate silk-fringed satin banner. By the outbreak of the Civil War, Negro graduates began to appear at commencement exercises. But the war brought dislocation as well as excitement to college life; many students marched south with the Union armies. Laura wanted to finish her course of study, but her father insisted that wartime conditions made continued study so far from home too difficult. She returned to New York to become a teacher and remained there until she married Stephen Pound.[25]

Pound and his bride stayed in New York for a brief time and then left Rochester on a westbound train. After spending a few days in Chicago, they continued on to Lincoln, crossing the frozen Missouri River in a wagon. On the train Pound asked his wife if she had any conception of what her new home would be like. The train had just passed through Tama, Iowa, a sleepy little village with a few weather-beaten one-story buildings. Mrs. Pound replied that she expected Lincoln to be much like Tama. "Good," said her husband, "but it [Tama] is better than Lincoln."[26]

Arriving at Lincoln in 1869 was an unsettling conclusion

to a honeymoon journey, but Laura Pound proved equal to the challenge. She was a small woman, but she possessed boundless energy, good health, and an unusual sensitivity to her environment. As the wife of one of Lincoln's most prominent lawyers, she quickly assumed a leading role in the life of the community. During the first few years of her marriage she devoted herself largely to her children. Her first child, Nathan Roscoe, was born in 1870. Two years later, Louise was born, and in 1874 her third child, Olivia, completed the family. But she still found time to be active outside the home, and as the children grew older, she invested more of her energies in civic and cultural pursuits. She was instrumental in establishing the city library and served on the library board for many years. When the city refused, for a time, to continue supporting the library, which consisted of a small room on the second floor of a downtown store, Laura Pound acted as a temporary librarian until she and other patrons persuaded the city to renew its support. She was also a charter member of the Hayden Art Club, an organization that later became the Nebraska Art Association. Of all the various social, literary, and civic clubs to which she belonged, she was known best for her work in the Daughters of the American Revolution. A group of women organized the Nebraska chapter in the living room of the Pound home, and Mrs. Pound became the first state regent. Not content with mere patriotism and ancestor worship, she prodded the local chapter to maintain a number of useful civic projects, such as the botanical garden in Lincoln's Antelope Park.[27]

Laura Pound taught in a Lincoln grade school for a short time, but left when a growing family brought additional responsibilities at home. Her experience had made her skeptical about the Lincoln elementary school, and she decided to teach the children herself. The neighbors were shocked when she had a large blackboard built into her living room wall, but she paid no attention to their criticism.[28] The products would justify the experiment soon enough, and those who scoffed would later nod approval. At her death a local newspaper observed, "Friends have credited much of the intellectual prominence of the family to the personal attention she gave their early mental development in the home."[29]

She began teaching Roscoe to read when he was three, and although he did not learn to read quickly, she later remembered that he had a remarkable memory.[30] He was not always a willing student. To relieve the boredom of his first lesson, he threw his primer into a water pail. That seemed to be one of his favorite pranks. Once when his parents were translating Horace, Roscoe, eager for attention, seized the book and consigned it to the water pail. Years later, when reading Horace at the university, he found a battered copy in the family library and indignantly asked, "What vandal ever did that to a book!"

His mother calmly replied, "His name was Roscoe Pound."[31]

When Roscoe was six, his mother began teaching him German. She had enrolled in a German course at the university and perhaps was able to impart the excitement of fresh discovery to her son. Another contributor to his mastery of the language was the German maid whom the Pounds hired when Roscoe was ten. She stayed with the family for several years, and he was able to practice the language while talking with her.[32] In addition to maid and mother, he came into contact with German from yet another source. The Pounds were not members of any church, but Roscoe attended a Methodist Sunday school in the local German community, and he often won prizes for reciting the most Bible verses correctly. Unfortunately, the

Sunday school experience also produced an unpleasant legacy. When he was twelve he returned from a church Christmas program with a case of measles that permanently impaired his vision.[33]

The German community of Lincoln added a cosmopolitan touch to his environment and made him aware of different people, different languages, different customs. There were many cultures in Nebraska during the 1880s, for the foreign-born outnumbered native Americans by three to one. Czechs and Bohemians and Scandinavians were scattered throughout the state, and Lincoln itself boasted a large population of foreign-born residents.[34]

Roscoe's early education also included Greek, Latin, and English literature. He began Latin at the age of eleven, and his father, who was quite adept at classical languages, shared the teaching responsibilities with Mrs. Pound. Judge Pound often read aloud to the children, and Dickens, Scott, Thackeray, and Shakespeare were among the family favorites. The children read the fairy tales of Grimm and Laboulage, Hawthorne's *Wonder Book* and *Tanglewood Tales*, and Froissart's *Chronicles of England*. Roscoe's favorite seems to have been *The Pickwick Papers*. When he was twelve, his parents offered him and his younger sister Louise a dollar to read Macaulay's *History of England*. They read together to ensure honesty, and they periodically asked each other questions. Tradition has it that Louise read faster but Roscoe retained more.[35] He had already begun to display the feats of memory that would amaze later audiences.

This mode of education was of immense significance for the intellectual development of the Pound children. Laura Pound was superbly equipped to give her children a sound course of instruction and one that, owing to the unusual intelligence of the children, could be keyed to a high pitch.

The children, for their part, provided one another with challenging classmates. They spurred one another on in an environment of friendly competition and mutual interest in learning. Friends of the family also contributed to this heady atmosphere. Mrs. Pound befriended many university students and faculty members. The poet George E. Woodberry, then an unhappy professor of English, was a frequent guest and stored up fond memories of Roscoe as a young student. George E. Howard, later a renowned social scientist and one of the original members of the Stanford faculty, found Judge Pound a great source of advice in his earliest ventures in scholarship.[36] The continual presence in the Pound home of such men reinforced the tendencies that the parents initiated. This intensive hothouse atmosphere undoubtedly gave the Pound children an intellectual boldness as well as an inclination to consider the life of the mind a normal function of everyday living. The high caliber of their living-room learning gave them a confidence with which to face future learning situations and a confidence in facing the future in general.

Roscoe Pound was a brilliant and increasingly studious youngster, but he also did most of the things common to all Nebraska boys in those years. The three children shared two armies of wooden soldiers "whittled out by Louise, dressed by Olivia, and given the proper military designations by Roscoe." Olivia remembered a home that was "always a gathering place for youth" rather than a "highbrow sanctum." The Pound children had many friends in common, and as they grew older, the living room of their home often resounded with the gaiety of dances and parties; Judge Pound, an excellent dancer himself, occasionally joined the fun. Roscoe and his friends sometimes held meetings of the Carroll Club, their "literary society," which they patterned after the late-nineteenth-century Browning clubs. At one meeting Roscoe, in mock solemnity, read a learned paper on the philosophy of the Bellman, a character in *Alice in Wonderland*, Louise enlightened the gathering on Lewis Carroll's theory of portmanteau words, and Derrick Lehmer, later a prominent mathematician, set "The Jabberwocky" to music, singing it with all the gusto of a seasoned performer.[37]

Roscoe's childhood revealed that Lincoln offered many opportunities and conditions for intellectual growth. It was obviously not a place that snuffed out the life of the mind and discouraged all culture but that of the businessman's luncheon. Nor was Roscoe a lone example or Lincoln an oasis in a stultifying region. At the same time young Willa Cather, according to a recent student of her work, "managed to find a good deal of cultural stimulation in the Red Cloud of the eighties—perhaps more than she would find in the same region today." Whatever may have become of modern village life, the experience of Pound and many of his contemporaries indicated that the small pioneer town offered many positive incentives for young artists and intellectuals.[38]

There was also the prairie, inviting a young boy to explore its untamed beauty and secrets. The prairie had the power to magnify personality traits. To a personality that was narrow, it was oppressive and it intensified that narrowness. The high degree of insanity among pioneer wives was a chilling reminder that life on the plains could be brutalizing. But to a person who was alert to life around him and could create meaningful experiences from it, the prairie offered an unexplored wilderness to discover. One became sensitive to variety and detail in that rich laboratory. It gave another set of interests and experiences to a young man who was enjoying a diverse and experimental life.

Roscoe often made field trips into the prairie in search of plants and insects, and Mrs. Pound, who later remarked that she refused to raise a bookworm or a "perfect little gentleman," encouraged his interest in the outdoors. She could also guide her youthful naturalist, for she was interested in Nebraska plant life and often sent native specimens to Asa Gray, the foremost American botanist of the era.[39] No one seemed to complain when Roscoe's large green worms escaped and began crawling where they were unwanted. The Pound library contained several volumes on natural science, and Judge Pound provided his son with all the necessary equipment. The investment brought many returns, for the boyhood hobby became a lasting fascination.[40]

The Latin School, the preparatory branch of the University of Nebraska, was Roscoe's first contact with formal education. Its primary purpose was to enable students from remote and isolated parts of the state to receive a high school education or correct certain deficiencies. It was, for many years, the largest division of the university, which left the latter open to the derisive charge that it was merely "the Lincoln high school." Staffed largely by the university faculty, the Latin School was quite stimulating and effective.[41]

Although he had a variety of courses and teachers, his fondest memories were of Ellen Smith, the registrar and his Latin teacher. He remembered her as a stern but sympathetic taskmistress, who

> endeavored to adhere honestly and faithfully to the very letter, and . . . expected the same fidelity fearlessly and impartially from others. No matter whether a rule of Latin grammar, a rule of punctuation, or a regulation of the regents or faculty was in question, it must be followed *in toto*, without inquiry or argument. Rules

existed to be obeyed: those who made them were to
debate them, those for whom they had been made were
to exert their best endeavors in compliance.

Both the Latin and the discipline served him well. Indeed,
Miss Smith's instruction was so thorough that Pound felt if
asked to repeat rule 302, he could "respond, as of old: 'the
supine in *um* is used after verbs of motion to express the
purpose of the motion.' "[42]

It was a different type of drill, however, that he preferred, and Friday afternoons found him on the parade
grounds issuing commands to his fellows on the drill team;
Lieutenant Roscoe Pound was the ordnance officer of the
university cadets.[43] But the drill team had to share him with
another campus organization. "The cadet band," a student
journalist reported, "claims the smallest drum major in the
country. Roscoe Pound is the young gentleman who has
been elevated to that position, and although he can scarcely
see over the bass drum he is better versed in military tactics
than the best six-footer in the ranks."[44]

Having spent two full and profitable years in the Latin
School, he entered the university in 1884 at the age of
fourteen. That same year J. Irving Manatt was appointed
chancellor, and under his leadership the university entered
an extraordinarily fertile period of development. Manatt
was an inspiring teacher and an important student of the
classics, and his scholarly instincts served him well in his
efforts to build a faculty. Many of the men whom Manatt
brought to Nebraska later achieved national and international reputations. A. J. Edgren, a brilliant philologist, later
returned to his native Sweden to become administrator of
the Nobel Prizes. Fred Morrow Fling, historian of the
French Revolution, began the problems approach to the
study of history in his undergraduate classes at Nebraska.

Charles E. Bessey, a botanist, became one of the most famous scientists of his era. And there were others who achieved distinction in their fields, such as the classicist Charles Edwin Bennett, the philosopher A. Ross Hill, the zoologist John S. Kingsley, and the literary critic Lucius A. Sherman.[45]

The university had not always been so fortunate. Sectional jealousies prevented it from enjoying security in the early years; internal wrangling among the regents also made the situation extremely unstable. Farmers condemned it as useless, religious groups condemned it as Godless. Good men would not remain on its faculty; spirited men were not allowed to remain. The Pounds' friend, poet George E. Woodberry, was dismissed for infidelity and an occasional drink. Also dismissed for similar reasons was Harrington Emerson, a gentle crusader who became a leading theorist of the efficiency movement during the Progressive era.[46]

Nor were the earliest chancellors of the university so able as Manatt. E. B. Fairfield, Manatt's predecessor, was hardly an overpowering intellectual. Fairfield supplemented his income by giving testimonials for Childs' Catarrh Specific. *Frank Leslie's Illustrated Newspaper* for 6 December 1879 carried the following advertisement:

THE CHANCELLOR OF THE
UNIVERSITY OF NEBRASKA CURED

Dr. Fairfield is well known all over the United States as a man of high standing, learning and great eloquence in the pulpit. He is at present Chancellor of the University of Nebraska. Prior to the use of Childs' Catarrh Specific, he had utterly lost the use of his voice and was compelled to suspend his daily lectures. . . .

Rev. T. P. Childs: *Dear Sir*: I think you have the true theory and practice for the cure of Nasal Catarrh and also for the treatment of the respiratory organs. My throat is now so well restored, that I lecture daily without difficulty, and I find no difficulty whatever in preaching. You are at full liberty to use my name for the benefit of others. Yours very truly, E. B. Fairfield, D.D., LL.D., Lincoln, Nebraska.[47]

Manatt's efforts went far toward overcoming the legacy of the Fairfield years, but the motivation and intensity of the students also played an important part. Many were aware that their parents had made great sacrifices to send them; others were there only through an enormous act of will. "Some of those boys," Willa Cather remembered, "came straight from the cornfields with only a summer's wages in their pockets, hung on through the four years, shabby and underfed, and completed the course by really heroic self-sacrifice." Most students felt that they must work hard and make great haste to learn. Student social life was simple and unsophisticated; student organizations were generally devoted to academic pursuits. "The University," recalled Alvin Johnson, a student in the 1880s who later founded the New School for Social Research, "in the eyes of the faculty . . . and also in the eyes of the more awakened students, had a mission: to bring the light of education and culture to the prairie."[48]

Pound enrolled in the classical course, the program that the most ambitious students chose. Yet the orientation of the classics at Nebraska, as at most universities of the era, was grammar rather than literature. There was too much gerund-grinding, too much of *hoti* and the enclitic *de*. The superior student was encouraged with the promise of eventual initiation into the mysteries of Sanskrit verbs. It was almost as if the whole procedure had been consciously designed to vex the flesh and dull the spirit. Few were encouraged to go on to the study of the classics as literature. "Of the hundreds, and thousands," Alvin Johnson insisted, "who had struggled and fought with Latin and Greek in the University of Nebraska, I knew only one who had penetrated into the real secrets of the literature, and that was Roscoe Pound, who would use his wonderful command of Greek and Latin literature to *épater les bourgeois*."[49] Doubtless Pound was not the only student to make the transition, but Johnson's observation shows how difficult the task must have been. Pound was not content with mere grammar. He was more than a classifier. His insight was more refined, more sensitive; his impulse was not confined to the analytical.

Much was available, however, to help him develop a capacity for analytical sharpness. Chancellor Manatt, forced into the classroom as an instructor in international law and political science, insisted that his students develop such tools. Years later, Pound recalled that "his [Manatt's] insistence on the student absolutely understanding a book and not merely reading through it, and his insistence that criticism must come after thorough understanding, was in my case of enduring value."[50]

The most enduring influence was provided by Charles E. Bessey, perhaps the most brilliant member of the talented faculty that Manatt had assembled. "No one man in America," wrote Andrew Denny Rodgers, the historian of American botany, "contributed more to the developing transitional period in North American botany than Bessey." He was a power among his fellow scientists, a founding member of the Botanical Society of America, an early president of that society and of innumerable scientific organizations, and, near the end of his career, president of the

American Association for the Advancement of Science. He was a marvelous teacher, kind, gentle, and popular. His enthusiasm was contagious.[51]

Bessey fits the script for the traditional history of the American college, a script that demands regents and faculty of noble proportions, gray-bearded founders who nursed the struggling university through tempest-tossed beginnings when the fate of learning was threatened. Because of this literary convention in older writings about the early development of universities, it is difficult to write about Bessey without making him appear a cliché. For the goateed, heavy-browed botanist was a man of great energy, wisdom, and vision.

Bessey became a botanist at a time when botanical studies were still in an observational stage and taxonomy was the supreme goal of all research. Bessey and his colleagues, critical of a preoccupation with taxonomy, were eager to establish botany as a science based on experimentation. Beyond a concern with the external structures of plants lay the uncharted fields of physiological botany and plant pathology. The "new botany" involved a conception of plants as living objects with a capacity for growth and development. It replaced a static conception of science and scientific inquiry with a dynamic one.

The new botany was consistent with the general revolution that the Darwinian hypothesis produced. Botanists who were inspired by the theory of evolution could hardly be content with gathering, mounting, and classifying. Bessey was profoundly influenced by Darwin and acknowledged his indebtedness with enthusiasm. "In . . . the proper work of modern botany," he insisted, "Mr. Darwin led, and where he did not enter himself, he pointed the way."[52]

Much of Bessey's early training was self-acquired and was

gained while searching for solutions to immediate problems. As a result, he displayed a preference for studying the
potential social utility of plant life rather than embarking
upon a quest for abstract principles. Farmers' institutes,
agricultural education, forestry, conservation, medical
botany, plant disease study, landscape gardening—all were
products that issued from his work. He took great interest
in agricultural experiment stations and wrote the section of
the Hatch Act dealing with the subject. But his motto,
"Science with Practice," and his emphasis on fieldwork were
balanced by an insistence that students develop a firm
foundation in theoretical science. He had studied with Asa
Gray, and the rigorous speculative training complemented
his native empiricism.[53]

As early as 1871, while teaching at Iowa State, Bessey was
making systematic use of the microscope in his courses. He
created the first experimental laboratory for purposes of
instruction in botany. Colleagues scoffed at him for emulat-
ing the methods of chemistry. But they have all been forgotten, whereas his textbook, *Botany for High Schools and
Colleges* (1880), became a landmark in modern scientific
literature.[54]

It was a profound experience to study under such a man.
An editorial appearing in the *Botanical Gazette* in 1886, the
year Pound began his studies with Bessey, suggested some
of the excitement that characterized the study of botany in
the 1880s:

> Botany in America was never in a more flourishing
> condition than at the present time. American systema-
> tic work, especially that emanating from Harvard, has
> long stood in the front rank, but other departments of
> the science have not until recently been so assiduously

or successfully cultivated. The study of the anatomy, development and habits of plants . . . was especially promoted by Bessey's Botany in 1880.[55]

Bessey and his students helped make Nebraska a major center for the study of natural science. At Nebraska one was in the vanguard of the new botany. At Nebraska one participated in the creation of the study of ecology in America. It was a situation designed to have a lasting effect on a brilliant and receptive undergraduate.

Pound came under Bessey's spell midway through his undergraduate career, and the experience was of critical importance to his intellectual growth. During his junior year he shifted his principal field of study from the classics to natural science. For the next two decades, Pound worked closely with Bessey, first as a student, later as a colleague, and the relationship deepened over time. Pound acquired insights from his teacher that he pursued as a botanist and that would later contribute to his ideas of law. Moreover, the intellectual bonds were strengthened by bonds of affection. Bessey quickly came to regard Pound as a son and watched his progress with near-parental enthusiasm as he advanced Bessey's ideas in imaginative ways.

Students of jurisprudence have often argued that Pound's early botanical studies gave him a taxonomical turn of mind, and that as a legal theorist he had a tendency toward excessive classification, overrefined analysis, and artificial categories.[56] His plethora of categories in jurisprudence was often labored, but this was part of his attempt to reveal the complexity in legal thought and the fact that different thinkers had molded their systems in conjunction with different social conditions and value judgments. Botany did not make Pound a legal Linnaeus.

Rather than leading him into rigid and artificial patterns

of thought, the new botany that he learned under Bessey's tutelage emphasized process, growth, and development. It was a dynamic study of living objects rather than a classifying of the inert and static. In introducing modern scientific methods to the study of botany, Bessey made experimentation the key concept. Hypothesis was only hypothesis and must be tested by experience rather than by the internal logic of the doctrine itself. This was the importance of the scientific method. In social philosophy the conception is a prerequisite for pragmatism, and both William James and Charles S. Peirce, the earliest pragmatists, were scientists before they were philosophers.

Hence the scientific method with its emphasis on experimentation, a method inherent in Pound's early botanical study, contributed to the molding of a pragmatic cast of mind. He would always be skeptical of absolutes. His empirical scientific viewpoint was reinforced by Bessey's avowed Darwinism, which encouraged Pound to see the world in terms of relativism and mutability. The influence of botany, in conjunction with his training at home, provided the foundations of a modern mind.

Bessey himself was a model for an advanced conception of the role of the intellectual. It was, above all, that of a scientist serving society, using the fruits of scientific discovery to advance the social welfare. And as a scientist had a social responsibility, so society was in need of the services of the expert. The day of the casual handyman approach to modern problems was passing rapidly. The intellectual must think in social terms as well as in terms of social utility.

Pound worked very closely with Bessey, but Bessey wanted no disciples; he urged his students to discover the answers themselves. Pound recalled somewhat wistfully:

I remember when I used to work in botany, that the

strength of Dr. Bessey's work with advanced students lay in his habit of drifting around quietly and sitting on the edge of the table where a student was at work and suggesting this thing or that, cross-examining him with an appearance of casually aroused interest, until before he knew it the student found himself engaged in long and difficult lines of investigation.

Pound's investigations bore fruit quickly; in 1888, the year he graduated, a brief note appeared in *The American Naturalist*. It was a quiet introduction to the career of scholarship that followed.[57]

Libraries and laboratories were a large part of Pound's college years, but they were only a part of it. He belonged to a number of campus organizations and was elected president of both the Societas Classica and the Union society. The agenda of the weekly Union meetings usually included an essay, recitation, or oration, and a musical program and closed with a debate. The meetings also served a social function. Both societies were open to coeds, who constituted about 40 percent of the student body. Both had standing rules that the coeds be escorted to the meetings. The organizations undoubtedly produced more successful marriages than classicists.[58]

There were many student achievements and honors in which Pound could take pride: he graduated at the head of his class, served as a class officer, excelled in debate and oratory. His junior-year entry in the university oratorical contest, an address that emphasized the modern scientific spirit of Lucretius' attack on superstition, was perhaps his only effort that netted a mere second place. Yet the accomplishment that pleased him most was decidedly extracurricular. In the university drill competition at the end of his senior year, Captain Roscoe Pound of Company A directed his unit to first place. It had been an arduous course to the position of company commander. When Pound entered college, he became a candidate for the cadet batallion. He was only fourteen and a rather small boy as well, and he was almost knocked over by the recoil of a Springfield 58, a rifle that was nearly as long as he was tall. He had to begin his cadet career as a marker.[59] Half a century later, he fondly recalled that the victory "does not look so big now, but it looked very big at the time."[60]

Pound graduated from the university in June 1888, and at the bottom of his final report card, Miss Smith, his former Latin teacher, wrote, "Good bye to term reports, and hearty congratulations from one who has watched your entire course with the interest of a friend." That summer he began reading law with his father, who had recently left the bench to resume an active practice. He also began to attend lectures at the Robbins "law school," which had been formed at the request of about two dozen young men reading law in Lincoln offices. C. A. Robbins, a lawyer with a penchant for scholarship and teaching, held classes two evenings a week in a room at the Lincoln Business College. There were two courses, one on Sir William Blackstone and another on torts.[61] Pound embarked on this new project with his customary enterprise, which pleased his father immensely.[62] In addition to assiting his father, he also collected bills for another firm of attorneys and sold tickets for the Burlington Railroad.[63] It was a busy and fruitful summer, but he was not yet ready to commit himself to the parental profession.

This refusal to embrace the law must have come as a profound disappointment to his parents, for although they had raised their children in an unusual fashion, there was still a strong conventional element in the Pound home. When he was a child, his mother had tied his left hand behind his back to ensure that he would become a "normal" right-handed boy.[64] When he graduated from college, his father expressed some doubt about the utility of his education. "Well," said the judge rather dolefully, as Mrs. Pound remembered the incident thirty years later, "the boy is through school and I don't know what he's good for."[65] Judge Pound did not fully understand the potential of this multifaceted education; he had no premonition that his son would develop one of the most comprehensive legal philosophies of modern times. He did know that his son was a bright boy who could become a fine lawyer if he would rid himself of the impractical desire to be a botanist.

Pound was a dutiful son, and he applied himself diligently to the task of learning the law. He enjoyed some aspects of the practice of law, but the study of law was not intellectually rewarding. The law seemed to be a ragbag of dull, lifeless details. As a college student, his reading of contemporary classics such as Holland's *Elements of Jurisprudence*, Cooley's *Constitutional Limitations*, and Savigny's *Roman Law* introduced him to major themes in nineteenth-century jurisprudence, but he did not find them compelling. His father started him with Blackstone's *Commentaries* and Walker's *American Law*, staple items for beginning lawyers. "Blackstone," he remembered, "made me very tired. . . . Then, as to Walker's American Law, I discovered that law was just a matter of rules. . . . Well, that didn't stimulate me very much." Such drudge work had little of the excitement that characterized his scientific studies. "It was not without anguish," recalled Justice Holmes of his own legal education, "that one asked oneself whether the subject was worthy of the interest of an intelligent man."[66] Pound's early probings in the law must have been equally anguished.

He continued to work in his father's law office, but when classes resumed at the university in the fall of 1888, Pound enrolled for graduate work in botany. He also accepted an appointment as Professor Bessey's assistant in the botanical laboratory, thus becoming the first of a series of remarkable aides. Bessey had recently become assistant chancellor, and the increased burden of his administrative duties forced him to turn to his favorite student for help with his scientific projects.[67] It was a golden opportunity for Pound.

As a graduate student he pursued a number of projects he had begun earlier. One of the most important of these was an attempt to make the Botanical Seminar a permanent organization. The Botanical Seminar, which soon became known as the Sem Bot, had its origins in the weekly meetings begun by a group of students in 1885. The group resented the superior attitude of the literary societies and wanted to promote field botany in Nebraska. It existed in an amorphous state until 1887, when Pound, as a college senior, organized it as the Sem Bot.[68] He nursed it through its infancy while a beginning graduate student; later the Sem Bot would achieve genuine importance in the history of both the university and the developing science of botany. As a graduate student Pound also made a number of personal contributions to science. He discovered and classified several new plants[69] and published nine articles in various scientific journals. It was an accomplishment that few scientists could claim at the age of nineteen.

Although he was a graduate student and Bessey's assistant, Pound had a number of friends who were still enrolled in the undergraduate programs of the university. They probably scoffed somewhat at his new exalted position, and the school paper took an opportunity to deflate whatever egotism he may have developed. A student journalist reported this incident of "mistaken identity," which allegedly occurred late at night after a baseball game and oratorical contest with the neighboring Doane College:

> Strange individual, "Come, its time to go to bed."
> Pound:—"Ah, come off."
> Doane student.—"Sitz, he's a prof."[70]

Pound's Nebraska boyhood had been uncommonly rewarding. The vital community in which he lived made him conscious of growth and development and of man's ability to shape his environment. His family and the university encouraged an attachment to the life of the mind, and his scientific studies impelled him toward pragmatism and a suspicion of absolutes. The diversity of his youth and the experimental life that it encouraged provided an unusual framework for his future.

He left the university in June, and the following September he left Lincoln for Cambridge, Massachusetts, where the Harvard law faculty introduced him to new and exciting developments in legal thought.

2

The Law at Harvard

Roscoe Pound entered the Harvard Law School in September 1889 with limited goals; he planned to stay for only one year before returning to Lincoln. He had come to Harvard because his father wished it, and he hoped to spend a substantial amount of time at the university herbarium, a botanical mecca. But the law school had a compelling quality about it. Within a year his doubts were transformed into a new dedication. The law school established the structure of his future, for at Harvard he developed his deep commitment to the law.[1]

The sheer novelty and adventure of traveling across half a continent provided a magnificent introduction to his year of study in the East. The train ride was long and arduous, and he complained that it was "the most detestable bit of traveling I ever heard of." His expressions of discomfort, however, were products of a feigned sophistication; he seemed much more excited by the countryside than disgusted by the day coach. Chicago was his biggest surprise, but he particularly enjoyed a few hours in Toronto and Montreal. He found his French adequate and the French-

31

Canadians fascinating, and wryly informed his parents that "they are very pious at Montreal and will allow nothing to be open on Sunday but churches and saloons."[2]

After arriving in Cambridge, Pound, apparently unaffected by homesickness, quickly adjusted to the routine of student life at Harvard. He took his meals at Memorial Hall and lived in a furnished room conveniently located less than two hundred yards from the law school. Yet his life did not fall into a monotonous pattern circumscribed by the paths leading from his room to Memorial Hall and the law school. The wholesome diversity that characterized his Nebraska boyhood was a guiding principle for his activities at Harvard, reinforcing his natural openness of mind and preventing the sterility that might have resulted from a single-minded pursuit of legal studies.[3]

Pound filled his idle hours in a number of rewarding ways. Although he had developed a fondness for the theater in Lincoln, the Opera House on O Street had not fully prepared him for the world of Boston theater. He took advantage of the seemingly endless round of plays, opera, and concerts. He saw the great Edwin Booth at least twice and marveled that a man so old could appear so young.[4] Boston and Cambridge also offered a wide array of sporting events, and the young law student frequently enjoyed a boat race on the Charles, Harvard football, and the Boston Braves. He found time for tennis and developed an interest in boxing, "with the result," he reported, "that my countenance presents a rather singular appearance." His exercise was not limited to athletics, for he occasionally shoveled snow and took other odd jobs.[5]

One activity for which Pound had little sympathy was the fraternity system. After an initial desire to join a fraternity, he decided, with characteristic enthusiasm, that one "could find no better way of cutting his social and political throat than to advertise himself as a frat."[6] Whatever the larger social and political considerations were, Pound preferred his private room, where he would "not be disturbed by callers." Yet he was not monkish; he formed a number of close friendships. Soon he was writing his father that "Hershey [is] my right hand man here." Omer F. Hershey, then an undergraduate in the college and later a leader of the Baltimore bar, was one of the earliest and most permanent of the Harvard friendships.[7]

Pound quickly developed an interest in Massachusetts politics, and his observations revealed at once a distaste for sham and pretense as well as a fondness for staunch Republican values. After attending a speech by Theodore Roosevelt, he reported that the commissioner "talked very virtuously and gave us considerable rot." He was contemptuous of many of the reform movements that stirred Boston in the 1890s.[8] Even so mild a measure as the Australian ballot was dismissed as "humbug."[9] Indeed, he complained that "everything is to be 'reformed.' . . . Whatever mugwumpy ideas I may have had before I came here have been thouroughly [sic] dispelled and I shall be content to be an offensive partisan the rest of my days." He took delight in the fact that the majority of students, in spite of being deluged with "free trade and mugwumpery," remained Republicans. Pound's politics would become more progressive in the years ahead, but his overall social strategy was always tinctured with the conventional wisdom of William McKinley's America.[10]

As a law student Pound was anything but conventional. He registered as a first-year student, but took only nine hours of first-year work. The dean might have allowed him to take a complete program of upper-division courses, but Pound decided that some of the first-year work would be more useful for Nebraska practice. He planned to remain at Harvard for only a year, and he wanted to make the most of it.[11]

The Harvard Law School in the 1890s was a place to test the mettle of the most ambitious and intelligent students. It was then at the height of its fame. Christopher C. Langdell, the wizened, white-bearded gnome who was its dean, had assembled a galaxy of legal talent into the most famous law faculty in Harvard's history. It was a faculty with a burning sense of purpose, both in scholarship and in teaching. "Enthusiasm," Arthur Sutherland comments, "rather than indoctrination, must have been Pound's most valuable endowment from his Harvard teachers."[12]

Every student who came to the Harvard Law School in 1889 fell under the influence of Christopher Columbus Langdell. Born in 1826, Langdell had been a student at Harvard in the 1850s, practiced law in New York City in the 1860s, and became the first dean of the law school in 1870. His conception of law and his contributions to legal education were, to a large degree, extensions of his personality. A shy man, he had led a rather secluded life as a lawyer in New York. He rarely appeared in court and could usually be found in the library of the New York Law Institute or his private office. A narrow, winding staircase connected the office of his firm to a secluded garret that served as Langdell's private office and quarters.[13] His practice was a prelude to a single-minded pursuit of the rules of law.

Langdell's contributions to legal education were varied. He initiated regular examinations and introduced nonpractitioners to law faculties, but his most important contribution was the case method of study. Langdell published his casebook of appellate court opinions, *Selection of Cases on the Law of Contracts*, shortly after his appointment as dean. By the 1880s the case method replaced the earlier textbook-and-lecture method of instruction at Harvard; by

World War I, casebooks had become the major tool in American legal education.

The basic assumption of Langdell's jurisprudence was that law is a science governed by a limited number of principles, and it was the task of the lawyer-as-scientist to discover the controlling principles of legal phenomena. Langdell thought that the principles, few in number, could be found in only one place—judicial opinions. In pedagogy as in jurisprudence, he found the focal point of legal learning in the critical analysis of appellate court opinions. Classroom time was spent discussing the rules of law contained in the assigned cases.[14]

The spirit of the scientific method permeated Langdell's work. Perhaps it was this cast of mind that appealed to Charles W. Eliot, the Harvard scientist and president who created the modern law school. The Langdell system also suggested the catholicity of science: in drawing on English as well as American reports for the development of legal principles, the case method made the university law school the voice of the Anglo-American legal tradition rather than the voice of Ohio, Wisconsin, or Massachusetts. To some critics, however, the approach was pseudoscience at best. Oliver Wendell Holmes, Jr., insisted that Langdell's work was a "misspent piece of marvellous ingenuity" that represented "the powers of darkness." His scholarship, Holmes charged, was the emptiest of formalisms. It revealed "the narrow side of his mind, his feebleness in philosophising, and hints at his rudimentary historical knowledge. I think he was somewhat wanting in horse sense." More recent critics have charged that the case method represented a narrow, technical view of the legal tradition that divorced the study of law from social and political realities.[15]

Pound was initially uncomfortable with the case system.

He was accustomed to the text-and-lecture method of the Robbins "law school." As an entering first-year student at Harvard, he expressed strong misgivings about casebooks and insisted in a characteristic burst of independence that he planned to read hornbooks "even if they do discourage such reading." Yet his opinion soon began to shift. "I must acknowledge," he confessed to his father, "that after the first month the case system seems to me better than any other." Certainly this way of learning law appealed to him more than learning it through Walker's *American Law* or the venerable Blackstone. He admitted to his mother, after several months of casebooks, "You might tell Father that I have not altogether given up my text book ideas yet, but they are shaken."[16]

Although he rejected Langdell's arid legalism, Pound continued to utilize the case method throughout his long career. When he became dean of the Nebraska College of Law in 1903, one of his first acts was the introduction of the system. His attachment to it revealed his assumption that the judiciary occupied the central position in the development of law, and that American law was part of the larger common law system. In a letter to Morris Cohen, a philosopher with a keen interest in jurisprudence, Pound wrote, "I can not think that the Case system of instruction has anything to do with the [underdeveloped] status of philosophy of law. . . . Moreover, I submit that there is quite as much philosophy of law to be found in Mr. Justice Holmes' opinions as in text books, and it is usually infinitely sounder."[17]

Pound's teachers at Harvard imparted the excitement of a novel method of study. James Barr Ames, one of Langdell's first students and a professor when Pound arrived, found the case method electrifying when Langdell introduced it. "We were made to feel at the outset that we were his fellow students," Ames remembered. "We very soon came to have definite convictions . . . and we were possessed with a spirit of enthusiasm for our work in Contracts, which was sadly lacking in the other courses."[18]

Ames, Langdell's most brilliant student, was a cultivated Bostonian who in 1873 became the first member of an American law faculty who had no prior experience in private practice. He was a favorite of the law students, and his great charm and classroom manner did much to popularize the case system. Joseph H. Beale, who studied under Ames, remembered that it "was Ames who really settled much the best method of teaching up to his time; that is, the teaching by free discussion between members of the class and between the class and the teacher." Felix Frankfurter, a law student at Harvard in 1903-1906, called Ames's method of instruction "teaching by combat." "Nothing pleased Dean Ames more than to have you disagree with him," said Frankfurter, "or to have you make him re-think his thinking. He didn't want followers. He wanted thinkers, independent ones."[19]

A series of exhaustive casebooks was Ames's principal contribution to legal scholarship. He also dug deeply into the yearbooks and reports to produce several articles on the development of legal doctrines. Ames's idea of legal scholarship was limited in scope, for his method discouraged going beyond the judicial opinion to understand legal growth and change. As a result, he developed the view that gradual adaptations effected during centuries of growth best expressed the peculiar needs of a people; he abhorred abrupt change.

He viewed legislation with particular alarm, insisting that the "power of legislation is a dangerous weapon. Every lawyer can recall many instances of unintelligent, mischievous tampering with established rules of law."[20] An occasional statute might be necessary to correct a minor evil, but for the most part, the slow, organic development of the common law would suffice. Ames represented a view that dominated the legal profession: statutes in derogation of the common law must be strictly construed. His thought was part of the climate of opinion that fostered judicial hostility to novel social legislation.

Ames declared that the failure to adhere to precedent produced an inferior judiciary. In Germany, for example, "too much regard is paid to the opinion of writers and too little to judicial precedents, with the unfortunate result that the distinction of the continental judges is far less than that of the English judiciary." Ames would have limited the jurist's role to clarifying the doctrines contained in the common law; only in this way could he help a judge properly decide a case.[21]

His fascination with the case method, his exclusive concern with the common law, his failure to appreciate social and economic forces that shaped law, and his distrust of legislation were symptomatic of the late-nineteenth-century view of the legal process. Although Pound eventually rejected much of Ames's view of law, the work of men like Ames had a tremendous impact on Pound and other twentieth-century legal scholars. Ames imparted a deep reverence for the common law to his students, and the patient attention that he gave to the proliferating body of the common law provided an invaluable foundation for scholars who followed him. If as a scholar he lived in an artificial and antiquated past, as a teacher and dean he was deeply involved with the future. Ames was a missionary devoted to the attainment of excellence in the law. His chosen instrument was the Harvard Law School. He seems to have conceptualized it in much the same terms as Jefferson did his University of Virginia; it was to produce a dedicated and capable legal elite—statesmen, professors, and administrators as well as practitioners. By 1937 even Morris Cohen, a critic of the case method, admitted that Ames had played a major role in providing the foundation for legal scholarship in the twentieth century. "Langdell and his followers," wrote Cohen, "especially Dean Ames, laid a broad foundation for legal scholarship in this country not only by their insistence on examining all the cases but by making law teaching a dignified profession and by training a group of scholars to regard the study of law as a worthy field of human interest apart from its aid to successful practice."[22]

The teacher who most influenced Pound at Harvard was John Chipman Gray. Gray was a giant of a man who, as a young Union officer, had galloped to Washington to tell Lincoln that Fort Sumter had fallen. A member of a prominent Boston family, he joined the faculty of the Harvard Law School in 1869 and remained there until 1913. He continued to practice law throughout his teaching career, arguing cases both before the Supreme Judicial Court of Massachusetts and the United States Supreme Court. He was an immensely learned man, and one of his books, *Restraints on Alienation*, was quoted by the House of Lords, a rare honor for an American authority.[23] He was a warm and witty man as well as an intellectual giant. During the Christmas vacation in 1889, Pound, unable to return to Nebraska, remained at Harvard. One afternoon Gray entered the library, saw Pound reading a book on Roman law, and told him that the volume was unreliable. On discovering that his student read German, he disappeared into the stacks, returned with a copy of Sohm's *Institutes*, gave it to Pound, and went about his work. Twenty years later, Gray attended his student's lectures on Roman law at Harvard.[24]

Gray used the case method, but it did not possess an aura

of sanctity for him. The very mention of the "Harvard
system" or "case system" disgusted him, for he opposed
dogmatism in legal education.[25] Even after adopting the
technique, he expressed his misgivings about Langdell's
mechanical conception of law. "The idols of the cave," he
wrote President Eliot, "which a school bred lawyer is sure to
substitute for the facts, *may be much better material for intellectual gymnastics than the facts themselves and may call forth more
enthusiasm in the pupils*, but a school where the majority of
the professors shuns and despises the contact with actual
facts, has got the seeds of ruin in it and will and ought to go
to the devil." His complaint was an interesting echo of the
major point that his friend Holmes had made in the Lowell
lectures two years earlier—"The life of the law has not been
logic; it has been experience."[26]

It was simply impossible, Gray argued, to reduce the law
to a series of logical consequences derived from simple
postulates. If immutable principles do exist, he wrote, "we
know very few of them, and these very elementary, entirely
insufficient with which to build the slightest legal
structure."[27] Such misgivings made it impossible for him to
use the case method as an exercise in abstraction. He assigned a series of judicial opinions to his students to illustrate the development of legal rules; moreover, he felt that
cases might make the law seem more real to students. "To
abstract law from facts," he observed, "is *the* thing that a
lawyer has to do all his life." Furthermore, attention to
actual cases "is an effectual corrective to unreal and fantastic speculation, which is the most dangerous tendency of
academic education."[28]

Pound was thoroughly impressed by Gray's erudition,
but he also appreciated his tough-minded approach. "One
can," he reported, "get more law and legal common sense (I
don't know how else to express it) out of his course" than

any other in the school. Perhaps he had in mind Gray's definition of an act of God—something disagreeable that no one could prevent. He also applauded Gray's stern treatment of classroom comedians. "Professor Gray is an ideal instructor and keeps down the funny men and other bores—so that we learn something." To foolish questions from his auditors, Gray would reply, *"De minimis non curat lex* [The law does not concern itself with trifles]."[29]

The emphasis on a slavish adherence to precedent was a commonplace in the late nineteenth century, but it was not a doctrine that Pound heard from Gray. Gray felt that a survey of rule by precedent, as practiced at different times and in different legal systems, indicated that the technique was not universal. The idea of rule by precedent had a limited scope in Roman law; in Germany, precedents had so little effect that lower courts did not follow the rulings of upper courts. Even in the English common law, the use of precedents did not make a significant appearance until Sir Edward Coke developed the practice in the seventeenth century. Gray noted that the use of precedents varied widely in the two great common law nations, England and the United States. The British House of Lords was more reluctant to reverse its decisions than the United States Supreme Court.[30]

As a definition of law, Gray often used a passage from a sermon that Benjamin Hoadly, the Whig bishop of Bangor, preached before the King in 1717. "Whosoever hath an absolute authority to interpret any written or spoken laws," said the bishop, "it is he who is truly the Law-Giver to all intents and purposes, and not the person who first spoke or wrote them." Gray believed that a court made law by interpreting statutes and that no doctrine could be considered law that did not receive judicial construction. If a "half-a-dozen old gentlemen form the highest judicial tribunal of a country," he wrote, "then no rule or principle which they refuse to follow is Law in that country." He considered only the judicial pronouncement to be law; all other rules were mere sources of law.[31]

Judicial creativity varied according to the definiteness of the sources of law. When a constitution, statute, or precedent was clear, it usually controlled the judge. However, when statutes were inadequate and unclear, or when precedents were confused, the judge enjoyed a high degree of freedom. He had almost complete freedom of decision when the only relevant source of law was custom. Gray challenged the common nineteenth-century assumption that custom played a vital role in shaping the common law, and insisted that "when the custom is one way and the judge's judgment of what is moral is another way, the judge follows the latter, and disregards the custom."[32] Pound incorporated this theory of judicial creativity into his own philosophy of law. In 1922 Pound, quoting Gray, told an audience that " 'the difficulties of so-called interpretation arise when the legislature has had no meaning at all; when the question which is raised on the statute never occurred to it; when what the judges have to do is, not to determine what the legislature did mean on a point which was present to its mind, but to guess what it would have intended on a point not present to its mind had the point been present.' "[33]

The law was not a body of timeless certainties, Gray argued, and the student of law must not treat it as such. Growth and change were very much a part of law; moreover, "growth and change is not a mere weaving of spider webs out of the bowels of the present rules of Law."[34] The student of law must deal with what the law "ought" to be as well as what it "is." Jurisprudence, Gray thought, had assumed a new meaning. "The supposed immutability of its

principles," he declared, "was what once gave it its dignity
and charm; today it owes them rather to its possibilities and
prospect of boundless development."[35]

Gray often appeared to be an amused observer of the
legal process, and he took delight in destroying the sand
castles of orthodox legal theory. It was, above all, this critical faculty that was his legacy to Pound. Gray never formulated a theory of legal growth or a guide for judicial
decision-making. He had no new system to impart. Indeed,
his criticism had some of the characteristics of a lovers'
quarrel. He called for realism in law, but it is clear that he
did not call for rejection of the common law tradition. As
Joseph H. Beale remarked years later, "Gray cannot get far
ahead of Austin as exceedingly cleverly corrected by Gray."
Although Gray was an imaginative lawyer, he was under the
spell of John Austin, whose writings dominated English
jurisprudence. The mature Pound would reject the
positivistic core of Gray's thought—the doctrine of Bishop
Hoadly. But he would, like Gray, become a legal scholar
dedicated to reforming a system to which he was deeply
committed.[36]

Pound had William A. Keener for contracts, and he considered Keener second only to Gray. Keener was awesome
in appearance. He had a bearlike figure, a full, red beard,
and predacious eyes. He carried a huge red bandanna that
served as a handkerchief and a stage prop, and he began
each lecture by blowing his nose until the rafters literally
echoed the explosion. Keener was brutal in the classroom.
His method was Socratic with a vengeance. He was quick-
talking, quick-thinking, and ruthless in his questioning.
Students frequently thought of themselves as prey being
stalked by a relentless quizmaster. Despite his exacting and
savage style, he never tried to stifle a student. He welcomed
questions and disagreement and was ecstatic when a stu-

dent could defend a contrary position with skill and determination.[37]

Although an early disciple of the case system, Keener was not content to follow Langdell blindly. Langdell had hoped that the method would enable the student to discover a number of fundamental principles, but Keener used the case system as a technique for developing a student's ability to analyze legal problems. It was this method of instruction that brought him to the attention of President Seth Low of Columbia. In March 1890 Pound wrote his parents that Keener, "who is generally regarded as the ablest young man here has got mad or disgusted with the fogies and is going to Columbia. It seems to me he will be a great loss." Low made an attractive offer at a time when Keener was engaged in a salary dispute with the Harvard Corporation, and he began teaching at Columbia the following year. It was a loss for Harvard, but not for the "Harvard system," for Keener brought the case method to Columbia, increasing the prestige and influence of the new technique.[38]

In 1889 the lecturer in constitutional law at Harvard was James Bradley Thayer. A master of his subject, Thayer had joined the law faculty in 1874 after several years of practice, and he remained at Harvard until his death in 1902. He was a student of both evidence and constitutional law, but it was his work in the latter field that had the greatest impact on Pound. Thayer's observations about the doctrine of judicial review would appear in the opinions of Holmes, Brandeis, Stone, Cardozo, and Frankfurter when they took their seats on the Supreme Court. Thayer's "rule of administration" for deciding constitutional questions was an early expression of the doctrine of judicial self-restraint.[39]

The frequency with which the Supreme Court invalidated statutes in the last three decades of the nineteenth century shocked Thayer. He argued that the court's mandate was too weak for the exercise of such power. The power of the court to invalidate an act of Congress was purely inferential; the authority for judicial review did not appear clearly in the Constitution. Yet Thayer agreed that historical evidence sustained the exercise of judicial review, and he did not quarrel with the legitimacy of the practice.[40] Judicial review, he argued, simply did not mean judicial supremacy; it was not an arbitrary power. Courts were not the only agencies that construed the Constitution. The legislative branch, in devising statutes, also construed the Constitution. Moreover, legislative construction was more immediate and more frequent. Judicial construction of constitutional questions was possible only when controversies came before the court; consequently, the judiciary had only a postponed and incidental control. This led Thayer to the conclusion that Congress should be the primary agent in questions of constitutional interpretation and that "a legislature, in construing the Constitution for purposes of legislation, may adopt any construction which is *reasonable* [italics added]."[41]

Although Thayer argued that Congress had a broad area of constitutional discretion, he did not deny that the Supreme Court had a checking function. But the court must exercise that function with extreme caution. "To set aside the acts of such a body [Congress]," he wrote, "representing in its own field, which is the very highest of all, the ultimate sovereign, should be a solemn, unusual, and painful act."[42] The Supreme Court, in considering the constitutionality of a statute, must resolve every reasonable doubt in favor of Congress. The court must not pass upon the wisdom of legislation; it was only empowered to pass upon the constitutionality of legislation and should invalidate only those laws that the Constitution clearly proscribed.[43]

Thayer felt that the expansion of judicial review in the

last part of the nineteenth century boded ill for the Republic. The new role of the court, he wrote in 1884, "has tended to bereave our legislatures of their feeling of responsibility and their sense of honor, and also to lead the community off into mistaken views as to the office of the judiciary."[44] By identifying constitutionality with propriety, the Supreme Court had assumed burdens that properly rested with Congress. In 1893, addressing the Congress on Jurisprudence and Law Reform at the Chicago World's Fair, Thayer reminded his audience that the "checking and cutting down of legislative power, by numerous detailed prohibitions in the constitution, cannot be accomplished without making the government petty and incompetent. . . . Under no system can the power of courts go far to save a people from ruin; our chief protection lies elsewhere."[45]

Although Pound later insisted that the courts must play a major role in adjusting law to social needs, he also accepted Thayer's doctrine of judicial restraint. An excessive exercise of judicial review usually indicated a misguided attempt to protect the people from imagined abuses of government. When the judiciary stood between the legislature and the electorate, it stood "between the public and what the public needs and desires, and protects individuals who need no protection against society."[46]

Pound left Harvard in the summer of 1890. "At the end of one year," he had predicted with confidence, "I expect to be able to show some of you something." He had tested himself against the best law professors and students of his time, and he had met the challenge. Had he chosen to remain another year he would probably have been selected for the *Harvard Law Review*. He was approached by an editor, but Pound replied that he must return to Lincoln. His father's health was failing, and he felt compelled to assist him in his practice.[47]

When Pound bade farewell to Harvard, he had no idea that he would return twenty years later, first as a professor, then as dean of the law school. He probably had little awareness of the profound way in which his year at Harvard had influenced his life and thought. At least he knew that he had become vitally interested in the mysteries of the law. Perhaps he also realized that he had formed a deep commitment to the common law system. From a careful consideration of cases, he gained both background and respect for the substance of law; from Gray he inherited the notion of judicial creativity and a healthy realism; from Thayer he learned to respect legislation and judicial restraint. And if he often heard Ames praise artificialities of nineteenth-century law, he also heard him scold the legal profession for its lack of professionalism. All of his teachers led him to a judge-centered view of the legal process, a position not uncongenial for the son of a judge. In short, Harvard encouraged him to challenge the legal system within the context of that system. Pound had acquired a foundation for his pursuit of law and its relationship to society.

3

The Lure of
Botany

In the summer of 1890 an ambitious young man embarked
on a long adventure in American law. Roscoe Pound returned to Lincoln to take his first professional steps in the
familiar surroundings of his birthplace. Although Judge
Pound's reputation provided security, the fledgling attorney was not seeking protection from challenge. Harvard
had fired his enthusiasm for the law, and the test it provided had strengthened the self-confidence that was so
much a part of his personality.

Pound quickly began to show his competence as an attorney. He had chosen the law as his profession, and he pursued it with characteristic intensity. Yet his early career as a
lawyer was not all-consuming; there were other outlets for
his enormous energies. The experimental character of his
life allowed him to supplement a demanding legal career
with forays into local politics, participation in the life of the
university, and further botanical study. Although he had
rejected a career in science for the practice of law, the lure
of botany was a strong one, and the proximity of the univer-

sity ensured that it would remain an important preoccupation.

The University of Nebraska had been a central influence in his youth, and it continued to exert a powerful attraction. He enrolled for graduate work and soon became one of the most visible of Nebraska's ninety graduate students. His fellow students elected him president of the Graduate Club and an officer of the Lincoln Microscopical Club.[1] He still enjoyed the extracurricular life of the university and was a frequent referee at the intermural football games as well as a devoted follower of the varsity eleven.[2] "Roscoe Pound succumbed to the inevitable," the student newspaper reported in an article on the 1891 Iowa game, "and went to Omaha to yell for the U. of N."[3]

The major attraction of the university was the gentle Professor Bessey and a brilliant group of young botanists. Even the compelling character of the Harvard Law School had not diminished his interest in science, and James Barr Ames later remembered that Pound's year in Cambridge would have been even more exceptional if botany had not distracted him.[4] It was not surprising that botany once again became very important to him in the congenial atmosphere created by the university, Bessey, and the Sem Bot.

The Botanical Seminar, more commonly known as the Sem Bot, began during Pound's undergraduate days as an informal group of seven Bessey students. In his senior year Pound molded the "Original Seven" into a formal campus organization designed to establish the academic respectability of science. The organization had no constitution or bylaws, an ironic product for a future lawyer. But the Sem Bot did have a clearly defined purpose and required new members to pass an extremely grueling examination. It was a thoroughly professional organization that offered its members an institutional focal point, group consciousness, and internal mechanisms of control. The Sem Bot provided a glimpse of Pound's later commitment to professionalism in law.[5]

It was a very unusual group of young botanists that Pound rejoined in 1890, when, after a year's absence, he resumed his leadership of the Sem Bot. It contained a number of students who would leave their mark on the development of botany in the United States. H. J. Webber began his career by making "fungus forays" with Pound and other Sem Bot members. Per Axel Rydberg, another member and perhaps Bessey's ablest student in systematic botany, became an outstanding taxonomist and a leading authority on Western flora. Albert F. Woods, a pioneer plant physiologist, became the director of scientific work for the United States Department of Agriculture. Woods was responsible for the early development of the Federal Bureau of Plant Industry and supervised the Department of Agriculture graduate school.[6] Conway MacMillan, one of the Original Seven, became a professor of botany at Minnesota and edited the *Minnesota Botanical Studies*, an early organ of the new botany.[7] Frederic E. Clements, one of Pound's closest friends, served the universities of Nebraska and Minnesota as a professor of botany before he joined the Carnegie Institute as a research associate. Clements became a master ecologist, and A. G. Tansley called him "the greatest individual creator of the modern science of vegetation."[8] Professor Bessey's son, Ernst, was also a member of the group; for him the Sem Bot was the beginning of a distinguished career in mycology.[9]

These students were only a few of the many aspiring scientists who were attracted to the Sem Bot, and it eventually surpassed the literary societies as the most prestigious organization at the university. Throughout the two decades of its golden age, Pound's talent and labor were the central factor in its success; indeed, it did not long survive after he left Lincoln in 1907.[10] But at its zenith the Sem Bot was an exciting organization, touched by a rare combination of seriousness and frolic that was so characteristic of Pound himself. He helped develop the elaborate ritual and farce that were a central feature of the Sem Bot, and he often won the club's pie-eating contests.[11]

In 1891 Pound and J. G. Smith, at the urging of Bessey, used the Sem Bot as a base from which to launch the Botanical Survey of Nebraska. Pound became the director and the Sem Bot became the working staff of an ambitious project to explore the flora of the region systematically. The Botanical Survey had the blessing of the state legislature, but the project was essentially private in nature, funded by the participants and friends of science.[12] The survey team divided the state to conquer the flora. Pound and Smith made the first foray themselves, spending July and August of 1892 exploring the vegetation of the Central Sandhills, a great grassland of nearly 20,000 square miles. The two men, accompanied by a patient mule named Moses, wandered for nearly five hundred miles, making notes of the plant life and collecting specimens for the university herbarium.[13]

The Sandhills trip was merely the first of a long series of explorations that lasted into the next century. Survey members fanned out across the entire state, subjected it to an extremely thorough investigation, and published their findings in two monograph series, *The Flora of Nebraska* and the *Reports of the Botanical Survey*. In 1900 Pound proudly informed the Nebraska Academy of Sciences that the Botanical Survey had discovered over one thousand new species native to the state, and produced a series of studies utilizing the techniques of the new botany. "In the course of the Survey," he added, "it has constantly been borne in mind that the ultimate object should be to ascertain all that might be learned of the *vegetation* of the state."[14]

Pound's emphasis on "vegetation" revealed his enthusiasm for the new botany, a dynamic study of plants as living objects with a capacity for growth and development. The new botany was a major departure from the dominant Linnaean tradition that limited research to a taxonomic trinity of gathering, mounting, and classifying plant life. This static view of science was particularly strong among American botanists in both the East and the Far West. Eastern botanists persisted in the familiar taxonomy of Asa Gray, little influenced by the Darwinian impulses that were a late addition to Gray's botany and an even later addition to his theories of botanical education. In the West there was more emphasis on fieldwork, but taxonomy reigned as supreme among Westerners as it did among the closet botanists of the East. They were virtually untouched by Darwinism and the cluster of new botanical interests that the theory of evolution had produced. Westerners were naturalists in the Emersonian tradition, glorying in the fieldwork that put them close to divine Nature. Their greatest reward was to lend their names to a new species.[15]

Since the 1870s Midwestern botanists had moved beyond their colleagues on either coast, and insisted that taxonomy, although necessary and important, was not the supreme goal of the science. Classification as an end was too sterile, and taxonomy often contained the false assumption that relationships in plant life were static and eternal. Fixity, said the new botanists, was an illusion; the focus of scientific inquiry must be on process. They were interested in the lower forms of plant life and micro-organisms, and they developed new fields of physiological botany, plant pathology, and ecology. They stood as botanists with the advance guard of the revolution that Darwin had wrought.

Darwin, who had given Midwestern botanists their distinctive sense of direction, regarded the natural world as plastic, dynamic, and intensely volatile, and consequently its continuous variation treated man to an endless parade of new forms and species. Life was inherently unstable, but the principle of natural selection, Darwin's most fruitful insight, lent definition to the chaos of nature. Each element of life struggled for existence within a threatening environment, and its survival depended on a successful accommodation to those forces that challenged and sustained it. But natural selection was not a neat, predictable formula; the developmental hypothesis that it offered was maddeningly inexact. A species that had survived the struggle owed its success to random and fortuitous adjustments that profoundly modified its former structure. There were no factors within the long process of development that guaranteed the success of individual struggles. Darwin's tentative and elusive key to the origins of life required a radically new approach to science, and he suggested that students eschew the static for the dynamic, substitute fieldwork for laboratories, and explore problems that had once been considered unworthy of scientific inquiry. In short, he called for a physiological experimental science rather than a taxonomical natural history.

Darwinian ideas inspired the work of the Botanical Survey, and the members accomplished their tasks with thoroughness and precision. They were concerned with relationships among plants, sought their data from experimental fieldwork, and regarded all forms of vegetation as legitimate, living objects of study. But the work as a whole was fragmentary; the basic research of the survey cried for a synthesis. The inspiration for such a project came in the spring of 1896, when Bessey gave Pound a copy of Oscar Drude's *Pflanzengeographie von Deutschland* to review for the *American Naturalist*. Pound had long been attuned to German scholarship by Bessey's urging and example, but Drude's masterful survey of the geography of German plant life struck him as a profound moment in science. The book inspired both a glowing review and the *Phytogeography of Nebraska*.[16]

The *Phytogeography of Nebraska*, published in 1898, was the first book-length study of its kind in the English language. It was a comprehensive statement of the developing field of ecology and became a landmark in American botany.[17] Pound persuaded his friend Frederic Clements, a fellow Sem Bot member, Botanical Survey worker, and instructor in botany at the university, to join him in the ambitious project. The two men began work in the autumn of 1896, and the venture was to serve as a joint thesis for the Ph.D. Neither man had time for the project during the day, so they worked at night in the university herbarium which, because of a regulation prohibiting its after-hours use by graduate students, they entered through a window carefully left unlatched in the afternoon. The project was completely a joint effort, and they even relaxed by whistling their favorite grand operas in unison. The music often brought an encouraging visit from Bessey, who knew that the work must be going well when strains of music floated down the hall. The thesis was completed and successfully defended near the end of the academic year, and Pound received the university's first doctorate in 1897. Clements' degree was delayed by an administrative tangle in the dean's office, but was granted the following year.[18]

The *Phytogeography of Nebraska* was one of the finest examples of the new botany. It encompassed the entire plant kingdom with chapters on fungai, micro-organisms, and the lesser varieties of plant life as well as the more complex specimens. It was an attempt, said the authors, to go beyond the mere cataloguing of species. Phytogeography was the study of "the vegetation of the earth as vegetation." It combined ecology with morphology and taxonomy in order to assess biological function and the interaction of plants with their environment. The method and the material combined to make the science of botany more sophisticated and more complete.[19]

Pound and Clements had to devise novel techniques to gather the data that the new botany demanded. One of the most important results of their study was the development of the quadrat method, a technique designed to eliminate some of the error to which this observational science was prone. Species that appeared most prominent even to careful observers were not always the most abundant. Plants like the prominent-flowered blazing stars and prairie clovers made a greater visual impression than species that were actually more abundant. To correct this problem in determining the distribution of species, Pound and Clements marked off a series of five-meter square plots, physically counted the number of plants in a species within each plot, and took an average of the several plots. The quadrat method guaranteed a more precise enumeration of the vegetation, which made it possible for botanists to define the boundaries of plant regions more accurately and to determine the changing degree of distribution within transitional areas.[20]

Ecological problems dominated the *Phytogeography*, and imaginative measuring techniques like the quadrat method allowed Pound and Clements to deal with them more effectively. A product of the Darwinian revolution, ecology focused on plant communities rather than individual plants

and explored the environmental dimensions of plant development. Pound and Clements thought of ecology as a
study that "deals with the life of a plant in its home . . . [and]
is best understood by regarding the habitat of a plant as an
aggregate of influences or factors acting upon the plant."[21]
This environmentalism stood in marked contrast to the
earlier interest in classification and replaced the sterility of
classical taxonomy with a larger conception of nature and a
more sophisticated understanding of process. It would
serve Pound in jurisprudence as in botany.

The interaction between the organism and its environment was only one of a vast series of organic relationships
that Pound and Clements saw in nature. They argued that a
plant formation was "a biological community in which each
factor has more or less interrelation with every other factor,
a relation determined not merely, nor necessarily, by the
fact of association, but also as a result of biological forces
induced by physiological and meteorological phenomena."[22] Their ecological investigations thus led them to the
conclusion that the natural world was a vast series of organ-
ically related parts, integrated biologically into a continuous
process of interaction. No organism, no unit of natural life,
was isolated from the larger whole. Critical of narrowly
defined taxonomical ventures, they condemned "hair-
splitting methods which dub every indivisible group a
species, in disregard of phylogeny."[23] Their use of the word
"phylogeny" was the key to a larger meaning, the idea of
the natural world as a single great branching tree of life.
Ernst Haeckel, the devoted German champion of Darwinism, had coined the words "phylogeny" and "ontogeny" (as
well as "ecology"), words permeated by organicism, to express the unity and interrelatedness of life. He discovered the biogenetic principle, the notion that the ontogeny of a living creature is a recapitulation of

its phylogeny, or, as he explained it, "the development of the embryo is an abstract of the history of the
genus."[24] The *Phytogeography of Nebraska* was squarely in
this tradition.

The organicism that permeated botany and biology in
the late nineteenth century becomes more understandable
when compared with pre-Darwinian conceptions. The
fundamental intellectual construct of the eighteenth century, a conception that had its origins in the distant beginnings of Western thought and survived to influence the
nineteenth century, was a doctrine known alternately as the
Scala Naturae, the Ladder of Perfection, *l'Echelle des Etres*,
and the Great Chain of Being. The Great Chain of Being
postulated a gradation of existence, but the links of the
chain had no organic connections. It was not subject to
evolutionary transformation, for the species that composed
it were immutable and timeless. Its levels of being were
static entities rather than stages of growth. Although the
search for new links fostered a comparative anatomy that
eventually led to ideas of evolution and phylogenetic relationship, the world of the Great Chain itself was a universe
made rather than a universe making. It was in this spirit
that botanists like Carl Linnaeus, the great Swedish
naturalist, erected vast taxonomical schemes to illustrate
the fixity and order of life.[25]

The Darwinian theory of evolution introduced a dynamism into natural history that shattered the static Chain
of Being, but, as Pound and Clements' work shows, parts of
the wreckage persisted to color the most advanced products
of nineteenth-century scientific thought. Naturalists destroyed its tight little world, but the notion of a unilinear
and continuous series ranging from the simple to the complex was reinterpreted in historical terms to become a unilinear and continuous chain in time.[26] Unable to accept the

purposelessness in the natural selection of fortuitous variations, many—perhaps most—naturalists began to see in evolution a developmentalism that allowed them to retain teleology in the face of Darwinism.

Teleology, the concept of ordered development toward a final end, has been a familiar element in Western thought. Christianity lent theological support to the idea. Aquinas made the teleological argument one of his five proofs for the existence of God—the existence of order in the world revealed an outside intelligence directing natural things to their end. The theological gloss, however, was not a necessary part of the argument, for the doctrine was complete in Plato's theory of forms, without theistic overtones. The fundamental point of all teleologies was that direction existed and life progressed toward some end, either by outside intelligence or by internal perfecting principles. Teleology played an important role in the Great Chain of Being. In an imperfect world each level of being, whether by outside direction or an internal dynamic, sought to attain the end of its development, its perfect form. The levels of being were rigidly separate, but within each level occurred movement toward some preexisting end.

It is difficult today, a century after Darwin announced his theory of evolution, to detect any teleology in a scheme based on the natural selection of accidental variations. Few modern scientists would disagree with the judgment of H. J. Muller that "this principle . . . cuts away the ground from under all teleology in the origination of the organic world."[27] Yet many distinguished nineteenth-century scientists (Darwin himself was an exception) disagreed violently with that conclusion and insisted as strongly that Darwinism was informed by design and direction.

Charles Darwin was simply all things to all men,[28] and

nowhere was this more obvious than in the effort to extract teleology from natural selection. Darwin was pleased to learn that Leo Lesquereux, the leading American paleobotanist, finally accepted the theory of evolution, but he must have been profoundly shocked when Lesquereux wrote that he had embraced the *Origin of Species* because it made the birth of Christ and redemption by grace more intelligible to him.[29] Asa Gray, the principal American defender of Darwin, saw a somewhat milder but unmistakably theistic principle of design in the theory of evolution. He implored men "to recognize Darwin's great service to natural science in bringing back to it Teleology; so that, instead of Morphology *versus* Teleology, we shall have Morphology wedded to Teleology."[30]

Darwin was understandably distressed by these developments. He did not intend "to write atheistically," but he found it impossible "to see as plainly as others do, and as I should wish to do, evidence of design and beneficence on all sides of us." In an observation that went to the heart of the matter, he wrote that "designed variation makes . . . my deity 'Natural Selection' superfluous." In 1868 he publicly disavowed Gray's interpretation, but the arguments for design in Darwinism persisted.[31] It was with unintentional irony that his son Francis later wrote, "One of the greatest services rendered by my father to the study of Natural History is the revival of Teleology."[32] Francis Darwin was echoing the judgment of Thomas H. Huxley, his father's leading British advocate, who had long argued that the theory of evolution contained a nontheistic teleology. Huxley insisted that Darwin replaced "the commoner and coarser forms" of teleology with "a wider teleology . . . actually based upon the fundamental proposition of Evolution." This fundamental proposition was that "the whole world, living and not living, is the result of mutual interaction, according to definite laws, of the forces possessed by the molecules of which the primitive nebulosity of the universe was composed."[33] Huxley's conclusion was one of the clearest statements of teleological organicism ever uttered. It meant that the natural world, an organic unity, had developed in an orderly and continuing fashion through the operation of internal laws that had directed the process since birth.

Like other early champions of evolutionary theory, Pound and Clements did not escape the urge to combine old certainties with the new uncertainties of natural selection. They were influenced by empiricism and environmentalism, Darwinian impulses that suggested variation and mutability, but they also accepted a teleological conception of natural development that introduced elements of inevitability. From the dynamism and instability of a world in flux, Pound and Clements discovered surprisingly definite conclusions in plant growth that revealed inherent direction. As a result, the *Phytogeography of Nebraska* exhibited the tensions that marked the reception of Darwinism among its most devoted followers.

The new fixity came in what Pound and Clements called "the principle of succession," the idea that an ordered progression of successive plant communities finally evolved into a stable community. "As a general rule," they argued, "each layer [of vegetation] vanishes as it becomes subordinate, and the formation [plant community] comes to be represented by a primary layer alone. . . . In the case of secondary formations, the complete occupation of the ground by the culture formations suppresses their development."[34] What Pound and Clements were describing was the notion of "climax" in evolutionary development, and it demonstrated the persistence of teleology in post-Darwinian science. After a plant formation had run its course of ordered progression, it attained a climax that produced a final stable plant community characterized by a high degree of equilibrium. Scientists now argue for a series of climaxes, and some question the existence of any climax, but all agree that the mature plant community is extremely sensitive to the environment and subject to variety, modification, and a great diversity of vegetational patterns. The *Phytogeography of Nebraska*, however, recognized only a single climax, one that established a relatively permanent pattern and ended the process of succession.[35]

The monoclimax theory of succession, which Clements would soon develop in greater detail,[36] was much more than an observation that forest land, once leveled, would return to forest. It meant in addition that a plant community, once formed, would develop within predictable limits toward a final stable end through an internal perfecting mechanism. This is the process that Pound and Clements were describing when they argued that mature plant communities, the products of succession, suppressed the development of secondary communities. The attempt to combine an ecological environmentalism with a teleological organicism was a dramatic preview of a conflict that later appeared in Pound's legal thought. In jurisprudence he argued that legal doctrines were responses to the environment and were shaped by the felt necessities of the time, but he also regarded the law as an organic unity that developed in an orderly fashion through the force of an inner dynamic.

Although modes of thought that later informed his jurisprudence appeared in his botanical work during the 1890s, there was no direct connection between Pound the scientist and Pound the lawyer.[37] His science provided Darwinian conceptions such as empiricism, environmentalism, organicism, and teleology, but it did not immediately determine the direction of his legal philosophy. "For my part," he wrote in 1895, "I am inclined to stick up for the analytical theory," and years later he recalled that sociological jurisprudence was the last in a long series of shifting allegiances to various legal theories.[38] Still, a man of ideas had lived daily with compelling ideas, and they were of larger importance than any immediate change in legal thought. The new botany did not produce a new jurisprudence, but it made his later philosophical positions easier to develop.

The new botany made Pound suspicious of classification as the central theme of the science, but it did not destroy his interest in taxonomy. As director of a botanical survey that had discovered hundreds of new species, he was forced to pay careful attention to problems of classification and nomenclature. Furthermore, progressive botanists everywhere were becoming aware of the pressing need for a uniform nomenclature. The fact that science had replaced a world of constancy with a world of change made it even more imperative that the language of science be stable and consistent. To eliminate the chaos that resulted from competing systems of classification, the Botanical Section of the American Association for the Advancement of Science, meeting at Rochester in August 1892, took the first steps toward the adoption of a new and systematic method of classification. A second meeting the following year at Madison, Wisconsin, strengthened the advocates of the Rochester Code.[39]

Pound became a supporter of the Rochester Code, although he recognized it as a tentative measure. True to the new botany's empiricism, he hoped that the suggested reforms would be thoroughly tested; it was solely through the application of the new rules that their soundness would be revealed. The dominant systems, both the Linnaean and the "natural system," were inadequate. The Linnaean system based its classificatory principles only on the sexuality of plants, and although the natural system focused on the whole plant, neither system questioned the constancy of species or sought to establish organic patterns of vegetation. Pound condemned a "superfine analysis of the floral covering" and insisted that "taxonomy must ultimately modify recent hair-splitting methods," or meaningless classifications would devour the science of botany.[40] As an ecologist, Pound argued that botany be studied as life rather than as logic. He wanted to prevent artificial constructs from obscuring the natural order. In attacking the existing systems of classification, he argued for a rigorous certainty in language rather than a rigorous certainty in life.[41]

Not all botanists, however, were eager for reform. Edward L. Rand and John H. Redfield, disciples of Asa Gray who resented any suggestions that challenged the latter's work, published a major attack on the work of the Rochester meeting.[42] Nathaniel Lord Britton, an advocate of the new code, implored Bessey to "admonish them to improve their manners." As editor of the botany section of the *American Naturalist*, Bessey was in a commanding position to strike back, and he chose Pound as his instrument.[43] Pound wrote a scorching review of the Rand-Redfield study, insisting that their critique of the Rochester Code demonstrated "a most wonderful ignorance of the whole subject." American botany was no longer in its infancy and should not follow a great man blindly; the invocation of Gray's name was not enough to justify uncertainty and vacillation. The critics of the code, he wrote, were really the ones who stood for disorder and confusion. They also stood for provincialism, and Pound displayed understandable pique at what he thought was Eastern snobbishness. "Boston," he fumed,

"still thinks herself the centre and focus of American learning in all branches, and . . . the authors regard all of those
poor mortals who do not live in the shadow of Cambridge as
intruders."[44]

Pound regarded the Eastern disciples of Gray as
literalists attached to an inadequate creed. Even the language of Gray's *Manual*, medieval Latin, was being made
obsolete by the general academic return to the teaching and
use of classical Latin.[45] The Rochester Code was, he admitted, a mere preliminary, but it could be used as the basis of a
more complete system. He urged American botanists to
rally to Otto Kuntze's call for an international congress.
Pound considered the German scientist a master taxonomist, but Pound's critical perspective prevented him
from becoming a disciple. He was opposed to Kuntze's
effort to honor a discoverer of a species at all costs. Kuntze
had created an interminable list of endings, prefixes, and
combinations with which to bracket personal names, and
Pound insisted that it would intensify the existing
confusion.[46] The criticism did not undermine their mutual
esteem, and Kuntze continued to recommend Pound's
work to the European scientific community. He even chose
to immortalize the young American botanist at the early age
of twenty-eight, when, with a fine sense of irony, he named
a fungus *Roscoepoundia*.[47]

Nor was *Roscoepoundia* the only recognition of his
achievements. He was appointed honorary curator of the
University of Nebraska Herbarium in 1898.[48] The following year the *Académie Internationale de Géographie Botanique*
awarded him their international scientific medal, and he
was elected to the Board of Directors of the Nebraska
Academy of Sciences.[49] He later became the first of the
Nebraska group to receive a star in *American Men of Science*,
an honor extended to only one hundred botanists.[50]

Pound was, in short, one of America's most creative botanists in the 1890s. At a time when there were fewer than a half-dozen ecologists in the entire world, his studies helped establish ecology as a major branch of the science.[51] Henry C. Cowles, a young scientist who would become a brilliant ecologist, called the *Phytogeography of Nebraska* "the pioneer work of its kind in America." Colton Russell, another botanist, predicted that the study was "destined to exert a far-reaching influence and act as a stimulus everywhere."[52] The reputation of the book did not dim in the succeeding half-century. In 1952 H. A. Gleason, a leading figure in the generation of ecologists that succeeded Pound, remembered Pound and Clements as the first genuine ecologists in America. The botanists who preceded the two Nebraskans, Gleason argued, provided no more than hints of the real work that came later.[53]

In helping to establish ecology as a new field of study, Pound revealed the experimental aspect of his personality as well as his ambition and drive, traits that he acted out with aplomb. He was a strong-willed young man who thrived on challenging problems, and he moved effortlessly into positions of intellectual and institutional leadership. As the central figure in the Sem Bot, a group of unusually capable young scientists, Pound was *primus inter pares*. He organized the Botanical Survey, a major regional enterprise, and nurtured it throughout the 1890s, giving it effective management, financial support, and a sense of purpose. Pound was an unstinting advocate of the new botany, and he carried the battle to the enemy with his unsparing attack on moribund taxonomists who had claimed the mantle of Asa Gray. His emerging international reputation was a testament to the imagination and effort behind his formidable list of accomplishments.

As a scientist, Pound was an aggressive and creative

thinker who enjoyed exploring the frontiers of knowledge and was eager to lead his fellow pioneers. But the botanical interlude also revealed an irreconcilable dualism in his thought that would, in time, create an intellectual impasse. The empirical, evolutionary themes in his version of the new botany revealed an appreciation of environmental diversity and change, but the teleological elements in his organicism introduced a fundamental predictability into Darwinian conceptions of growth. Organicism, in short, placed definite limits on the relativism and range of his evolutionary conceptions. But, for the moment, the vitality of his thought was more impressive than its dualism.

Pound's record in science would have been impressive for any botanist, but it was incredible for a part-time botanist. Science was an avocation that he pursued with intense dedication, but it was still only an avocation, and it merely supplemented his other great strides in a more conventional calling. He was an energetic, highly motivated botanist, but he was an even busier lawyer.

4

Years of Growth: Law and Politics In Nebraska

The legal world of Nebraska to which Pound returned in 1890 was not the most promising environment for a young attorney's professional debut. The boom-time opportunities that his father had enjoyed were disappearing with the passing of the frontier, and the host of lawyers that had flooded the capital city forced newcomers to compete in a crowded bar. The Panic of 1893 introduced new complicating factors and sent attorneys scurrying after vanishing legal business. The panic was particularly severe in Nebraska, and the most vital parts of its economy—agriculture and transportation—suffered alarming dislocation.[1]

A lawyer who entered practice under such conditions had to be resourceful and relentless. Pound was prepared to be both, and from the beginning he was forced to assert himself. His bar examination lasted almost three hours, an unusually lengthy inquiry prompted by the committee's curiosity about his Harvard background. After satisfying

the bar examiners, Pound quickly won the confidence of
Lionel C. Burr, an important Lincoln attorney who hired
him as a stenographer but made him a partner within two
years. He became a solo practitioner in 1895, and near the
end of the decade he joined two other Lincoln attorneys to
form Hall, Woods & Pound, which became a leading center
of corporate practice in the state.[2]

The problems of carving out a career in the Nebraska
legal profession were formidable, but Pound's assets were
equally formidable. His pioneer family was one of the
state's most distinguished, and his father was a respected
judge. Pound had talent, ambition, and a capacity to accept
change that allowed him to respond effectively to the tur-
moil of the decade. Yet his sense of life's mutability and
dynamism, born of his botanical studies and the frontier
experience, was balanced by an enthusiastic acceptance of
the legal profession's fundamental propositions, an attachment that allowed his penchant for change to be
dramatic without being controversial. Finally, the environment of the 1890s was not uniformly bleak. The law no
longer offered instant success, but the bar was still fluid and
it welcomed candidates with talent and tenacity. Those who
survived the hardships of the panic found new opportunities as the depression lifted in the last years of the
decade. Pound's debut as a lawyer also occurred at a critical
time in the development of the bar, for it coincided with the
birth of the modern legal profession in Nebraska and the
nation.

Throughout the 1890s Pound pursued a very general
practice, and he established a widespread reputation by his
eagerness to accept a diverse range of legal problems. He
followed the circuit court as it made its way through one
Nebraska town after another, and he gained a wealth of
experience as a trial lawyer. In his first successful jury case,

a rising Nebraska politician named William Jennings Bryan appeared as opposing counsel. Pound became familiar with the ubiquitous justice of the peace and learned, as he later told a Texas audience, that "the initials J.P. were popularly taken to represent 'Judgment for plaintiff,' partly because the plaintiff was wise enough to select for a defendant a party who could pay the costs."[3] He frequently represented the Burlington Road and the Union Pacific, practiced in appellate as well as trial courts, and appeared for both plaintiffs and defendants. In time, however, his practice was limited to the appeals courts, commercial law, and advising other attorneys.[4] As the economy grew stronger in the closing years of the nineteenth century, corporate enterprise renewed its conquest of the Great Plains, and Pound proved adept at capturing a share of the growing practice in corporate law. He had clients throughout the region, and he was highly regarded by businessmen.[5]

Pound's practice gave him a clear understanding of law at the grass roots, and this early experience was a source of strength in his later efforts to make legal theory more comprehensive. At the same time, there was nothing particularly unusual about the nature of his practice. He rose to the top of the Nebraska bar quickly, but he did so by performing his conventional tasks well. He did the right things, and did them in the right way. He won the respect of the elders in the profession, and they made him an appellate judge at the tender age of thirty. This was not the tribute that came to rebels.

Pound was aware of this conventional aspect of his life and thought. A few years after his return to Lincoln, he observed, in an unusual moment of self-awareness, his tendency to accept existing institutions and conventional standards. "Why am I in the law?" he asked. "Why because my father wished it. Why do I make a pretense of being civilized when I am at heart one of the most uncivilized creatures at large? Because I have a certain family standard to maintain. Fashion, convention and a wholesome fear of the laws; there you have the explanation of everything in my life."[6] Convention would almost always establish the limits of his experimentation. It explained, in part, his choice between science and law, and the decision to reject a career that brought him sudden international recognition for a pursuit in which he enjoyed only local fame. Science had not yet acquired its twentieth-century glamour and was not a suitable profession for an ambitious young Nebraskan.

Respect for fashion and convention also explained his early enthusiasm for the "cult of the robe," the ritualism of the bench that Judge Jerome Frank condemned as a cheap device to make judges appear "touched with divinity." Pound realized the symbolic power of the judge's vestments, and he applauded when the judges of the federal circuit courts decided to don robes. "Everything which tends to restore the judiciary to its true position," he argued, "which tends even in slight manner to give to it in the eyes of the public those long lost attributes of dignity, authority, and eminence, which belong of right to the common law judge, is opportune and welcome." His apologia for the robe, framed during the turbulent 1890s, was part of a familiar call to restore the dwindling prerogatives of American judges.[7]

The legal profession faced disturbing challenges in the 1890s, and the problems of lawyers extended beyond the mere search for business. Trade union militancy, agrarian radicalism, and corporate arrogance lent an unusually dramatic appearance of social instability to the era, and the battles over trusts, tariffs, and monetary policy assumed the dimensions of mortal combat. The agitation for reform ranged from the alien socialism of Daniel De Leon to the native Populism of Tom Watson, but the diverse prescriptions were uniformly alarming for a profession so deeply rooted in the established order. Most lawyers met the challenge by closing ranks and putting aside their internal differences in the struggle against a common foe. Some feared the collapse of public order, others were primarily concerned about the narrow interests of their corporate clients, and still others trembled at the intellectual and social irresponsibility that they saw in the strident demands for change. A brooding fear of anarchy united the disparate impulses of the bar as lawyers joined in an apotheosis of the profession and the judiciary as the last institutional agencies of reason.

As early as 1887 Christopher G. Tiedeman, a leading laissez-faire theoretician, established the theme for the legal profession in the politics of the coming decade, when he argued that "the efforts of the courts . . . is our only means of defense against the inordinate demands of socialism." By 1892 even the moderate John F. Dillon, who had once considered Tiedeman's strictures alarmist, now argued that the most unsettling problem in an age of unsettled problems was "whether the bench is able to bear the great burden of supporting, under all circumstances, the fundamental law. . . . This is the only breakwater against the haste and the passions of the people." And five years later, in Populist-torn Nebraska, Roscoe Pound offered a celebration of ceremonialism that revealed the lengths to which a groping bar was driven in its quest for security.[8]

His testament to the robe, with its ringing defense of judicial perquisites, came less than a year after the political battles of 1896, dramatic battles that had intensified his attachment to the ideological preferences of an embattled bar. As a young lawyer rising in the profession and the son of a prominent Republican judge, Pound had naturally joined the forces of sanity and McKinleyism. But unlike many of his stalwart Republican colleagues, Pound was not an advocate of laissez-faire, the Gilded Age message that linked Social Darwinism, natural law, classical economic theory, and the Protestant Ethic with the interests of industrial capitalism. Pound was more troubled by attacks on judges and lawyers than by attacks on business and empty abstractions, and the irresponsible rhetoric that he detected in Populism reinforced his mistrust of its program.

The campaign of 1896 was a memorable experience for Pound, and he frequently peppered his later speeches to bar associations with blistering criticism of the Populists. He remembered them as narrow, stupid men, fit only to serve as the butt of his jokes to audiences of nodding legal worthies. The Populist crusade, with its frenzied attack on courts, suggestions of class war, and carelessly constructed arguments, alarmed Pound, for the movement challenged institutions, social arrangements, and values that he cherished. Years after the Bryan campaign, Populism remained an epithet. He reminisced with his sister about its blind partisanship and reminded her of the "arrant nonsense" with which agrarian radicals opposed the award of a judgeship to lawyers who had served large corporations. For Pound the quality of a lawyer transcended the character of his clients, and he scored the hard-pressed farmers who translated all associations into ideological commitments.[9] He found the raw protest of lower-class reform distasteful: it lacked dignity, it was not respectable, and its arguments were unsound.

Pound joined the struggle by writing a major campaign article for the *Nebraska State Journal*, the leading Republican daily in the state. The article was a dispassionate attack on the principal heresy of Populism and Bryan's

Democracy—the free-silver argument. Nebraska silverites argued that the declining price of wheat was due to an appreciation in the value of gold. Unlimited coinage of silver would restore wheat prices, which had fallen from $1.25 per bushel in 1871 to $.49 in 1894. In a frontal attack on the silver argument, Pound insisted that the state of the currency since 1870 "had no more to do with the price of wheat than it has had to do with the prevalence of cholera." The price fell simply because surplus increased while demand remained constant. In 1870 the United States and Russia controlled over two-thirds of the world export market in wheat. After 1870 Romania, Serbia, Canada, Argentina, Chile, Uruguay, and India entered the market with a vengeance.[10]

Pound sought to affirm his point by comparing wheat with other commodity prices. The American corn crop, he noted, was over three times as large as the wheat crop. If the monetary system affected the price of wheat, surely it would affect the price of corn. But corn had maintained its price since 1870, because most of the crop was consumed at home. This proved conclusively, he insisted, that the farmers' plight was caused by shrinking foreign markets rather than a rigged monetary system.

An impressive array of statistics made Pound's argument seem impregnable. He gleaned his information from a variety of sources, including the reports of the Department of Agriculture, consular statistics, reports of the French ministry of agriculture, and a circular of the Russian finance ministry. The article was one of the most successful versions of a widespread Republican ploy. Throughout the farm belt, party strategists sought to connect depressed agricultural conditions with the laws of supply and demand rather than the gold standard.[11] Pound advanced the argument with great forcefulness and contributed a meas-

ured appeal to reason in an unusually emotional election
year. His statement, he admitted, made "dry reading," but
there was a suggestion that he strove to appear objective
and dispassionate as a matter of strategy. "Declamation," he
cautioned, "will fill convention halls much more easily than
it will fill our pockets."[12]

The article became a major campaign document, and the
Republican press of Nebraska showered it with accolades.
"No intelligent reader," the *Nebraska State Journal* ventured,
"can look over these official figures without being convinced that the conclusions reached by Mr. Pound are deci-
sive and incontrovertible." The *State Journal* continued to
keep his conclusions and name before the public in the
ensuing weeks. Another Lincoln newspaper, the *Evening
News*, took Pound's article as a model for campaign literature and maintained that the silver heresy could best be
eliminated by "literature . . . that states the propositions
clearly and discusses them logically." In Omaha the *Daily
Bee* carried a lengthy synopsis. The article came to the
attention of Frank Irvine, a Republican judge of the Nebraska Supreme Court, who sent Pound a note of congratulations and expressed the hope that his work would receive
wide circulation. "Sometimes I distrust the capacity of vot-
ers to reach intelligent conclusions," mused Judge Irvine.
"If, however, sound reason has any sway among them,
there can be no doubt your article conclusively meets and
answers one of the most dangerous sophistries which the
Populists advance."[13]

The favorable response by leaders of the bar and the
party encouraged Pound, and the campaign publicist became a campaign speaker. He addressed the Lincoln
Seventh Ward Young Ladies' McKinley Club and the
Fourth Ward Republican Club, and appeared at a number
of party functions. He was a member of the Lincoln McKin-

ley Club and was selected as a delegate to the state convention. After the election Pound continued to be active in state and local politics, and he served two terms as chairman of the Republican central committee of Lincoln.[14]

There was a parallel between Pound's professional and his political activities. His professional career, which advanced rapidly from a general practice to appellate work and commercial law, corresponded to the conventional standards of successful career development, and his defense of ceremonialism and McKinleyism advanced some of the bar's ideological conventions. Both his political service and demonstrated mastery of the law appealed to established attorneys like Judge Irvine, and soon after the campaign of 1896, Pound's role in the internal politics of the legal profession eclipsed his activities as a Republican politician. In October 1896 the Nebraska Supreme Court selected him as a member of the commission to examine applicants for the bar. It was an unusual honor for a man who had been a lawyer for only six years, and it demonstrated his stunning rise in the law. When the commission of five met later in the month, Pound, predictably, was elected secretary.[15] The bar examination was an increasingly substantive element in the law's rites of passage, and as such was a fitting symbol of his developing concern with professionalism.

Pound also served the bar through his participation in the movement for a modern Nebraska State Bar Association. There had been efforts at organization in Nebraska shortly after statehood; Pound's father was the first president of the Lancaster County Bar Association. But the early ventures had long been moribund when, on 22 January 1900, Nebraska lawyers met at the federal court building in Lincoln to form a new professional organization.[16] Pound was chosen to serve on the important Committee on Organization, and he helped draft a constitution that was adopted the following June.[17] As the organization's first secretary, a position he held for the next six years, Pound devoted an enormous amount of time to the fledgling association and came to its aid in several early financial crises.[18] "It used to be said years ago," remarked John N. Dryden, president of the association in 1916, "that Roscoe Pound, when he was Secretary, was the Nebraska State Bar Association."[19] The nature of the organization to which he devoted so much energy reflected some of his deepest commitments.

The preamble to the association's constitution contained a dual statement of purpose. The association was to be "an organization for the promotion of the administration of justice according to law, and for the advancement of the honor and dignity of our profession and encouragement of cordial intercourse among the members thereof."[20] The standing committees also provided a clue to its character. There were committees on law reform, judicial administration and remedial procedure, legal education, and legislation affecting the profession.[21] Although the organization possessed a conventional common law hostility to legislation, it did not hesitate to seek legislative support for its two goals: serving the interests of justice and promoting the welfare of lawyers. Yet it was apparent from the beginning that the primary goal was not public service. "For the advancement of the honor and dignity of our profession" was the preambular passage quoted in the opening sentence of the first two annual presidential addresses. The fact that both early presidents used this as a text indicated that internal professional objectives were more important to the organization than its obligations to the public.[22]

The new professional consciousness that Pound advocated for the Nebraska bar was being sought by professional and occupational groups throughout America at the turn of the century. A complex set of factors forced a new group consciousness upon some of the most stubbornly individualistic members of a society that extolled individualism. In the preindustrial cities and towns that dotted the American landscape, occupational identifications meant little to doctors, bankers, laborers, and lawyers, who located themselves within the autonomous communities in which they lived. But the new industrialism of the Gilded Age, with its demand for a more specialized division of labor, robbed traditional communities of their homogeneity, while the revolution in communication and transportation allowed individuals to develop long-range associations and interests. As their cities and towns grew less traditional and less isolated, and as functional specialization intensified, those persons who possessed unique skills in common discovered a larger occupational kinship that transcended geographical and political boundaries. An awareness of common skills and common goals allowed the new professional identifications to be institutionalized, and new organizations emerged to give their memberships a lever of control in a changing society.[23]

Although new collective identities were becoming a common feature of the emerging social order, the transformation of medicine was a particularly dramatic example of how Americans replaced their class, financial, and regional identifications with new occupational loyalties. The practice of medicine, which had been undermined by quacks, nostrums, and a contempt for expertise, regained its stature in the 1890s, when doctors banned together to consolidate spectacular advances in medical science. There was a burst of organizing activity throughout the decade as doctors created the scores of local medical societies that provided a grass-roots foundation for the reorganization of the American Medical Association in 1901. The AMA and its local affiliates launched feverish membership drives, demanded higher standards of medicine and more effective licensing, campaigned for improved medical schools, and secured authority from state legislatures to supervise and regulate health care. At the same time, other occupations responded to the lure of professionalism, and social scientists, teachers, and social workers sought to improve their skills, establish more effective patterns of recruitment, and create organizations and procedures to sustain their new professional identities.[24]

American lawyers were thus part of a major reorientation in middle-class attitudes. After decades of witnessing the deterioration of their craft, lawyers in the 1890s developed a new enthusiasm for professional cohesiveness and a new fondness for highly articulated standards, internal mechanisms of professional control, and lengthier periods of preparation for a career. In part, the fear of labor violence, agrarian reform, and imported radicalism provided an incentive for collective effort, but there were also positive factors that lent a more optimistic note to the new professional identity. As the economy grew more complex, there was a greater demand for carefully trained lawyers. The elite law schools, whose professors had a missionary zeal to make legal study a learned discipline, provided another impulse for professional improvement. Lawyers were also discovering that their interests crossed local boundaries, and men whose vision of the profession had been limited to a local practice sought communion with their colleagues in distant regions. In 1880 lawyers supported only 16 isolated state and local bar associations, but 35 years later there was a vast professional empire of 48 state and 623 local bar associations echoing the ABA's plea for deeper professional identity, improved professional schools, and increased professional control over the administration of justice. Lawyers, like other occupations and interest groups, learned that new collective efforts were required to meet the challenge of industrialism.[25]

Although lawyers everywhere had a growing concern with professional standards and professional security, there were peculiarly local conditions that encouraged the creation of the Nebraska State Bar Association. Throughout the country, no legitimate occupation had a more tarnished reputation, but the practice of law stood in particularly low public repute in Populist-torn Nebraska. Much of the Populist criticism was justified, but the low state of the Nebraska bar stemmed, in part, from the same lack of institutional restraint that farm-belt rebels praised. When Pound entered practice in 1890, almost anyone willing to read law for a few weeks could become a lawyer. The democratization of the bar had undermined professional standards. But Populist criticism and the virtual absence of professional standards were only two factors that affected the Nebraska bar. The rapid transformation of the state in the last years of the century created a need for new institutions that could introduce order and direction into the confusing novelty of urban-industrial growth.

Elements of Nebraska's brief past also worked to the advantage of attorneys who sought to create and institutionalize a new professional identity. The circuit-riding days were a recent memory; much of Pound's early practice involved pursuing the law business that followed the judge as he made the rounds of his circuit. Circuit-riding gave some structure to the Nebraska bar. It created friendships, channels of communication, and standards of behavior that lent cohesiveness to the profession. The cohesiveness of the circuit made it easier to implement the updated corporatism of the bar association.

In both the camaraderie of the courthouse and the professional identification of the bar association ran a similar theme of exclusiveness and elitism. Perhaps all groups that possess specialized knowledge and skill exhibit some exclusiveness, but lawyers cultivate those tendencies into a more thorough elitism because their skills touch society at so many sensitive spots. It was to this elitism that E. Benjamin Andrews, chancellor of the state university, appealed at an early meeting of the Nebraska State Bar Association. He insisted that lawyers provided the vital answers to pressing public questions, and that the administration of justice as well as "a worthy judiciary is absolutely dependent on a worthy bar."[26]

If the Nebraska legal profession had elitist pretensions, it was not secure enough to be smug, and the Committee on Legal Education urged that formal academic training replace the less systematic method of reading law in a private office. The committee agreed that there had been many able self-made lawyers in the past, but an increasingly complex society called for increasingly rigorous methods of preparation for the bar. At the same time, it cautioned students against fly-by-night schools and specifically condemned correspondence schools.[27] This recommendation had special relevance for Pound. He had taught Roman law at the university since 1895, and he was appointed assistant professor in 1899.[28] Both Pound and the bar association realized that education was the most crucial factor in the creation of a profession.

Although the Nebraska State Bar Association was primarily a watchdog of the lawyer's welfare, it did not entirely neglect its public role as caretaker of the administration of justice. The state supreme court was struggling with a crowded docket, and the increasing volume of litigation overwhelmed its three judges. On 18 September 1900 the association recommended that the legislature create a special agency to help the court clear its docket. The state responded the following year with the Nebraska Supreme Court Commission, a temporary body of nine commissioners to be appointed by the judges. The commission heard appeals to the state supreme court, and its decisions, once approved by the court, had the authority of a final judgment. The commissioners operated as three-man courts, which were for all practical purposes divisions of Nebraska's highest bench. The judges, at the urging of Pound's former partner, Lionel C. Burr, selected him as one of the commissioners in April 1901. The youngest of the nine men, Pound had reached the top of the Nebraska legal profession at the early age of thirty.[29]

The appointment to the commission was a magnificent opportunity for Pound. It provided him with the title, professional standing, and perquisites of judicial office, the common law role to which, he insisted, "dignity, authority, and eminence" belonged as a matter "of right." He spent two and one-half years in the pleasant role of appellate judge, for the commissioners and judges were virtually indistinguishable, and judicial office proved to be a congenial setting for his intellectual development. The cases that came before him seldom had great social significance or dramatic appeal, but he often found meaningful questions in ordinary problems, and the opinions he wrote revealed the direction of his emerging legal philosophy.

An unresolved dualism appeared in Pound's judicial opinions, and it would persist as his ideas matured in the years ahead. His intellectual loyalties, divided between competing themes, were at once instrumental and organic, catholic and parochial, venturesome and defensive. Clad in the robes he had celebrated, Pound displayed a passion for common law fundamentals. At the same time, his opinions showed movement toward some advanced positions, and there were suggestions of the sociological jurisprudence to come. He was a pragmatist who argued that man could actively mold his legal system, but he also insisted that common law traditions and modern professional imperatives provided self-contained mechanisms for structuring legal change. The ambivalence, however, was not immediately apparent, for Pound's ideas lacked the systematic development that would place him in the vanguard of modern jurisprudence. His opinions as a commissioner were merely glimpses of the future.[30]

The most advanced theme in Pound's work on the court was his denial that the law was a fixed body of immutable rules to be applied regardless of social consequences. He insisted that legal rules were and ought to be responsive to social change, a position that challenged current professional assumptions. In a mundane case involving a disputed will, he paused for a moment to consider the nature of the legal system in which a common law judge decided controversies. The theory underlying the Anglo-American legal system, he announced from the bench, "is that the law consists, not in the actual rules enforced by decisions of the courts at any one time, but the principles from which these rules flow; that old principles are applied to new cases, and the rules resulting from such application are modified from time to time as changed conditions and new states of fact require."[31] Each doctrine in a legal system was related to its social universe, just as each plant in the floral covering was related to its larger natural environment. There was life in law as in botany, and both were characterized by continuous development. These ideas stood in marked contrast to the accepted wisdom of Langdell, that the law was a self-contained and gapless system from which an inexorable logic derived inevitable conclusions.

Darwinism gave Pound a sense of dynamism in nature, and in combination with his study of Roman law and continental legal systems, encouraged him to accept diversity and mutability in law. He realized that the common law did not alone constitute the legal universe. Shortly after he became a commissioner, he drew on this insight when a Catholic bishop sought to enjoin a priest from exercising his clerical functions. Pound insisted that a "religious organization must determine its own polity" and held that the bishop could obtain an injunction to prevent the priest from acting contrary to the demands of his superior. He settled the issue by examining the intricacies of canon law, and noted that it borrowed many of its rules and methods from the inquisitorial system of Roman law. Within its restricted sphere, the system enjoyed legitimacy, even though it violated legal principles "which, through familiarity, we are prone to think part of the order of nature."[32]

In these two opinions, involving such diverse problems as disputed wills and disputed clerical obligation, Pound's assumptions were both traditional and innovative, and he demonstrated a tendency to employ daring conceptualization in the service of ordinary, accepted conclusions. His arguments contained vital elements of his later sociological jurisprudence: legal rules were flexible, required adjustment to a changing environment, and were not uniformly fundamental. But fundamental principles did exist. The rules and their application might change, but "the principles from which these rules flow" were more permanent. Furthermore, Pound used the most liberating elements in his thought for limited purposes. In the case involving dissent within a Catholic diocese, he employed uncommonly sophisticated insights to defend a common legal position. Most nineteenth-century American judges sustained the church hierarchy against internal challenges in suits involving religions with elaborate ecclesiastical structures. Pound's opinion introduced a new subtlety and a broader perspective into that conclusion, but it did not alter the conclusion. Thus, at an early stage in his development, Pound linked his most unconventional insights with conclusions that either defended, or only slightly changed, established practices.

The pragmatic element in Pound's thought did not guarantee any specific substantive conclusion, but it prevented him from falling victim to an arid literalism. He knew that law must be reasonable if it were to be sound. Nebraska had a statute requiring a person who purchased land at a tax sale to pay the county treasurer immediately. Pound refused to accept an argument that penalized a buyer for late payment simply because the county treasurer was not ready to collect. He declared that the statute "must be given a reasonable construction consistent with the exigencies of business." County treasurers had to file innumerable papers in what often seemed an interminable process before they were prepared to receipt the purchaser's payment. "It must be apparent," he concluded, "that there is a limit to the number of payments any treasurer and his deputies can receive in any one day under these statutory requirements. We ought not to ask purchasers to pay faster than the proper officials can take their money."[33]

The testing of legal doctrine by its actual impact rather than by its internal logic—this approach reflected methods that Pound had developed in botany. In both law and natural science, he challenged narrowly deductive schemes of analysis, and urged an inductive approach that assessed neglected relationships and consequences. It was in this pragmatic spirit that Pound successfully eliminated from the law of trusts a troublesome fiction that was sound in logic but ludicrous in life.

In the early nineteenth century, English courts had introduced two novel assumptions into a familiar principle of fiduciary obligation. There was universal agreement among lawyers that a bank could be held liable for participation in a breach of trust if it knowingly accepted an unlawful deposit of trust funds. But courts also concluded that money could not be traced after it had been deposited, and that the initial withdrawal that a bank made following a particular deposit consisted of the bank's corporate funds. Those conclusions had a measure of credibility, but situations emerged in which their mechanical application neutralized accepted standards of liability. When, for example, a bank successfully invested the first withdrawal from wrongfully mingled funds, but liquidated the rest of its holdings, its liability for accepting an unlawful deposit was meaningless. If the beneficiary could not reach the product of the first withdrawal, there were no assets left to attach.[34] Nebraska law followed the English practice and gave Pound an opportunity to attack the triumph of legal logic over legal consequences.

A Lincoln bank knowingly accepted an unlawful deposit of five thousand dollars in municipal funds. After the money was unlawfully mingled with the other assets of the bank, it spent a portion of the deposit for the purchase of securities. A few months later, the bank failed and went into receivership. Its only remaining assets were the recently purchased securities, and the receiver sold them for $3,334.37. The city, as beneficiary, sought to obtain these funds, but the trial court ruled unfavorably. On appeal, Pound held that the funds from the sale of the securities belonged to the city. He replaced confused Nebraska precedent with a new rule of law, attempting "to wipe out the old dogma that money had no earmark, and to substitute the sensible rule that whenever trust property enters into a mass . . . so long as the trust property remains in or forms a part of such mass, [the beneficiary] has a claim or charge thereon to that extent."[35] Thus when the bank changed its assets from cash to securities, wrongfully mingled funds went into the purchase of the latter. The city of Lincoln could trace its funds to the securities, and since Pound ruled that the beneficiary could reach the product of the first withdrawal, it collected the total amount from the sale of the securities. This was a doctrine that would enjoy widespread acceptance in the future, and one of its first exponents was a young judge on an obscure appellate court in a jurisdiction not far removed from the frontier.

Pound was anxious to eliminate unreasonable fictions, but he was more enthusiastic about reforms in the administration of justice. Modern society required some modifications in substantive law, but an improved legal profession was the best guarantee of legal reform. As a commissioner, Pound continued to encourage the development of effective trial practice, a logical extension of his work in organizing the state bar association. He was quick both to compliment able attorneys and to condemn incompetent attorneys who pleaded cases before him. In one instance he remarked with great pleasure that "we have been furnished with unusually careful and elaborate briefs in which a number of points . . . are exhaustively discussed."[36] But he had no patience with careless work. In another case that came to his attention, the losing party moved for a mistrial on the ground that his attorney had not represented him in court. The attorney had been present at a preliminary hearing at which the judge set the date of trial, but he either misunderstood or forgot when the trial was to be held. Pound refused to grant a new trial, arguing that the "business of the courts must move, and counsel must take notice of orders duly made and entered."[37] Uniform standards of practice were indispensable elements in the development of a cohesive bar, and courts could act as a regulatory mechanism for ensuring an emerging professionalism.

Providing a measure of discipline for the bar was not the only important judicial function. As the central agent in the legal process, the judge gave law its basic character, direction, and definition. Pound's view of the judge's role was similar to the position taken by John Chipman Gray, one of his professors at Harvard. Gray argued that the judge played an extremely creative role in deciding the merits of a case. Pound, like Gray, accepted judge-made law as a fact of life. "We have only to turn to the annotations of our public statute books," he announced from the bench with unusual frankness, "to see that scarcely less law is made by construction and interpretation than by direct legislative enactment."[38]

In addition to his continued concern with bar reform as an instrument of legal reform and his approval of a judiciary that dominated the legal process, Pound's attitude toward the legislature also showed his affection for common law fundamentals. Legislators, he believed, stood in the shadow of the men wearing robes. Most lawyers at the turn of the century were hostile to statutes and took the position that they represented alien intrusions into the common law. Ralph W. Breckenridge, a Lincoln attorney, echoed the conventional wisdom when he argued that "the less of legislative ignorance and inexperience that is crystalized into statutes the better."[39] Pound was not so hostile to the legislature, but he was no friend of statutory law. In construing an amendment to a statute, he noted that "the restatement and amendment took the usual unfortunate form of tacking on a new provision without endeavoring to reconcile it to the original section."[40] Pound's subdued sarcasm indicated his disdain for the lawmaking qualifications of a legislature. His description of the "usual" legislative technique in amending statutes as a process of careless addition made clear his feeling that legislatures decided without deliberation. The judge-centered view of law to which Pound had been exposed at home and at Harvard had taken effect.

Although Pound was critical of statute law, he was less suspicious than most lawyers, and he accepted the legislature as a legitimate agency of the lawmaking process. He recognized that not all legislative initiatives were attacks on the bench, and he adopted generous canons of constitutional construction when reviewing challenges to Nebraska statutes. Nebraska had a law that made it illegal for individuals or businesses to form combinations to restrain trade, but it specifically exempted labor unions. When the Nebraska Retail Lumber Dealers' Association, charged with violating the law, protested that it was unconstitutional class legislation, Pound sustained the statute in a tone recalling James Bradley Thayer's injunction that reasonable doubts be resolved in favor of the legislature. Pound agreed that the legislature could not make an unreasonable classification and arbitrarily exempt persons and groups from statutory prohibitions that operated upon others engaged in similar activities. The statute in question, he argued, was a proper exercise of legislative power; the exemption of labor unions was a reasonable classification. The statute attempted to restrain conspiracies designed to control the manufacture, sale, and transportation of goods. "Labor and skill," he declared, "are not articles of commerce,—at least not in the same sense as the articles thereby produced; and we think the classification which distinguishes between them, and provides for a diversity of legislation with respect to them, is reasonable and proper." Moreover, Pound felt that the provision exempting labor unions was not really necessary; the spirit and intent of the statute led clearly to such an exemption. "The section in question," he concluded, "is inserted, rather, out of abundance of caution, to prevent judicial extension of the terms of the act beyond its scope and purpose, than to grant a privilege or immunity to persons who would otherwise fall within its terms."[41] He was probably thinking about the federal judiciary's construction of the Sherman Act, in which a statute designed to prevent monopolies was used to undermine trade unions and collective bargaining.

Pound was willing to give a broad construction to the police power, the authority of a state over the health, welfare, and morals of its citizens. Omaha had an ordinance, passed under the authority of a Nebraska statute, that made it unlawful to distribute handbills or literature on any "public street, alley, sidewalk or public grounds." Violators could be fined up to twenty dollars. A person was fined under the measure, and he charged that it violated freedom of speech. On appeal, Pound denied that the ordinance placed an unconstitutional burden on free speech. It was "manifestly a police regulation" designed to prevent the accumulation of trash, a problem that was growing acute in Omaha and other American cities. He reasoned that an exercise of the police power was not invalid if it merely affected some constitutional right in an incidental manner. These rights were not absolute; they admitted of some compromise where questions of public health were involved. Pound was not an enemy of civil liberties, but he was impatient with the casuistry that marred constitutional debate at the turn of the century. He looked behind the abstractions of legal argument and rejected the mechanical application of constitutional principles to situations in which they had only marginal relevance. "The test in such cases," Pound contended, "is whether the regulation in question is a *bone fide* exercise of the police power or an arbitrary and unreasonable interference with the rights of individuals under the guise of police regulation."[42]

Nebraska experienced dramatic changes at the turn of the century, and Pound had to consider the relationship between social change and traditional legal arrangements. Technological advances like the expansion of telephone service often had a profound impact on private interests. A property holder sought an injunction to prevent a telephone company from installing poles and lines because the construction workers had injured some of her trees. After a lower court dismissed her demand, she appealed to the Nebraska Supreme Court. Pound held that she had a legitimate complaint and could sue the company for damages if her property were seriously injured. But property holders were not entitled to enjoin such construction and impede social progress. "To hold otherwise," he observed, "would probably prevent many useful public improvements."[43]

Pound insisted that property rights must be considered within the context of social welfare, but he did not believe that there was an inherent conflict between property and the public interest. In some cases, social progress required adjustments by vested interests, but for the most part, it was wise social policy to guarantee the stability of property and contracts. In cases involving competing property interests and commercial relations, where no overwhelming public interest was present, he thought that existing law should be applied rigidly.

A case involving a contested will provided a vehicle for this argument. A husband had given a land title to his wife.

When she died, her children inherited the property. The husband sued to recover it on the ground that he and his wife had made a verbal agreement that the property, at her death, would pass to his daughter by a former wife. Pound decided that the will conveying the land to her children was strong evidence of the wife's intentions; only evidence to the contrary that was "clear, unequivocal and convincing" could modify the language of the will. Pound argued:

> Much more certainty and conclusiveness are requisite than in ordinary cases. . . . If, as there is much to indicate, he acted under a mistake of law in supposing that . . . the property would pass to his daughter . . . yet such mistake did not and does not constitute any legal ground for withdrawing his completed gift. Neither does it authorize us to impress the property with a trust which the parties themselves did not create.[44]

Property and commerce required such a high degree of stability that Pound virtually refused to recognize the possibility of unreasonable precedents. It seemed that in these branches of law no consistency was a foolish one, an attitude that Pound revealed in two cases regarding unenforceable contracts. A Nebraska farmer placed his cattle under the care of a second farmer. The two men signed a contract stating that if the cattle were injured, they would arbitrate the extent of the damage before taking a case to court. This was a recognized practice in many jurisdictions. An impressive series of decisions held that although a contract could not provide that the whole question of liability be arbitrated, contending parties could reach a preliminary agreement on the amount of damages before seeking a judicial determination of liability. Many American courts followed this position, but Pound held that such contracts were improper in Nebraska and could not be enforced in its courts:

> Whatever distinction may be made elsewhere between arbitration generally and arbitration as to damages only, it is well settled in this state that a provision in a contract requiring arbitration, whether of all damages arising under the contract, or only of the amount of damages sustained by the parties thereto, will not be enforced, and that refusal to arbitrate is not available to the parties in an action growing out of the contract.[45]

His abrupt disposition of the issue became clearer in a similar case where, in a concurring opinion, Pound questioned the wisdom of the rule but refused to sanction a judicial change. "Were the question a new one," he admitted, "I do not believe this court would take the stand to which it is now committed. . . . [But] where these peculiar doctrines work no harm, certainty and consistency are no less important than agreement with other courts."[46] Pound's willingness to bow to the binding force of an unreasonable precedent revealed a sympathy for stability in the law of property rather than a generous attitude toward idiosyncrasies in local law.

Pound preferred a rigid application of precedent in cases involving property, but he was not willing to torture an old rule in order to adapt it to novel, inappropriate circumstances. When it was necessary to fashion a new rule of commercial law for Nebraska, he seemed to strive for a principle consistent with the exigencies of business life. A Nebraska lower court had held that a promissory note requiring a debtor to pay exchange costs was not negotiable. This type of instrument obligated the debtor to pay a specified sum of money or some other object of value; the exchange clause created the additional obligation of paying the costs of transferring the promised item that a bank or commercial clearing house might charge. In refusing to uphold such an instrument, the lower court assumed that the exchange payment rendered the amount of the note uncertain. Pound reversed the lower court decision, arguing that the exchange requirement did not impair the negotiability of the note. He observed that American business activities were "carried on more or less in subordination to certain financial centres, to which and from which money is constantly flowing." Those financial centers were important agencies in the economy, and the law should account for their existence. Pound insisted that the exchange charge was merely incidental to the amount payable, and did not affect the size of the debt itself. "These questions," he maintained, "are primarily questions of business and business usage, and so far as not foreclosed by any established course of decision, ought to be resolved in a liberal spirit, to promote the interests of business."[47]

The problems of procedure provided another important staple of legal controversy for Pound, and his opinions demonstrated the tendency to use fresh insights in the service of traditional values. He was unwilling to follow the bar in its blind acceptance of antiquated practice rules, and he criticized procedural artificiality as he had earlier criticized the sterile taxonomy of pre-Darwinian botany. But Pound's defense of procedural innovation allowed him to combine an attack on empty abstractions with an attempt to strengthen the common law judiciary. He sanctioned significant changes in the mechanics of legal argument and discovery because exaggerated procedural requirements strangled the judiciary and diverted its attention from substantive issues. The reputation of judges suffered when their energies were exhausted on procedural questions.

American procedural law, Pound realized, required a systematic reexamination, and he winced at the cavalier treatment it often received. He was particularly critical of the shoddy, free-for-all methods that characterized frontier Nebraska and abhorred the once-popular tendency to blink at serious procedural error if the verdict were "substantially just." Chief Justice Samuel Maxwell of the Nebraska Supreme Court, who was especially fond of that doctrine, refused to grant new trials if "substantial justice" had been done. "It was the feeling of the bar," Pound observed wryly in later years, "that substantial justice *according to law* would have been a better and safer criterion and that the phrase was sometimes used to cover up disinclination to go into the case [italics added]."[48]

Pound demanded a new precision in procedure, but he objected to an exaggerated literalism. He regarded both carelessness and sophistry with contempt and wanted litigants protected from a thicket of artificial technicalities. Throughout his tenure as a commissioner, Pound adopted a generous attitude toward pleadings (the pretrial documents defining a cause of action). A defeated party in a case that he reviewed sought reversal of a judgment on the ground that his opponent's pleadings were defective. The opponent had originally initiated the suit in his capacity as a guardian. He had described himself as "Levi Bennett, guardian of Emery W. Tuttle" but had not expressly stated that he was suing "as guardian." Pound refused to reverse the verdict, arguing that "so long as the plaintiff describes himself as guardian, alleges his appointment as such, and . . . shows clearly an intent to sue in his representative capacity, we may fairly so construe his pleading, notwithstanding his failure to say expressly that he sues as guardian."[49] In another case involving challenged pleadings, a party who omitted essential elements of fact in his pleadings had corrected the omission through allegations during the course of the trial. Pound again refused to upset the verdict, thereby sanctioning an amendment to pleadings during the trial itself.[50] Amendments to pleadings were by no means allowed by all contemporary judges, but Pound realized that the practice imparted greater flexibility to trials and made it easier to dispose of a case at the trial level.[51]

Another aspect of procedure in which Pound demanded less artificiality involved the use of depositions, written documents containing testimony taken out of court. Both parties to a suit had taken depositions from a single witness. One party introduced in evidence a deposition taken by his opponent; the latter objected, but the trial judge overruled his objection. On appeal, Pound held that the judge had properly denied the objection. Either party, he declared, could use depositions taken by his opponent. Pound overruled a contrary precedent, and Nebraska became one of the earliest states to employ this procedural innovation. He observed that "the common law originally was very strict in confining each party to his own means of proof, and . . . regarded a trial as a cock-fight, wherein he won whose advocate was the gamest bird with the longest spurs. But we have come to take a more liberal view and have done away with most of those features of trials which gave rise to that reproach."[52]

His acceptance of amendments to pleadings and his treatment of depositions revealed a deep concern for the performance of trial courts, an unusual interest at a time when legal philosophers preferred to theorize about a purer law at the appellate level. But Pound realized that trials must be more than preludes to an appeal if the lower court were to play a useful and respected role. As an enemy

of both inadequate performance and artificiality in procedure, he saw clearly that the standards of the bar and the
trial bench suffered when procedural issues triumphed
over substantive questions. Pound was unwilling to allow
methods of appealing a verdict that encouraged incompetent trial practice. An appellate court should exclude evidence and issues that had not been raised in the lower court
but appeared for the first time on appeal. "It is fundamental in our practice," he wrote, "that a cause must be tried
upon appeal on the same issues on which it was tried in the
first instance."[53] An appeal was merely a reexamination of
the issues presented in a lower court; it did not give an
appellant the right to present a new case. Pound seemed
disturbed by the possibility that attorneys might be less
efficient if they were allowed to present a different case on
appeal. "While we ought to be very liberal in construing
objections to claims made in the county court . . . it would be
most unfortunate to make the proceedings in the county
court formal and farcical." He concluded that "no opportunity should be afforded for mock contests in which
neither side develops its case in good faith, followed by a
substantial trial for the first time on appeal."[54]

As a former trial lawyer, Pound knew that excessive procedural technicality in lower courts merely exaggerated the
inherent anarchy of the jury. He wanted greater precision
in law, but he insisted that the law must not be so precise as
to be incomprehensible, particularly when jurors must understand and apply it. In a case where the judge had read
the pleadings as his instructions to the jury, Pound declared
that such a practice warranted reversal of the verdict if the
judge's action resulted in prejudice against the losing party.
"The pleadings," he said, "are supposed to be drawn in a
more or less artificial and technical style, addressed to the
understanding of trained judges. The instructions are sup-

posed to be drawn in a plain, direct and simple style, addressed to the understanding of laymen."[55] The juror, unfamiliar with the language of the law, could not be expected to understand the subtleties of the pleadings. Furthermore, a lack of guidance merely compounded the nascent rebelliousness of the jury, for as Pound shrewdly observed in a later case, "juries, as a rule, need no encouragement to take such a line as they think will lead to a just result."[56]

Pound's experience as a jury lawyer in the 1890s had given him many insights into the nature of jury-made law. He was not a victim of the comforting illusion that the refined wisdom of appellate courts informed the entire administration of justice. Although theory held that the jury found the facts and then applied the appropriate rules of law, jurors often made their own law when they disagreed with the instructions. An incident on the circuit had left Pound with a vivid impression of a jury's capacity for disregarding instructions. He was arguing a case for a railroad that was suing a private party. Railroads usually appeared as defendants being sued for negligence by dissatisfied shippers, but here a road appeared as plaintiff. Pound was rather unsure of his case but the jury promptly returned a verdict for his client. After court had adjourned he talked with the foreman, a huge Scandinavian farmer, and asked how the jury had reached its verdict. The foreman laughed and, warming to his subject, told Pound that they had decided to find for the plaintiff and soak the railroad. They knew better than to follow the judge's instructions, because it had been obvious that he had tried to confuse them. The judge said that the railroad was the plaintiff, but everyone knew that was impossible.[57]

The work of the Nebraska Supreme Court Commission was completed in November 1903; it had cleared the docket and performed its duties with skill and efficiency.[58] Pound's brief tenure as a commissioner gave him an invaluable opportunity to observe the operations of a court and enabled him to bring judicial experience as well as the experience of teaching and practice to the study of law. Although his legal philosophy did not yet possess its ultimate sophistication and depth, Pound's maturing insights provided a framework for his later sociological jurisprudence. But not all of Pound's suggestive ideas were complementary. Some of his intellectual commitments were instrumentalist and relativistic, whereas others were organic conceptions that sustained the timeless, self-regulating mechanisms of a received tradition. His legal theory lacked internal cohesiveness, and the divisions would haunt him in the future.

Pound's family, education, and career provided a complex, contradictory background for his intellectual development. His parents encouraged an experimental, questioning attitude, and taught him to value the life of the mind, but they urged him to pursue a conventional career and to adopt established political values. His Harvard days were exciting, but his most unusual professors were still servants of the common law tradition. His career as a lawyer in a rapidly developing state impressed him with man's potential to shape his surroundings, but Pound's electrifying success corresponded to the conventional definition of career development. As a leading member of the Nebraska State Bar Association, he participated in an important movement for institutional change, but the reform was designed to allow the legal profession to control legal development. He accepted the need for change and urged that law be considered in terms of its social consequences, but his common law enthusiasm gave him a suspicion of statutes, a presumption that social welfare and the security of property were synonymous, a belief that there were fundamental principles from which flexible rules were derived, and a fondness for the judiciary as the dominant mechanism in the administration of justice. Finally, his science contained similar contradictory impulses. The "new botany" was an evolutionary, empirical science that focused on dynamic environmental relationships rather than taxonomic abstractions, but there were deterministic themes in the Botanical Survey and the *Phytogeography*. The internal, self-regulating mechanisms in law had a parallel in botany, where a "climax" gave natural selection a teleological fixity.

The unresolved dualism in Pound's thought did not emerge as a problem during his tenure as a commissioner. His ideas were still in a formative stage, and none of the elements had received the systematic exploration that would reveal their inherent incompatibility. He was unaware of his contradictory intellectual loyalties and did not consider the potential impasse between his instrumental and organic impulses. For the moment, his optimism, self-confidence, and visible success made any doubt impossible, and he left the Nebraska Supreme Court Commission with complete assurance of continued intellectual and professional triumphs.

5

The Law at Nebraska

On 13 June 1903 the regents of the state university notified Pound that he had been elected dean of the Nebraska College of Law. He received the call with some misgivings, for the offer had certain troublesome features. The salary of $2,500 was far less than he could have earned in practice; his marriage three years earlier and his father's poor health made financial considerations more urgent. But Pound's primary concern was his fear of being isolated. The job might be too limiting for one who had such boundless energy, and it might prevent him from playing the wider professional role to which he was accustomed. He had no intention, he confided to a friend, of retiring at thirty-three.[1]

But the deanship was not a professional graveyard. By the early twentieth century the law school was coming into its own, and the bar no longer considered it a useless adjunct to apprenticeship. Arthur F. Mullen, a Democratic national committeeman in the 1930s, recalled that formal training was indispensable for an aspiring Nebraska youth of the late 1890s. "The old days of hit-and-miss admission to the bar were gone. Ten years earlier I might have gone into practice without formal education or definite examination. Now I had to have them both."[2] Since the Nebraska State Bar Association had given its blessing to academic legal training, a dean of the state law school could operate well within the established professional power structure. Pound would not have taken a position that made him an outsider, and his acceptance of the deanship signified the coming of age of legal education in Nebraska.

Improving the quality of the College of Law was a challenge to his imagination and endurance. The college was only a two-year school, and it was staffed largely by part-time teachers, Lincoln attorneys who gave one or two courses of lectures. Pound's predecessor, M. B. Reese, was satisfied with existing conditions and saw no reason to alter them. "It is believed," he argued, "that the arrangement of studies and topics could not be improved by any radical changes, and I know of no disposition to make the attempt." Although better law schools were instituting three-year curriculums, Dean Reese insisted that the program at Nebraska should remain a two-year course because its attractiveness to prospective students would lead to increased enrollments. Additional students would help accomplish the dean's primary mission—to make the college a source of revenue.[3] "While this college is not yet self-supporting," he reported in 1899, "a consideration of the revenues now being derived from it, clearly demonstrates that, could it receive a liberal support from the state for a few years, it could soon be made to yield handsome returns, financially."[4] Dean Reese's final recommendation to the regents, significantly, was that tuition should be increased; the traffic could bear a higher charge.

But not all of the university's administrators saw higher education as a business proposition. Certainly E. Benjamin

Andrews, the dynamic chancellor, did not have such an entrepreneurial attitude. Andrews had previously been president of Brown University, and he had transformed it into a modern institution. He increased the faculty four-fold, introduced a vast array of new subjects, created the women's college, and made the graduate school a reality. "My impression," wrote Alexander Meiklejohn, another imaginative college president, "is that no one in the last half-century has so captivated, so dominated an American college community as he did."[5]

After becoming chancellor at Nebraska in 1900, Andrews established the medical college and the teachers' college, and in the eight years of his administration increased the faculty eight-fold. Many of the most renowned scholars in the school's history came during these years. In addition to Pound, Andrews recruited prominent social scientists like Edward A. Ross and George E. Howard as well as younger men like Hartley Burr Alexander, the poet, and the versatile Alvin Johnson. Under Andrews' able leadership, Nebraska became an exciting institution with great presence as well as great potential. "Whatever he touched," recalled Edward A. Ross, "he freshened with his exuberant personality. I found him an unfailing source of inspiration."[6]

Consistent with the dynamism of Andrews' leadership, the new dean of the law school brought a fresh spirit to a complacent division of the university. He advanced a reform program that would transform legal education and, consequently, determine the development of the profession itself. The first task was to eliminate "the strange notion of an inherent natural right of the citizen to practice law." Pound had witnessed the damage that ill-prepared attorneys could inflict. He urged lawyers to realize that their collective future depended on the success of the professional school. Although the organized bar was no longer hostile to formal legal education, the sentiment persisted in some quarters that office-taught law was superior to school-taught law. Pound realized at the outset that he must encourage the profession's growing identification with the mission of the law school.[7]

Many problems facing legal education were generated from within the academy, and Pound acknowledged that law schools must put their own houses in order. Friends of legal education must eliminate the "money-making school." One could not learn law in an institution devoted to profits rather than professionalism. Even the more respectable institutions often suffered from an excessive reliance on part-time professors. Law schools needed a trained staff of teachers who devoted their efforts to students and scholarship rather than to practice. Pound was extremely conscious of the Harvard example; the business of teaching, he insisted, was "too serious and too exacting an undertaking to be an appendix to the daily tasks of a practitioner."

Pound's demand for a full-time faculty of scholars to replace a part-time staff of practitioners did not represent an attempt to create a school that would ignore practical problems. He was determined that the school should "teach primarily the principles by which courts decide controversies" and not mislead students with artificial systems and imaginary doctrine. True scholarship was not an investigation of the obscure, and scholarly teachers brought genuine expertise to their classes. The part-time teacher was only a partly prepared teacher, one who too often substituted expediency for expertise. Law schools could not elevate the profession by encouraging carelessness parading under the banner of practicality.

The teacher-practitioner symbolized a preoccupation

with routine affairs that Pound deplored, for he was convinced that the law school must do more than "teach law and make lawyers." In order to produce graduates who were more than technicians, legal study had to be informed by disciplines such as history and philosophy. "Doubtless many will smile," Pound mused, "when I speak . . . of philosophy." Yet attitudes about law merely reflected more fundamental assumptions that were often unexpressed and unrecognized. Laws were not created in a vacuum, and they must not be studied in a vacuum. "To-day the philosophy of law is the philosophy of the law that is." Pound was not arguing for a lifeless jurisprudence; he was arguing for pragmatism in law.

Pound did not consider academic innovation an end in itself. His program for reform in legal education was an attempt to introduce major changes in the larger world of law. The law school was to be the principal mechanism for giving the bar a new professional cohesiveness and more sophisticated modes of analysis. By making recruitment and training more systematic, the law school would be an indispensable element in the drive for professional consolidation. The new prestige of legal education would make the teaching of law a respected professional role, and faculties would develop more depth, expertise, and impact. A pragmatic jurisprudence would eventually replace existing mechanical conceptions, for the new corps of professors would give students an appreciation for the social dimension of law.

Legal education offered a medium for eliminating the fragmentation and outmoded ideas that plagued the bar, and it could provide lawyers with the vision that would make them creative agents in legal reform. Pound was convinced that one can not expect more than the conventional patchwork amendment and haphazard code-making from a bar of practical lawyers, educated in nothing beyond the exigencies of practice. However diligent, however patriotic, unless they are trained to more than accurate application of the existing law to such facts as are presented to them, they can not be expected to make the legislators whom the next stage of our law imperatively requires. If the law schools fail us here, whither shall we look?[8]

The reconstruction of the Nebraska College of Law began immediately, and by the conclusion of his first year as dean, Pound had made so many changes that the school was hardly recognizable. A revision of the entrance requirements exchanged quantity for quality. The school now required applicants to possess a high school education, a policy that caused a decided reduction in numbers, for the former standards of admission asked only an ability to read and write. Edith Abbott, who had been a law student at Nebraska, recalled that Pound acknowledged the ability of all to write, but questioned the ability of many to read. He argued that a high school education was neither an unreasonable nor a burdensome requirement. Since secondary schools were now readily accessible throughout the state, the requirement could not deter any reasonably ambitious student.[9]

The course of study was extended from two years to three. The additional year made it possible to introduce new subjects, and it also gave professors more time to improve existing courses. It enabled Pound to introduce the case method of study that he had learned at Harvard. Within two years he had established the technique throughout the school, thus contributing to the growth of the "Harvard system" in American legal education.[10]

Pound frequently reminded his students that a good lawyer must be more than a good advocate. He tried to balance the fascination of courtroom dramatics with a number of new courses in legal history, Roman law, international law, public law, and jurisprudence. There were some things, he insisted, that a lawyer cannot learn in an office; it was the task of the law school to provide them. The students recognized Pound as an example of his own teaching; the law school yearbook for 1906, dedicated to Pound, included a drawing of the dean standing with his hand on a stack of thick volumes bearing the titles Pedagogy, Languages, Architecture, Ancient History, Science, Medicine, Philosophy, and Literature.[11]

In addition to the general areas of legal education, a student also needed training in local practice and doctrine. To meet parochial needs Pound instituted elective courses in conveyancing, the Nebraska code, probate practice, and practice in the Nebraska Supreme Court.[12] He also created an elaborate system of practice courts in which all students were required to participate. The practice courts, modeled after the judicial system of Nebraska, included three justice courts, a district court in two divisions, and a supreme court. Students served as parties, witnesses, jurors, counsel, judges, and court officials. Pound attempted to make the practice courts as realistic as possible, reflecting the exigencies of actual practice rather than an ideal set of conditions. He supervised the activities with great care, and his background as a jury lawyer and appellate judge enabled him to give students a rare and realistic preview of the law in action.[13]

Throughout the Pound reforms ran a single theme

—although a lawyer must be a technician, he must be more than a technician, and he must never be isolated. A lawyer had to assume a vantage point outside the immediate problem and even outside the law itself to realize the full potential of his craft. Pound was determined to prevent a conflict between the law in books and the law in action, and he was equally determined that "students do not go forth with the notion that all the eccentricities of merely local practice are immutable portions of the legal order of nature. We must be careful," he cautioned, "not to give an enduring character to what is purely provincial."[14]

Pound's legal thinking kept pace with his reform activities. His ideas and attitudes, still relatively shapeless at the beginning of his tenure, matured rapidly during the Nebraska deanship. The first edition of his *Outlines of Lectures on Jurisprudence*, published in 1903 as he assumed his new duties, demonstrated that his progressive impulses still lacked systematic development. The volume was rather sparse, particularly when compared with later editions, and it disclosed little of its author's creative genius. It bore the revealing subtitle "Chiefly from the Analytical Standpoint," and the book was clearly the product of conventional systems of legal theory. Jurisprudence, declared Pound, "might be called: the comparative anatomy of developed systems of law."[15] There was no revolt here from the generally accepted view of John Austin, the nineteenth-century English jurist who limited the scope of jurisprudence to the internal operation of an existing legal system. In outlining the various theoretical positions, Pound presented as most important the analytical, the historical, and the metaphysical; by "metaphysical" he meant a vague collection of legal theories evincing larger philosophical concerns. He did describe a new theme that he called "critical jurisprudence," a method that dealt with "the ideal future of law in view of philosophy, analysis, and history, and of the nature, constitution, needs, and ideal future of society and of the state." Yet he buried the glimmer of sociological jurisprudence under a detailed examination of established traditions in legal philosophy.[16]

If the *Outlines* reflected an addiction to analytical jurisprudence, Pound's educational reforms revealed the creative potential of his mind. He stood at a crossroads as he began his duties as dean, committed to an established tradition in jurisprudence, but willing to experiment and ever open to the intellectual stimulation of the university community. The advanced positions he had explored as a judge could be pursued with less hesitancy at the law school, where fewer traditional restraints existed.

The University of Nebraska at the turn of the century was an extraordinary academic community, quite capable of influencing the subtle chemistry of ideas. Although many American universities were centers of complacency and caution, Nebraska offered a rare haven for dissent. Chancellor Andrews had had a controversial career as an economist, and he drew similar rebels to Lincoln.[17] Thus there were other minds at Nebraska against which Pound could test his own, and from two social scientists, Edward A. Ross and George E. Howard, he received significant shoves in the direction of sociological jurisprudence.

Ross came to Nebraska in 1901 shortly after he had been eased out at Stanford for advocating free silver and attacking business control of government. The outspoken scholar, a militant crusader for social science and social reform, was the leading public spokesman for modern American sociology. Ross was a disciple of Lester Ward, who was a constant friend and counselor. Like his mentor, Ross emphasized social interaction and social change rather than institutional sociology. A flinty man who loved an argument, he delighted in trying to convert others. But Ross was no dogmatist; he prefaced his textbooks with the hope that they would soon be obsolete, and the sooner the better. In his missionary work he was a zealot only for the spirit of the new social science with its pragmatic emphasis on process rather than finality, the actual rather than the Ideal, and life rather than logic.[18]

Ross and Pound had become friends when the latter was a supreme court commissioner, and the friendship ripened after Pound became dean. Both were members of "The Ten," a group that dined together once a month, and at which the two were frequently locked in debate over the merits of the existing system of law. Ross recalled Commissioner Pound as a "champion of judges and courts [who] pounced on me whenever I swung at the current administration of justice."[19] As a social reformer, Ross was critical of the judiciary's hostility to reform; as a social scientist, he was critical of the tendency to subordinate experience to logic.

At first Pound seemed impervious to Ross's suggestions. "I did not," the sociologist remembered, "imagine I was 'making a dent' on him."[20] Doubtless his criticism of the courts was more general and more harsh than Pound would ever be willing to accept. But Pound was moving toward the position that law was a product of social forces and social philosophies, and that courts, as social institutions, must adapt law to the changing requirements of the era. Ross was not the key to Pound's intellectual development, but his was an important voice at a time when Pound was searching for a new sense of direction in jurisprudence, and Pound never forgot his contribution. "I believe," he wrote Ross in 1906, "you have set me in the path the world is moving in." Later, when his academic star was rising, he told Ross that if he produced a genuinely modern legal theory, he would "not fail to state from whom all my inspiration has come."[21]

Pound was particularly impressed with *Sin and Society*, a popular essay in which Ross urged Americans to think of morality as a social phenomenon rather than a series of abstract vices. "I have been especially interested in your 'Sin and Society,' " Pound acknowledged, "because of the collateral legal problem." The impact of law, like morality, was often a function of social dynamics. Pound also encountered Ross's organic conception of society, which provided a parallel to evolutionary ideas Pound had learned as a botanist. "We have grown into an organic society," declared Ross, "in which the welfare of all is at the mercy of each." Society was a composite of interdependent forces rather than a collection of independent actors. There were "viewless filaments of interrelation," he wrote, "that bind us together." Because the game of life was a product of the social environment, Ross insisted that "the establishment of the rules of the game lies within the province of society." The public had a right to identify its own requirements and to create an appropriate code of behavior. Men, he believed, could exert a measure of control over their collective destiny. The intellect, he had learned from Lester Ward, was the supreme product of the evolutionary process, and as a result, social planning was a way of giving continuing significance to the evolutionary hypothesis. Although Ross was a democrat, he accepted Ward's injunction that modern society required expert guidance, and he declared that "social defense is coming to be a matter for the expert."[22]

George E. Howard was another faculty member from whom Pound drew fresh insight. Howard, an old friend of the Pound family, had been lured away from Nebraska as one of the fifteen professors who formed Stanford's first faculty. He favored a socially productive intelligence and insisted that the pursuit of science for its own sake was "very much of a humbug." While at Stanford, he urged that university to "adjust itself to the changing needs of an advancing civilization" and called for a "new humanism" defined in terms of social utility rather than aesthetic appeal.[23] Howard resigned from Stanford in response to Ross's dismissal, which he considered a violation of academic freedom. He returned to Nebraska at the urging of Chancellor Andrews and continued his productive career as a historian and social scientist. His insistence that knowledge must be of social value echoed a theme that Pound had first heard from Bessey, and it was perhaps for this reinforcement that Pound remembered Howard as an important influence on his intellectual development.[24]

Not all of his inspiration came from Nebraska sources. While he was sparring with Ross and Howard, he was also learning from a new school of jurists. He had once drawn inspiration from German botanists, and now, as a lawyer, he returned to German scholarship for new insight. Creative German jurists in the late nineteenth century had been developing effective challenges to the dominant legal theories. The most important of the new philosophers was Rudolf von Jhering, whose influence began to loom as a major factor in Pound's maturing thought. Although Pound had mentioned Jhering in the *Outlines*, the jurist had not occupied a prominent place. But his experience as dean and the stimulation of Ross and Howard provided more favorable conditions for Jhering's philosophy to work its magic. By the middle of 1904, his presence was an important element of Pound's legal progressivism.[25]

Jhering was the most creative legal thinker in the nineteenth century and the godfather of the American school of sociological jurisprudence.[26] The context in which he operated made his achievement seem even greater, for the German legal system was considered the most backward in western Europe, and German scholarship consisted of brilliant but sterile debates between Romanists and Germanists. The reigning historical school, led by Friedrich Karl von Savigny, taught that a nation's law was a unique product of its peculiar development. Historical jurists did not conceptualize law in the timeless categories of natural law theory, but law nevertheless became timeless in Burkean terms. Although the present legal system had evolved, the process of evolution seemed to have no continuing significance. Furthermore, purposive human effort could have little good influence on such organic development, and Savigny condemned legislation and codification as alien intruders in a process best fulfilled through the unmanipulated accretions of time.[27] Since the present could take care of itself, little attention was paid to the needs of practical jurisprudence. "Little was said," Max Rümelin recalled of his student days in the 1870s, "on the subject of how legal precepts originate in the needs of practical life and how they in turn affect practical life. . . . Only when the student turned to Jhering's writings . . . was he guided toward thinking in these terms."[28]

Jhering had been trained in the historical school, but even his earliest work, *The Spirit of the Roman Law* (1852-1865), rejected its extreme chauvinism. He insisted on a comparative approach spanning many legal systems and held that the study of law should be anthropological as well as analytical.[29] The seeds of revolt contained in the *Spirit* were nourished by Darwinism, and Jhering felt that his own research confirmed the existence of evolutionary principles in the development of law.[30] Contrary to the prevailing notion that legal growth was a seamless, effortless, and unnoticed process, he argued that "the life of the law is a struggle,—a struggle of nations, of the state power, of classes, of individuals."[31] Although sometimes misunderstood as an advocate of litigiousness and jungle ethics,

Jhering merely wanted to dramatize the fact that law responded to purpose, that it was a product of manipulation and competing interests.

The central concept in his jurisprudence was Purpose: "there is no legal rule which does not owe its origin to a purpose, i.e., to a practical motive." Purposes created Interests, which became the basis of law. Thus Purpose was the source for the rights that Interest asserted. Jhering's determinants of law were human actions rather than operations of the *Volksgeist*. The centrality of egoistical self-assertion in his system indicated an intellectual kinship with utilitarianism. "By means of pleasure and pain," he argued, in familiar Benthamite terms, "nature is able to guide us in the paths we should follow."[32]

Jhering was influenced by Jeremy Bentham, but he added a novel dimension to utilitarianism. Jhering was less sanguine than Bentham that men would serve social purposes by the enlightened pursuit of their own interests, and he insisted that enlightened self-interest must be made to serve larger social purposes. "Our whole culture," he asserted, "our whole history rests upon the realization of individual human existence for the purposes of the whole." He even developed a scheme of social interests which, although prolix, discursive, and incomplete, must have seemed suggestive to Pound, who later developed an elaborate theory of social interests.[33]

One of the continuous themes in Jhering's writings was the challenge that lawyers "abandon the delusion that it [law] is a system of legal mathematics, without any higher aim than a correct reckoning with conceptions." In addition to its artificiality, the "jurisprudence of conceptions" exhibited a fatal absolutism. No legal doctrine was timeless, and jurists must never overlook the "relativity of purpose." "The idea of the law," he wrote, "is an eternal Becoming;

but that which has Become must yield to the new Becoming."[34]

Pound regarded Jhering as the most creative theorist in the "new school of jurists" that was redefining legal theory, and he credited the Austrian intellectual with being "the pioneer in the work of superseding this jurisprudence of conceptions (*Begriffsjurisprudenz*) by a jurisprudence of results (*Wirklichkeitsjurisprudenz*). He insisted that . . . the first question should be, how will a rule or decision operate in practice?"[35] Jhering helped Pound develop a general sense of direction, but Pound was too independent to become a disciple. His early excursions into sociological jurisprudence bore the stamp of his unique mind and personality. The first philosophical fruits of the Nebraska deanship were clarion calls to action but not to revolution. They expressed dissatisfaction with aspects of the existing order, but offered no invitation to alter it in a radical fashion. Possessing the hesitancy of first steps, these new directions in Pound's thought were made more hesitant by the curious blend of boldness and caution that informed his very being.

His developing jurisprudence began with an established assumption, the familiar hostility of the common law to legislation. Unlike many lawyers, Pound was not consumed by this animosity, but he was suspicious of statutes. "There is little in legislation that is original," he avowed. "Legislatures imitate one another."[36] As a creature of the common law tradition, Pound chose to place his faith in judges rather than assemblymen. Legal history as he understood it had alternated between periods of development by judges and periods when legislators were dominant, and he concluded that law had been more vital when guided by the judiciary.[37]

The command theory of law, according to Pound, was an inevitable companion of legislation. When legislation dominated legal development, the command theory dominated legal philosophy. The doctrine, also known as legal positivism, held that law was simply a command given by a political superior to a political inferior. Pound considered the notion an amoral monstrosity that prevented the healthy growth of law. He argued for an alternative view that emphasized the conjunction of law and morals. Such theories of law had usually accompanied periods of development by judicial activity. "No conception," he insisted, "has been more fruitful in legal history than this notion that the foundation of law is in ideal or natural justice."[38]

Natural law theorists argued that there were absolute, unchanging principles to which temporal laws must correspond. This doctrine of a higher law provided an alternative to the moral neutrality of the command theory, which accepted the legitimacy of any existing pattern of legal obligation. Natural law theory, however, was no longer available for service. As early as 1895 Pound, captivated by the dynamic environmentalism of the new botany, had declared that natural law was dead.[39] Darwinism had undermined its mechanical, formalistic elements, and apologists for business had discredited its claims to superior morality. But Pound was optimistic about the future development of law in spite of the return of the initiative to legislatures at a time when natural law theory, the traditional opponent of positivism, was a shattered doctrine. A new jurisprudence, the sociological school, made the prospects of a legislative regime more promising.

Sociological jurisprudence emphasized the social forces in legal development, the relativity of legal doctrines to time and place, and the need for men to use law as an instrument for securing changing social interests. It substituted social requirements for *a priori* abstractions as the goals of the legal system and thus preserved the normative element in natural law without accepting its timelessness and formalism. Sociological jurisprudence could provide a new theoretical basis for legislation, and by freeing it from a dependence on a debilitating positivism, could make legislation more creative. "Law is not an end," wrote Pound with a phrase borrowed from Jhering, "but a means. A school which studies it as a social mechanism will do no little service if it but deliver us from the condition of dry rot which juristic thought has hitherto contracted in periods of enactment and codification, and preserve or restore the juristic ideals of reason and justice, which, for a time, we seem fated to lose or to forget."[40]

This defense of the new jurisprudence revealed Pound's attachment to the common law tradition, for he urged it as a method of preserving ideals inseparable from judge-made law. If the ideals were preserved, legislation would be more palatable. As an advocate of the new jurisprudence, he would not stray far from old traditions. Nevertheless, Pound was not a captive of every common law dogma. He admired the system, but he recognized the need for pruning such superfluous dogmas as individualism.

Almost every feature of the common law in the nineteenth century revealed the impact of individualism. The common law had long made the individual a focal point for the development of doctrine, but nineteenth-century lawyers had framed new applications of individualism that Pound regarded as accidental rather than essential. The trial court, particularly in the United States, merely provided a public setting for inherently private combat. Public law questions were treated as mere controversies between private litigants. Pressing social needs were sacrificed to conceptions like "liberty of contract," which undermined labor legislation on the grounds that such laws interfered with the employee's right to bargain with an employer.

Pound did not object to the protection of individual rights, but he felt that the common law's excessive concern was anachronistic. "Men have changed their views," he declared, "as to the relative importance of the individual and society; but the common law has not." Where common law individualism was not anachronistic, it was frequently misplaced. Liberty of contract, conceived in the name of individualism, served only to aid in the exploitation of the individual. There was a time when individual interests required more careful attention, "but times have changed. The individual is secure and new interests must be guarded. The common law renders no service to-day by standing full-armored before individuals, natural or artificial, that need no defense but sally from beneath its aegis to injure society."[41]

The most effective way of eliminating such anachronisms was through an improved system of legal education. It was to the law schools that Pound assigned primary responsibility for the necessary reformation. The remedy lay in "training the rising generation of lawyers in a social, political, and legal philosophy abreast of our time. . . . [It must be] a better and sounder philosophy of law than the average practitioner imbibes from Blackstone, or from Coke by way of Story and Cooley and Miller."[42]

In spite of his dedication to the improvement of legal education, the uphill struggle often seemed overwhelming. In January 1905, during the second year of his deanship, Pound submitted his resignation. The student newspaper speculated that the position was too demanding for the small salary it carried, but financial considerations did not dictate his decision. Building a law school was lonely and frustrating work, and Pound felt he was not getting enough support from the regents.[43]

The announcement of his resignation shocked the university community. The chancellor immediately called a special meeting of the regents to consider the matter. The *Nebraska State Journal* wrote a glowing editorial about Pound and urged the university to find some way to retain him. But the most impressive reaction came from the student body. The students were genuinely concerned that the resignation of Pound would be a serious loss to the law school and to the campus. The editors of the school newspaper staged a series of mass meetings, which were attended by a large number of students from all divisions of the university. They implored Pound to reconsider, and they petitioned the regents to stop the "disastrous 'brain leakage' from the University of Nebraska."[44]

The campaign was not successful. The regents accepted Pound's resignation in March, but when they made another appeal in July, he reconsidered and agreed to return as dean. In the interim the regents had made additional strides in meeting some of his requests for improvements at the law school. They had authorized the addition of two new full-time professors, George D. Ayers and George Costigan, both graduates of the Harvard Law School. Two other men were appointed as part-time faculty members. In addition to the new men, Professor W. G. Hastings returned to the school, and thus the staff grew to almost twice its former size. The regents also authorized the creation of a law library, and many new sets of reports were purchased. Law students in the past were forced to rely on the holdings at the state capitol, and this had long been one of Pound's most insistent complaints. The improvements indicated a willingness by the regents to increase their support of the school, making the deanship much more attractive to a man who had feared it might simply be a place to retire.[45]

Of all the groups that welcomed the return of Pound, none applauded louder than the student body. During the crisis over his resignation the school newspaper called him "one of the most popular professors that the University has ever had."[46] Pound was deeply interested in the welfare of the students. When the university refused to buy much-needed lockers for the law students, Pound offered to purchase them himself.[47] He judged innumerable debate contests and accepted frequent requests for lectures on contemporary affairs.[48] Once when a delirious student had escaped from a hospital, Pound spent an entire night searching for him in the cornfields south of Lincoln.[49]

Among those who followed the fortunes of the university athletic teams, none was a more devoted fan than Pound. He was the complete enthusiast. Year after year he served on baseball and football committees. He was a perennial toastmaster at the annual football banquet, and he often underwrote banquets for the neglected baseball team himself. Pound was a great friend of college athletes and deplored the tendency to label them mindless gladiators. No football rally was complete without the exuberant dean. "Every student," remarked the school newspaper, "knows Dean Pound's ability to get enthusiasm out of a crowd."[50]

Pound also commanded great prestige among his colleagues. When serious divisions within the faculty threatened to shatter the university community, Pound gathered the entire faculty together in an assembly room of a Lincoln hotel. "The program," Alvin Johnson remembered, "was song and 'reaming swats that drink divinely.' " Pound started the festivities with the ballad of bold Dick Turpin. Other songs followed, and one by one all the professors warmed to the occasion, dissolving their animosities in old college tunes.[51]

Although countless activities made tremendous demands on his time, Pound still continued to read, to think, to develop his own creative approach to law. A few of his articles began to appear in law reviews, but his reputation still remained a local one. Then, at the 1905 meeting of the Nebraska State Bar Association, Pound delivered a paper that so impressed George R. Peck, the visiting president of the American Bar Association, that he immediately secured Pound's promise to address the next annual meeting of the national organization.[52]

The Twenty-Ninth Annual Meeting of the American Bar Association, held in St. Paul, Minnesota, during August 1906, was a historic convention. Pound gave the principal address, "The Causes of Popular Dissatisfaction with the Administration of Justice." Most of the 370 delegates were present in the spacious auditorium of the state capitol, although few had heard of the Nebraska professor who was to address them. It was an audience accustomed to eulogies on the common law or lucid expositions of familiar legal principles. The delegates may have been mildly curious about an address that found fault with the American legal system, but they were completely unprepared for Pound's skillful blend of scholarship and public policy. "As the 1900s opened," wrote Robert W. Millar, looking back from the perspective of a half-century, "he were a bold man who would seek to disturb . . . the existing order in anything more than its peripheral detail." Still more bold was the man who would challenge the existing order in that citadel of the status quo, the American Bar Association.[53]

Pound started on a mild note. His topic, he said, was not a new one; there had always been dissatisfaction with the administration of justice. Certain problems were inherent in any legal system. The mechanical operation of the law created discontent, particularly in a transitional period when existing laws became anachronistic. Furthermore, many people did not realize that the administration of justice was a difficult task, and they failed to insist on proper standards. And in every society there had been people who simply disliked restraint.

But in addition to the problems inherent in all legal systems, the common law system had its own peculiar sources of dissatisfaction. Foremost among these was its extreme individualism, a tendency that ill agreed with the collectivistic character of the industrial age. In the trial courts the tradition of contentious procedure seemed designed to obscure all issues. *Stare decisis* also contributed to popular dissatisfaction with the law, because the rage for precedents often seemed to produce a mere "citation match between counsel, with a certainty that diligence can rake up a decision *somewhere* in support of any conceivable proposition." The practice of deciding important public questions as mere incidents of private controversies created political jealousy of the courts. Behind many of these problems was the absence of a general legal philosophy, so characteristic of the common law, which "gives us petty tinkering where comprehensive reform is needed."[54]

Pound also enumerated specifically American problems that cried for comprehensive reform. The multiplicity of courts, the generous provisions for appealing minor error, and overrefined jurisdictional niceties elevated procedural questions over substantive questions. The concurrent jurisdiction that resulted from the federal system made it too easy for a cause to hang in limbo between two sets of courts. Judicial energy was cruelly wasted by the American system. Rigid jurisdictional lines left certain courts idle while others struggled with burgeoning dockets; an emphasis on mere points of practice consumed countless judicial man-hours in appellate courts; unnecessary retrials took their toll in the trial courts.

There was a further set of problems that Pound attributed to the larger climate of opinion in which courts operated. A lack of popular interest plagued the administration of justice; most people, for example, considered jury service a bore. A tendency to make law do the work of morals at a time when morals were changing placed a double burden on the judiciary. The bench was cheapened by forcing judges into politics. Sensational newspaper coverage of judicial business created a misinformed public. Legislatures ill equipped to perform their tasks created innumerable difficulties for judges by giving them unclear laws to administer. Finally, changes in the legal profession itself had transformed the client-attorney relationship into an employer-employee relationship.

Pound admitted that many of the problems in the administration of justice were beyond the power of courts to rectify, but there was much that could be done to modernize judicial organization and procedure. As he enumerated the multitude of deficiencies, his speech bristled with harsh language: "Law is often in very truth a government of the living by the dead." "Common law dogmas have . . . put [courts] in a false position of doing nothing and obstructing everything." The "sporting theory of justice" had encouraged "the modern American race to beat the law" and made courts "agents or abettors of lawlessness." "Our system of courts is archaic and our procedure behind the times." There was an "obsolete Chinese Wall between law and equity." In his native state, Nebraska judges were "organized on an antiquated system and their time is frittered away on mere points of legal etiquette." The bar everywhere suffered under a "yoke of commercialism."[55]

This was a harsh diagnosis, one designed to impress the leaders of the bar. The audience was stunned but courteous. They dutifully applauded and perhaps were willing to let the matter rest until one of their number, Everett P. Wheeler, a tireless worker for the reform of legal procedure, moved that four thousand copies of the paper be struck off immediately for distribution to lawyers and Congressmen. The Wheeler resolution required unanimous consent, but James D. Andrews, a prominent New York attorney, blocked the motion. It had been difficult for him to listen to such heresies; he could not be expected to endorse them. "A more drastic attack," he declared, "upon the system of procedure employed by the courts in the United States, as a whole or *in toto*, could scarcely be devised." He offered to prove at a later business meeting that Pound's criticism was totally incorrect. Other delegates wanted to suppress the whole matter, and an abortive motion was submitted to eliminate the address from the forthcoming *Annual Report*. After many rulings on points of order, an amended resolution referred the address to a committee, where most delegates hoped it would be buried.[56]

At the business meeting two days later Pound's address was again the subject of angry discussion. It was not a debate; with the exception of Wheeler, no one rose to Pound's defense. There were like-minded men at the meeting, but they were silent. Andrews opened the proceedings with an impassioned defense of "the most refined and scientific system of procedure ever devised by the wit of man." He deplored incendiaries like Pound and ventured that "among the chief causes for dissatisfaction and alarm are just such utterances as are contained in this paper, for, instead of stilling popular clamor, they arouse public dissatisfaction and encourage it." Andrews even accused Pound of advocating both the elimination of appellate courts and, horror of horrors, the substitution of codes for the common law.[57]

When Pound rose to defend his paper, the chairman refused to allow him to speak, arguing that the question was not the merits of the paper, but rather what should be done with it. These standards apparently did not apply to M. A. Spoonts, who condemned that paper as "an attack upon the entire remedial jurisprudence of America. . . . It is the old effort of seeking to destroy rather than to build up." Then, after a flurry of motions and amendments, the address was referred to the Committee on Judicial Administration and Remedial Procedure with the instructions that it prepare a report for the next annual meeting.[58]

Pound was shocked by the immediate response to his address. "Probably one should be amused at the extreme persistence of this legal illiteracy", he informed Ross, "but I must confess I am alarmed by it."[59] He had certainly not considered the address a radical one, nor was the tone irreverent. But lawyers like Spoonts and Andrews, Pound's most vocal critics at St. Paul, regarded any criticism of American law as radical, irresponsible, and destructive of public order. The 1890s, with its parade of political unorthodoxy, had made most lawyers uncritical defenders of the bench and bar, and a decade of controversy left them incapable of accepting any reform suggestions.

The St. Paul address, although an indictment of the law's deficiencies, was also an endorsement of the legal system. It revealed not a hatred of the common law, but rather a hatred of what was happening to it. Pound reserved some of his sharpest barbs for the nineteenth-century procedural codes and chaotic organization of courts that paralyzed the judiciary. He also pointed to new and vital institutions that would rescue the common law from collapse and would restore the lost eminence of the bench and bar. "With law schools . . . to promote scientific study of the law; with active Bar Associations in every state to revive professional feeling . . . we may look forward to a near future when our courts will be swift and certain agents of justice, whose decisions will be acquiesced in and respected by all."[60]

Pound presented no radical prescription, and the rigorously analytical character of his address may have been an unconscious effort to make the presentation unemotional. He called for restoration rather than revolution; he urged only that certain anachronisms be pruned in order to strengthen the common law. He was plainly hostile, after the fashion of a common law enthusiast, to the growth of executive commissions. He agreed that legal change must lag behind other forms of change and that friction was inevitable. He obviously tried to be a friendly critic. "Our administration of justice is not decadent," he had said. "It is simply behind the times."[61] That the address was considered revolutionary revealed more about the legal profession than it did about Pound. It was a path-making paper that became "the catechism for all progressive-minded lawyers and judges,"[62] but it was not an address that a revolutionary would have given.

The criticism did not end with the close of the meeting. Typical of the remarks that followed Pound back to Lincoln was a letter from a judge who insisted that government existed solely for the protection of "individual rights *as against* public rights" and that delay was beneficial and allowed courts to protect the individual from society. The critical judge expressed the hope that courts would never become "partisans in the case of society against the individual," a sentiment that betrayed a common assumption that the bench and bar were the last barrier against an onrushing tide of socialism and anarchy.[63]

Yet Pound had not been shouted down forever. His official position in the association guaranteed him a valuable forum. He had served on the Committee on Law Reporting and Digesting, a standing committee, since 1904.[64] At the St. Paul meeting he was appointed chairman of the important Section on Legal Education, a position previously held by some of the leading members of the profession. After the St. Paul address many lawyers flocked to Pound's standard, for the association contained men who longed for a call to action. John H. Wigmore, the distinguished dean of the Northwestern School of Law, remembered that he and others "had begun to feel a thrill of interest, a prognostication of promise. Here was something really comprehensive, yet practical—maybe a program for effort." After the address Wigmore met with a small group that swore to implement it.[65]

Shortly after the St. Paul meeting Wigmore sent Pound a note offering encouragement and support. He must have felt some kinship with the much-maligned attorney from Nebraska. His own treatise on evidence had been criticized for introducing novel terminology.[66] Pound was delighted to receive praise from such a source, for he found Wigmore's work impressive and he had repeatedly used Wigmore's famous phrase, "the sporting theory of justice," in the St. Paul address.[67]

Wigmore's message eased some of the sting of St. Paul, and his subsequent offer of a position on the Northwestern faculty provided further therapy for one who felt rebuffed by his profession. Doubtless Wigmore sensed Pound's feeling of isolation, and he asked Judge Jesse Holdom of the Illinois Appellate Court to urge Pound to come to Northwestern. Judge Holdom encouraged him to accept the offer and assured him "that a hearty welcome by Bench and Bar awaits you."[68]

The Northwestern offer was a fitting sequel to St. Paul. Pound's address had given him a national reputation, and Nebraska must have seemed a shrinking stage. Furthermore, Wigmore's offer of a six-hour teaching schedule promised him new opportunities for creative effort, and Pound was delighted with the prospect of such freedom.[69] "Having been my own fasces and lictors," he wrote, "I shall not miss any of the insignia of authority. I have wasted as much time on petty administration as I can justify, and am heartily glad to be rid of it."[70]

In addition to the positive features that lured him to Northwestern, there were also forces pushing him from Nebraska. The crusading days at the university seemed to be drawing to a close. There were fewer students motivated by that high sense of purpose so characteristic of Nebraska youth in earlier years; they seemed less serious about their studies and more concerned about frivolities and fraternities. Some of the stronger members of the faculty were leaving. Ross had already gone to Wisconsin, and Frederic Clements and Alvin Johnson were making preparations to leave. Perhaps he had some premonition of the intellectual rigor mortis that would set in when Sam Avery became chancellor the following year. In 1907 Nebraska was beginning to lose some of the excitement of its adolescence; it was entering middle age at the same time that Pound was at the threshold of his most creative years.[71]

Once again Pound submitted his resignation. This time there was no turning back. Even a rousing student demonstration did not persuade him to reconsider. The news that he was going to Northwestern was announced during the last week of the academic year, a time when college students are rarely in a crusading mood. Nevertheless, the *Nebraska State Journal* called the reaction to this announcement "the most emphatic and spontaneous affair of its kind ever seen on the campus."[72]

On the morning of 24 May 1907, classes were dismissed for a colorful rally. The band led a grand march through the campus. After many speeches by professors and students extolling Pound, the crowd adopted a resolution urging the regents to persuade him to remain at Nebraska. Someone even wrote a song for the occasion:

DEAN ROSCOE OF NEBRASKA
(to "Auld Lang Syne")

We'd have you know, our Dean Roscoe,
   That it would give us woe,
To feel the blow of having you go
   'Way from Nee-brasko.
Dean Pound, D.P., D.P., D.P.,
   D.P., D.P., D.P.,
D.P., D.P., D.P., D.P.,
   D.P.,—stay with us
      (Last three words yell)[73]

Pound must have been deeply affected by this demonstration. It was a moving farewell to a revered professor, doubly moving because Pound himself was so fond of the students. Their disappointment must have made him a little sad, but he could take pride in their expressions of gratitude and respect. This was surely the spirit in which he left Nebraska for Chicago—a little sad at leaving familiar surroundings, proud of the work he had accomplished, and excited at the prospect of new worlds to conquer.

6

Chicago Years: Emergence of a Reformer

"Pound is coming to Chicago to be with us, body and spirit," Wigmore announced triumphantly to Justice Holmes. "If you haven't yet read his 'Causes of Popular Dissatisfaction with the Administration of Justice' . . . pray do so. Under a modest guise he conceals the most erudite and clear-seeing mind aged 37 now in this country." Chicago's most important legal organ also reported his arrival enthusiastically, noting the impressive effort of both the university and the Nebraska press to retain him as "evidence of the value of such a man to the community." For his part, Pound was eager to join the law faculty at Northwestern. The St. Paul address had given him a national audience, and Northwestern was an institution with a national constituency.[1]

The Northwestern University School of Law was one of the finest law schools in the country. Its excellent library, commitment to scholarship, and light teaching schedules enabled the faculty to pursue ambitious research projects.

The law faculty of eleven professors and thirteen lecturers included Albert M. Kales, a pioneer in the reform of procedure and judicial administration, and Charles C. Hyde, a leading authority on international law. In 1907, the year Pound joined the faculty, Albert Kocourek received an appointment as a lecturer. Kocourek later became one of the most imaginative analytical legal theorists in this century. But the towering figure at Northwestern was the dean.[2]

John Henry Wigmore was an urbane, brilliant, and restless man. He was already a leader of the American bar in spite of his reform impulses which made many lawyers suspicious of him. His limitless energies transformed the Northwestern School of Law into a major institution, and he had such a lasting effect on its growth that the history of the school is written in terms of his tenure.[3] By 1907 he had organized the *Illinois Law Review*, served as a commissioner of uniform state laws, and completed a monumental treatise on evidence that is perhaps the most important contribution to legal scholarship in the twentieth century. In 1908, while conferring a Doctor of Laws on him, Harvard President A. Lawrence Lowell called Wigmore "a jurist in a day when lawyers are many and jurists are rare."[4]

Wigmore considered a strong faculty the most important element in the institutional life of a school, and although Pound's appointment caused much lifting of eyebrows, he was delighted to obtain "one of the most eminent and promising of the younger legal thinkers of this country."[5] The two men soon became fast friends. They had similar intellectual interests, and they enjoyed working together.[6] Doubtless Wigmore encouraged Pound's increasing attention to criminal law, a field that he began to explore after moving to Chicago. Their mutual interests were not confined to intellectual matters. At innumerable bar association meetings Pound would delight the gathering with a stirring rendition of "Dives and Lazarus" while Wigmore accompanied him on the piano.[7] Wigmore was famous for his clever lyrics, set to well-known tunes, with neat digs at professors, legal theories, and important cases. For a Christmas greeting in 1907, shortly after Pound joined the Northwestern faculty, the dean sent his newest addition the following jingle:

> All hail the newest star,
>   now fixed amidst our constellation!
> A brilliant varied spectrum
>   marks your lofty stellar station.
> As sociologic jurist,
>   may the message of your pen
> Widely spread a mighty influence,
>   from your editorial den!
> When Pharaoh set the Israelites
>   to make bricks without straw,
> He didn't know how harder
>   'twould be to reform the law;
> But Pharaoh had his Moses:
>   *you're* the Moses by whose hand
> Our common law will pass from bondage
>   to the promised land.[8]

When Wigmore joked about an editorial den, he was not speaking of a cozy study in the Pound home. Pound was the editor of the *Illinois Law Review*, and within two years he molded the *Review* into one of the more important law journals in the country.[9] He did everything but set type: he made all final editorial decisions, prepared an editorial section, and wrote most of the book reviews as well as an occasional article and note.

In addition to his continuous responsibilities on the *Review*, Pound served as acting dean for a few months while Wigmore took a leave of absence. Curiously, he never taught a course in jurisprudence while at Northwestern. His classes consisted of contracts, quasi-contracts, trusts, code-pleading, and Roman law, a variety of subjects that indicated the wide range of his talents and interests.[10]

Soon after Pound came to Chicago, he began to recreate the pattern of his life in Lincoln; as he grew in importance within the university community, he also established a larger public presence. Reporters frequently sought his opinion on current legal topics; the *Chicago Evening Post* wrote that he "added to the intellectual forces of the city a mind of uncommon strength and interest-compelling power."[11] He became a prominent figure in the Illinois State Bar Association and served as chairman of the elite Chicago City Club's Committee on the Administration of Justice.[12] His many activities led the city's principal legal newspaper to comment that "Prof. Pound is an admirable example of the union of the legal scholar and the law reformer. He brings the learning of the cloister to the live, practical legal problems of the day."[13]

Chicago provided reformers with a congenial atmosphere and a host of associates. Jane Addams was finishing her first twenty years at Hull House. Charles E. Merriam, a political scientist at the University of Chicago, was leading a dramatic crusade for municipal reform. The atmosphere was especially engaging for a legal reformer, for the Chicago bar was active in efforts to improve the administration of justice. One could secure support and reinforcement from men like Kales and Wigmore at Northwestern and Ernst Freund and Julian Mack at Chicago. Indeed, just before Pound arrived in Chicago, the city had achieved a quiet revolution in the administration of justice. In December 1906 the Municipal Court, a product of the home-rule movement, began its operations. It quickly emerged as the best-organized judiciary in the United States, replacing a woefully inefficient and corrupt fee system employing justices of the peace. The Municipal Court had a great deal of power over its internal administration. It controlled its calendar, officers, clerks, and judges. The chief justice could assign judges to the calendar and audit the court's business. Most important, the court could develop its own system of procedure, which provided much-needed flexibility and helped place procedural questions in a properly subordinate position. The grant of rule-making authority to the courts was a reform for which Pound would labor long and arduously. He was much impressed with the example of the Municipal Court and declared that it was "teaching thoughtful students of judicial administration that many things are possible in this country which it had been the fashion to say were impractical and utopian."[14]

Pound found this general pattern of reform activity highly encouraging. During the year before his arrival at Northwestern he had expressed his first misgivings about the possibility of reform from within the legal profession. The response to his address in St. Paul made him feel a quiver of professional rejection, which was particularly frustrating for a man who was so deeply committed to the traditions of the common law. In November 1907 Pound advised Ross that the only available method of reforming the law was "*via* the public." The legal profession was in no mood to promote substantial changes. "The profession," Pound remarked caustically, "is persuaded that its conceptions are the legal order of nature and looks on one who doubts that proposition as visionary or else as a charlatan."

He told Ross that he was planning a book called *Sociological Jurisprudence*, which would popularize the new legal theory.[15]

Ross was eager to help Pound, particularly if the effort were to reach a mass audience. He put Pound in touch with Richard T. Ely, who was editing a series called the *Citizens' Library*. The reform-minded economist was enthusiastic about the project and wanted to secure the manuscript for his series. Pound responded to his offer with the observation that public demands were essential for current legal reform. "The profession," he repeated, "is so prone to ignore everything that does not run along conventional lines, that I do not care to write for it—yet." In spite of his pessimism, the "yet" was a qualification that exposed Pound's basic assumptions and his strategy as a reformer. He had no desire to cut himself off from the legal profession, for regardless of its weaknesses it was the medium through which the common law tradition was passed on to subsequent generations, and Pound would not for a moment reject that tradition. Although momentarily discouraged about the possibility of changing the attitudes of the bar, he hoped that his message would be heard by lawyers in the future. Furthermore, even when he considered writing for popular consumption, he was incapable of muckraking. "What I desire," he informed Ely, "is to bring before the public a more accurate statement of the bad and the good sides of our legal system."[16] On the eve of his emergence as a major legal reformer, at a point when he was most discouraged and critical of the existing law, he was still insistent that there was a "good side" that must also be considered.

Pound regarded the common law system as a vital one and objected only to the banal arguments that sustained it. He wanted a central role for the judiciary in the legal process, and a central role for the legal profession in the larger social process, but he considered the conventional apologia, with its formalistic, mechanical, and lifeless orientation, to be intellectually barren. The system needed to be refreshed, or society would reject it. Inertia and defensiveness were currently the law's greatest enemies, for the law could be strengthened by broadening its frame of reference, recognizing its social dimensions, and encouraging its inherent creativity.

Given his sympathy for the existing institutional framework and his willingness to work within it, Pound joined the established, respectable Chicago Bar Association rather than the more militantly reformist rival that Clarence Darrow and other advanced social critics had formed.[17] His strategy of reform demanded that he avoid alienating the bar. When he was criticized by a Chicago attorney for attributing the origin of written instructions to "lawyers of a loud-mouthed variety," he cautiously changed the invective in a later version to "eloquent counsel of a bygone type."[18] Pound's personality and strategy prevented him from being a lonely critic like Darrow, a man who stood apart from established institutions.

Pound was simply not capable of any fundamental suspicion of the legal system. In his most despairing moments, there was always a residue of optimism. The Chicago years increased the level of that optimism and strengthened his commitment to the common law. The kindred spirits that he found in Chicago were matched by increasing numbers in the American Bar Association. Although the Committee on Judicial Administration and Remedial Procedure, charged with examining his St. Paul address, did not endorse his ideas wholeheartedly, its report to the 1907 convention exonerated Pound of the charges made the previous year. The committee found that the address was "neither iconoclastic nor anarchistic." It was an attack on the administration of justice, but "who shall say that the attack is not at this day and in a measure justified? The evils herein complained of are real evils."[19] It suggested that a special committee investigate those evils and make recommendations for their correction. The association adopted the report, created the Special Committee to Suggest Remedies and Formulate Proposed Laws to Prevent Delay and Unnecessary Cost in Litigation and appointed Pound as one of its members. It was the first time the association had taken a genuine interest in the reform of judicial procedure. It represented a triumphant sequel to the St. Paul address and marked the beginning of the crusade for procedural reform.[20]

This new turn of events within the legal profession gained momentum when, in 1908, the association adopted some of Pound's proposals for improving the administration of justice. "It must be evident," he observed of the annual meeting, "that the Bar of America is in no wise to be counted as an anti-social force."[21] At the 1909 convention he was further encouraged by Frederick Lehmann's presidential address, a stirring message calling for a sociological conception of legislation. The association also gave renewed support to the reform of procedure. This pattern of activity revealed, Pound wrote, "that the Bar ... is no longer to be counted reactionary, and that the better class of lawyers are not committed to any doctrine of legal bars to social progress." The events of these years had acted to renew his faith. Less than four years after he had written Ross that the only hope for legal reform was "*via* the public," he informed him that "the time for a small book of merely propagandist character on sociological jurisprudence has gone by."[22]

During the Chicago years Pound reaffirmed his intent to operate within the contours of the common law tradition, but he wanted to make that tradition relevant to the twentieth century. Chicago provided associations with men who both reinforced and contributed to his development of a sociological jurisprudence. Ross continued to write encouraging letters from nearby Madison,[23] and local social scientists and other nonlawyers were equally encouraging. Pound became acquainted with several advanced social thinkers through the Social Science Club at the University of Chicago. He won the esteem of no less a figure than Albion Small, one of the most creative sociologists of the era. Small was particularly impressed with an address Pound had given at a meeting of the club. "On my way home," wrote Small, "I reflected that . . . one of the securest guarantees that the sort of evolution you were pleading for will in due time come about is the work that you yourself are doing in brushing cobwebs from the sky."[24]

Another group, the social workers of Hull House, contributed even more to Pound's intellectual growth. It was through an association with Hull House that John Dewey had developed nascent philosophical impulses into a program of social reform, and the social workers, adept at stimulating a heightened sense of social consciousness, exerted a similar influence on Pound.[25] He came into contact with them shortly after his arrival, perhaps through a friendship with Edith Abbott, a former Nebraska student who was dean of Chicago's School of Civics and Philanthropy. Pound gave lectures at Hull House and served as a member of the Juvenile Court Committee, an agency organized by the Hull House group to assist the Juvenile Court.[26] He had taught criminal law and had already developed some interest in criminal procedure, but it was only through conversations with the social workers that he became interested in the larger problems of the criminal process.[27]

Pound immediately began to act on this new interest. In December 1907, at a meeting of the American Political Science Association, he made a provocative speech about deficiencies in criminal justice. He expressed serious doubts about the central concept of criminal law—the fear of punishment as a deterrent. "The venturesome will always believe they can escape. The fearless will always be indifferent whether they escape. The crafty will always believe they can evade, and enough will succeed to encourage others." He also condemned the effort to make the criminal law do too much, to make it "a general agency for propagating morals." Pound argued that the most important reforms were of an extralegal nature. Much would depend on a "better general education in sociology, leading the public to abandon the retributive idea and . . . desist from [the] demand for revenge." He was encouraged by the emergence of institutions like the legislative reference bureau in Wisconsin, and he hoped for special advisers who could provide judges with a more scientific understanding of each case.[28]

Pound had already begun to develop a conceptual framework for legal theory that emphasized an interdisciplinary approach; now he also urged the introduction of extralegal techniques into legal institutions to make them more vital and contemporary. He used these suggestions in his own classes and advised the law students to attend the lectures given by Charles R. Henderson, a Social Gospel chaplain who doubled as a criminologist.[29] An interdisciplinary theme also dominated his plans for a national conference on criminal justice.

The First National Conference on Criminal Law and

Criminology was held at Northwestern in June 1909 to celebrate the fiftieth anniversary of the School of Law. Wigmore had proposed the conference, but the burden of organizing it fell to Pound, and he spent many months preparing for it.[30] The demanding preliminaries yielded impressive results, for the national conference was a landmark in the development of American criminology.[31]

The purpose of the conference was to unite all disciplines relating to criminal law and criminology, to formulate joint programs, and to eliminate misunderstanding. It was attended by lawyers, judges, criminologists, prison officials, parole officers, social workers, psychologists, and sociologists. The participants included Edward A. Ross, Jane Addams, Clarence Darrow, Ernst Freund, Julian Mack, and Graham Taylor. The goal of unfettered interdisciplinary discussion "was realized," commented *The Survey*, "beyond the most sanguine expectations of the committee of organization."[32]

Pound set the theme for the conference in his opening remarks to the participants. Those involved in the administration of criminal justice, he noted, were constantly working at cross-purposes, but the tasks of law reform required a unified approach. Intellectuals must become "social engineers," he declared, and he challenged each discipline to enrich its understanding and creative potential through

a comprehension of the point of view of all; that instead of the alienist and the psychologist and the sociologist and the jurist and the economist going their several paths and throwing each his individual light upon our system of punitive justice, the light of all these be concentrated into one ray which shall throw upon our system of punitive justice the combined wisdom of all those who are entitled to bring scientific knowledge to bear upon it.[33]

Social engineering demanded an open mind, and Pound urged a generous examination of new proposals. Although he could not accept certain suggestions made at the conference, he encouraged discussion of any proposal that a participant might advance. When Ross suggested a survey of criminals to define a "criminal type," many participants, particularly the lawyers, tried to hoot him down. Pound insisted that the suggestion be given a trial. He was dubious about the existence of a criminal type, but no one had ever proved it was impossible, and a survey of criminal statistics would be useful for many purposes. Pound thus demonstrated his willingness to encourage new ideas, even if he did find them somewhat misguided.[34]

The tenor of debate at the conference was generally impressive and advanced, the agenda bristled with every conceivable topic, and the proposals adopted by its committees were ambitious. The Committee on Causes and Prevention of Crime suggested a system of industrial education, better wages, hours, and working conditions, more effective public regulation of tenements, the creation of playgrounds, and the general improvement of the urban environment. The committee said very little about punitive measures. The general theme of the conference was an emphasis on "the *complex* factors combining to encourage and establish the persistent offender [italics added]."[35]

The most important result of the conference was the creation of the American Institute of Criminal Law and Criminology. It was the earliest organization of its type in the United States, and *The Outlook* expressed the hope that it would become "a vigorous and effective agent for social service." The institute immediately developed an active educational program and soon generated a great deal of interest in the reform of criminal law. Five years after its creation George Alger, a New York attorney long active in legal reform, noted that "lawyers who, ten years ago, considered it beneath their dignity to know much about criminal law, are now interested in it and active in promoting its reform."[36]

The conference also provided for a journal, and the following year the *Journal of the American Institute of Criminal Law and Criminology* began publication. It was the first English-language periodical of its kind, although twenty-five similar ventures were published abroad. It was broad in scope and conception, mirroring the diversity and eclecticism of the conference, and it avoided the limitations of traditional law reviews. As an additional measure, the conference recommended the translation of foreign treatises on criminology, and by 1917 the *Modern Criminal Science Series* was completed. It contained translations of the principal works of leading European criminologists and encouraged American students in a neglected and misunderstood field.[37]

Many of the themes that emerged during the conference corresponded to initiatives that Pound was pursuing in jurisprudence. As the principal organizer of the event, Pound had demonstrated his enthusiasm for exploring the diverse social dimensions of legal problems. The participants, drawn from a wide range of social science disciplines and social service occupations, responded eagerly to Pound's injunction to treat law as an exercise in "social engineering." The *Modern Criminal Science Series* also represented a parallel between the work of the conference and Pound's developing jurisprudence, for he had long urged the importance of continental scholarship, and he continued to advise the editors of the series in later years.[38]

Finally, the public character of the conference must have been a major factor in his decision to invest so much time and energy in it. He did not want to limit his professional role to teaching and scholarship, and he had a compulsion for organizing conferences and bar associations as well as courses and manuscripts.

The conference was Pound's swan song to Northwestern, for he joined the University of Chicago School of Law in 1909. Albert Kocourek, a colleague at Northwestern, recalled that Wigmore had managed to match the salary offered by Chicago, but Pound refused to accept a salary higher than that of the dean. Northwestern actually outbid Chicago and offered Pound an unprecedented salary of $6,500, to be raised in two years to $7,500. Pound still found the Chicago offer more attractive.[39] Perhaps he was drawn by its faculty; he had made many friends among men in both the college and the law school.

Ernst Freund and Julian Mack, two of his ablest new colleagues on the law faculty, were interested in the larger public problems of law. This was an attitude that William Rainey Harper, Chicago's dynamic president, considered a vital ingredient of legal education. "A scientific study of law," he argued, "involves the related sciences of history, economics, philosophy—the whole field of man as a social being." Harper instituted courses in systematic and comparative jurisprudence, legal history, and principles of legislation, all of which were closely associated with the departments of history, political economy, and sociology. Chicago provided a congenial atmosphere for Pound, and he accepted the first appointment to a recently created professorship. Charles F. Amidon, a federal district judge in North Dakota, wrote Pound that the decision was a wise and judicious one. "To have both you and Professor Wigmore in one lawschool in Chicago," he observed, "was perhaps an unlawful monopoly of talent."[40]

Chicago had not been the only suitor for Pound's attentions. The University of Wisconsin had tried unsuccessfully to add him to its growing list of reform-minded professors, and he also refused an attractive offer from the Yale Law School.[41] The University of Nebraska continued the effort to persuade its wandering son to return. In 1908, when the chancellorship fell vacant, Pound emerged as a leading candidate for the office. President Harris of Northwestern implored him to refuse the appointment, and Wigmore even offered him the deanship. The courtship persisted throughout the year, but Pound did not return to Nebraska.[42]

The most consuming of Pound's activities during these years was the crusade for procedural reform. When he delivered the St. Paul address in 1906, it seemed unlikely that it would be "the spark that kindled the white flame of progress." Most lawyers were either apathetic or antagonistic to procedural reform. Judge Charles F. Amidon was roundly condemned for suggesting that it had been "one of the serious faults of the legal profession throughout its entire history . . . to exalt matters of practice above matters of substance." George Whitney Moore, a Detroit attorney, dismissed this charge as "a most gross libel upon our civilization" and insisted that any inequities produced by adjective law were "not enough to cause more than a ripple in the social sea."[43]

Many lawyers considered common law procedure to be part of an enduring order of natural law, and Pound encountered this attitude time and time again. In response to a speech he had given outlining a program of procedural reform, a hostile lawyer advanced the notion that "the law cannot be simplified, because in the broader sense it is not made. It arises out of relations, and courts and legislatures merely declare what those relations are and what rules must govern them."[44] Other factors made it difficult to mount a crusade for procedural reform. The movement had to be an entirely disinterested one, for procedural reformers could claim no interest group as a base of support. And it was no secret that astute lawyers welcomed complicated systems of procedure as devices for endless obstruction. Even the "average lawyer," argued Charles B. Letton, a Nebraska attorney, "feels that if much of the form and many of the formulas of practice are dispensed with he will be disarmed of his weapons of war."[45] This was the attitude Wigmore had condemned as the "sporting theory of justice."

Procedural reformers also had to overcome the contrived argument that procedural inefficiency produced a beneficial delay. Moorfield Storey, a law reformer of sorts, was one of many who tried to convert the law's delay into the law's deliberation. He explained:

> Men in hot blood rush to their lawyers with some complaint. They want something done at once, and a writ is issued. Then they ask what comes next, and are told that in perhaps thirty days the case will be entered, that the other side has then thirty days in which to file an answer; and that very likely the case may be reached in a year or more. They have time to cool; and many a suit which would be tried, if it could be tried in a week . . . is settled before it is reached. Such delay is extremely useful.[46]

The argument was reminiscent of Rabelais's Bridlegoose, who decided cases by a cast of the dice but insisted on an elaborate system of procedure designed to leave the litigants so exhausted that they would accept any decision with relief.

In spite of these traditions, there was a growing movement within the legal profession that favored procedural reform, and Pound supplied the organizing principles that had long been absent. The St. Paul address was a catalytic agent, a rallying point for reformers, and Pound's tireless efforts in the following years gave a sense of unity and direction to the movement. A modern code of civil procedure in Kansas, a unified municipal court in Chicago, and the developing concern of bar associations were isolated gestures until the magic of the Pound message molded them into a coordinated program.[47]

The reform of legal procedure was Pound's first major sustained attack on a particular problem in the law. Trial practice in Nebraska made him realize the great need for removing the burden of artificial rules from lower courts. As a commissioner of the Nebraska Supreme Court, Pound had dealt generously with procedural issues: his decisions allowed greater flexibility in amending pleadings and eliminated excessive artificiality in instructions. Procedural law also appealed to him as a lawyer-intellectual. Lawyers have always had a special interest in procedure,[48] but Pound, who was capable of a high degree of abstraction, took an even greater interest in procedure than most. As a matter of personality, he enjoyed doing things in a rigorously proper way. As a politician, he preferred that his issues be pure. As a reformer, he abhorred the murky products of sentimentality and moralism. He seemed always to have a regard for ground rules and tidy methods. But he was always resolute that procedure must not dominate substantive questions.

Although procedural reform did not have universal appeal, it was a program that could be developed within the legal profession and it attracted lawyers of varied ideological dispositions. There was a widespread concern that some criminals hid behind technicalities of criminal procedure,[49] and this interest was transferred to civil procedure as well. Lawyers like William Howard Taft embraced procedural reform while rejecting virtually all other reforms.[50] The parameters of its appeal were demonstrated by a lawyer who, during a heated discussion of Pound's program for reform, rushed to his defense with the observation that "we have almost a perfect system of law on the statute books, but the trouble is with the practice and the pleadings."[51] Thus the issue was a happy one for Pound, for he could secure many allies with it. Procedural reform was an acceptable reform, and one with which he could establish a foundation for further efforts within the legal profession.

Pound provided his generation with both the classic diagnosis of an ailing administration of justice and the classic prescription for correcting its defects. In the years following the St. Paul address he prepared a comprehensive program of procedural reform and devoted ceaseless effort to popularizing it. He was the most active and creative member of the American Bar Association's Special Committee,[52] and his reports for the committee became a major guide for all who were interested in eliminating procedural abuses.[53] He addressed countless bar associations and civic groups; he also published many articles and editorials indicting existing evils and suggesting remedies for correction. He was both the leading propagandist and the leading theoretician of the movement.

The central theme of Pound's message was that procedure existed only for the sake of substance. He was indignant that the "etiquette of justice" was so often preserved at the expense of justice. A frightening number of cases turned on mere points of practice rather than the merits of the case. The reports of American courts at the turn of the century resembled the notorious numbers of the English reporter Saunders, who once thought it worthy of special notice that the error in a case dismissed on a procedural defect actually corresponded to a defect in the cause.[54]

The emphasis on overrefined procedure had a debilitating effect on trial courts. The trial judge was forced to be so rigorously scrupulous about procedural niceties that he was able to devote little attention to the merits. Judges became so cautious that they were reduced to the role of mere umpires, focusing their attentions on keeping the record free of error. Courts of appeals, aloof in their majestic isolation from trial courts, reinforced artificial attitudes toward procedure. At every level, the judicial process seemed more concerned with the record than with the actual controversy, and Pound insisted that this misplaced priority weakened judicial influence in the development of substantive law.[55]

"One of the most untoward results of the spirit of formalism in our procedure," wrote Pound, "is the attitude of what I may venture to call record-worship. We try the record, not the case." Both law and logic agreed that a record should merely preserve a permanent account of what happened, but courts frequently invested it with a life of its own.[56] Judicial priorities had been summarized most dramatically by Chief Baron Parke, who, from his vantage point on the Court of Exchequer in the mid-nineteenth century, devoted his great abilities to heightening all the absurdities in the English system of procedure. When someone suggested that appellants be allowed to amend the pleadings in order to clarify the issue, Baron Parke replied in horror, "Good Heavens! Think of the state of the Record!"[57]

The trial lawyer became an eager ally of appellate judges in forcing a preoccupation with procedure upon trial courts. Frederick W. Lehmann, Solicitor General during the Taft Administration, declared that lawyers plead their cases to the court of appeals rather than the jury.[58] In the heat of trial judges occasionally made mistakes, and when every error became reversible error, lawyers were often more concerned with setting traps for the judge than with arguing the merits of the case. A railroad attorney admitted this strategy with revealing cynicism when, at the time for his summation, he said, "I do not care to address the jury, your Honor. I have two objections to your Honor's rulings, which are perfectly fatal to any judgment that may be rendered against my client. It is, therefore, a matter of indifference to me what verdict the jury brings in."[59]

Appellate judges and trial lawyers united to force trial judges into issuing artificial and meaningless instructions to the jury. The preparation of these guides for the jury had once been a fine art, for it required an able judge to summarize the issues of a complex case and explain the applicable rules of law. But the appetite of appellate courts for error led trial judges to read written, appeal-proof instructions of a refined, technical nature. The result was a ritualistic babble that twelve laymen simply could not understand, and in many jurisdictions where the instructions preceded the closing arguments of counsel, the oratorical cross-fires further impaired their value.[60]

The consuming quest for error undermined the integrity and confidence of trial courts, and Pound argued for the sane policy of refusing to set aside judgments for procedural defects unless the error produced a miscarriage of justice. By narrowing the categories of reversible error, appellate courts could encourage better trial practice as well as increased public respect for the law. The same spirit would eliminate the use of meaningless instructions. Written instructions had undermined the authority of the judge, for jurors ignored what they could not understand. Pound felt that oral instructions alone were effective, for they enabled a judge to gauge the jury's response with greater assurance. The stenographer could provide a record of the instructions, so there was no need for a judge to reduce them to writing.[61]

The demand for simplicity was a central theme in Pound's program for procedural reform, and to that end he attacked the pitfalls of pleading with particular zeal. The sole function of pleadings, he argued, should be to give notice of an issue, and counsel should not be allowed to try the cause at this stage. The elaborate artifice of most American jurisdictions encouraged unnecessary allegations that merely served to obstruct the speedy settlement of disputes. The laborious process of "declaration" (complaint) by the plaintiff, followed by the "plea" (answer) of the defendant, and then a "replication" by the plaintiff, a "rejoinder" by the defendant, a "surrejoinder" by the plaintiff, a "rebutter" by the defendant, a "surrebutter" by the plaintiff, all in an attempt to define an issue, could be reduced to a simple complaint and answer.[62]

Other procedural reforms would ensure that adjective law remained subordinate to substantive issues. The indiscriminate granting of new trials must be eliminated. If a new trial was necessary, Pound felt it should consider only those questions decided wrongly rather than the entire cause. If, during the course of a trial, the judge was uncertain about a point of law, he should be allowed to reserve that point for further consideration and later decision; the elimination of haste would also lessen judicial waste.

Structural changes in court organization could do much to eliminate judicial waste and procedural tangles, and Pound hoped many abuses would disappear in a unified judicial system. A unified court would transform independent courts of limited jurisdiction into divisions of a single court empowered to hear all causes. This would eliminate the burden of forum-shopping, which a plethora of separate jurisdictions encouraged. The very names of courts were misleading. There were "courts of appeals" that did not hear all appeals, state "supreme courts" that were not supreme, and courts of "general" jurisdiction that were not omnicompetent. A mistake in choosing one's court was fatal to a cause, and if much time were consumed, the statute of limitations may have run out and defeated the claim. A unified court could eliminate these problems, for a cause could be transferred and all previous proceedings could be saved. A unified court would also permit a more efficient utilization of judicial manpower, for idle judges could be easily transferred to divisions with crowded dockets.

The most important single proposal for procedural reform, an innovation that Pound considered indispensable for the success of all other measures, was a statute that sketched the general outlines of procedure while allowing courts to fill in the details. It would give courts enormous power to develop their own rules of procedure, and they could increase their prestige while making the rules more flexible and responsive. New techniques could be tested under the careful supervision of men who were best equipped by tradition and temperament to understand the law's requirements. The rule-making power, like so much of Pound's program for procedural reform, was designed to liberate the judiciary for genuinely creative work, to give judges new power over trials, to restore respect for the bench, and to allow it to fulfill its common law functions.

The central position of the rule-making power in Pound's blueprint for change illustrated his fundamental traditionalism. He was certain that the device, once an unchallenged judicial prerogative, could again release the judicial creativity that was the essence of law reform. The ultimate solution to existing procedural chaos could not come from legislatures; detailed codes simply prevented experimentation and froze dubious practices into permanent form. Yet although he condemned the "legislative Juggernaut," Pound recognized that the clumsy nineteenth-century codes were responses to real needs. What he deplored most of all was that courts had allowed the vacuum to develop. "Would not a more active interest in the details of practice on the part of judges," he asked, "and a reasonable activity on their part in using their common-law powers tend to obviate the petty legislative tinkering of which complaint is made so generally?" It was in this spirit that he urged lawyers to correct anachronisms in judicial organization and procedure "before the layman starts the legislative steam-roller upon its destructive course and levels the good with the bad."[63]

Although Pound was considered a bold advocate of change, he always advised caution in executing programs for procedural reform. After discussing a comprehensive scheme before the Illinois State Bar Association, he was quick to remind his auditors, "It is not intended that every one of those [recommendations] necessarily shall be put in force tomorrow or day after tomorrow."[64] His argument for granting rule-making authority to the courts suggested the familiar gradualism of the common law. The key reform of his program would enable courts to "bridge over the change from the old to the new and, by gradual and progressive development of the details through periodical revision of its rules, make it possible to achieve a revolution without too violent a shock."[65]

Pound was far in advance of the legal profession, but his distance from the crowd obscured the traditionalism and caution in his message. His radicalism was largely the creation of a backward bar. "I disclaim," he insisted, "any intention of making an 'attack' upon the courts."[66] It was a disclaimer he had to make frequently. Suspicious and unimaginative lawyers were always leveling charges of disloyalty, and they gathered at every major address Pound gave. At a meeting of the Illinois State Bar Association in 1910, a reporter noted that Pound's appearance "fill[ed] the large audience room with eager lawyers and judges, and with the thermometer crowding ninety degrees they all stayed on till adjournment."[67] Most of these eager lawyers were more eager to condemn than support him. In failing to recognize how much Pound operated within traditional patterns, they revealed the inertia of the legal profession.

At this meeting four justices of as many state supreme courts conducted a full-scale attack on Pound's program of procedural reform. Justice Oscar H. Montgomery of the Indiana Supreme Court acknowledged the need for some reform, but he thought that Pound's suggestions were the wrong ones. He was particularly horrified by the prospect of vesting more power in the trial judge. The American people had a distaste for arbitrary authority and would oppose any effort to establish a discretionary power in trial courts. Perhaps Justice Montgomery was unaware of his own discretionary power as an appellate judge. Justice Joseph B. Moore of Michigan was not convinced that any reform was necessary; Chief Justice John B. Winslow of Wisconsin was convinced that it was not. "We in Wisconsin," he said with an air of weary cynicism, "have been reformed so long that we have forgotten how it seems to be unreformed."[68]

The most biting criticism of Pound's program came from the chief justice of the Illinois Supreme Court, Alonzo K. Vickers. "It seems idle," said the outraged Vickers, "to talk about striking down all accumulated wisdom that experience has brought us since the government was founded and substituting therefor some new and untried experiment in the name of reform." He thought Pound was "the most radical reformer" he knew, a man "with a cynical determination to find some fault." Chief Justice Vickers was contemptuous of the argument that the law must adjust to a changing industrial civilization; rather, he contended, the law had created the glorious progress that modern America enjoyed.[69]

Other attacks followed the assault by the judges. One attorney suggested that existing procedural rules were adequate; all that was needed was lawyers who could understand the rules. Justice Orrin N. Carter of the Illinois Supreme Court took the proposals as a personal attack on himself and his fellow justices. At the end of the meeting the president of the Association, Edgar A. Bancroft, seemed reluctant to grant Pound a customary vote of appreciation for addressing the annual meeting.[70]

Pound faced an extremely vocal opposition, but there was also a nucleus of law reformers at the meeting. Edward C. Kramer, a judge who had long advocated changes in Illinois practice, spoke in favor of Pound's proposals. I. N. Bassett, an old and distinguished member, reminded the supreme court justices that they were not infallible men. Albert Kales was busy shaping certain of Pound's suggestions into a bill that the Committee on Judicial Administration would recommend.[71] Pound himself was working with the Committee on Law Reform on the draft of a major report.[72] The old order in Illinois had been challenged. Of Pound's role in the movement for procedural reform in Illinois, George Costigan assured him, "you can go away feeling that you have given the biggest push in the right direction in that matter that has been given in this state, and that some kind of reform is bound to result."[73]

Pound played a similar but larger part on the American Bar Association's Special Committee. Its first report in 1908 precipitated some of the sharpest debates in the recent history of the association.[74] The report suggested three changes in federal procedure. First, no judgment should be reversed for error unless the error created a miscarriage of justice. Second, the Supreme Court should not issue a writ of error or habeus corpus unless the accused were unjustly convicted or the petitioner unjustly held. Third, the judge should be able to reserve questions of law for later decision. The first two proposals were adopted; the third was referred back to committee. Many lawyers feared that allowing a judge to reserve questions of law would undermine jury trial, but the recommendation was adopted the following year. "In truth," Pound insisted, choosing his ground of argument with care, "it is not in any wise radical."[75]

The recommendations were incorporated into a bill that the Special Committee drafted and introduced in Congress in 1909. Members of both judiciary committees expressed interest in the bill as it stood, and the House committee conducted a full-scale hearing on the measure. Pound drafted the association report, and its recommendations, although not adopted completely, were incorporated into the revised Federal Equity Rules of 1912. Wisconsin had adopted many of the suggested reforms in 1909, and several states followed suit in succeeding years. Support also came from outside the law as *The Nation* lavished its editorial praise on the Special Committee.[76]

Much work would be necessary before a comprehensive program of procedural reform was widely enacted, but the basic outlines of this brand of legal reform were firmly established. No one has yet altered Pound's recommendations in any significant way. "Adjective law," he insisted, "is but an instrument; its categories of actions and proceedings were not stamped upon legal science by the Creator."[77] Pound had given life to a movement that would in time make this sentiment a commonplace.

7

An Indictment of American Jurisprudence

During his years as a law professor in Chicago, Pound was known primarily for his work in procedural reform, but he also began to acquire a reputation as a legal philosopher. The campaign for a modern procedure was merely a phase of his searching examination of the entire system. It enabled him to test his ideas and himself in the world of affairs, an experience he often missed as a scholar, but his attention never left the fundamental questions of jurisprudence. He had pondered the larger issues of the law for many years, and by 1910, the last of the Chicago years, he had formulated a systematic critique of American law. The central theme of his criticism was that the deductive method and nineteenth-century legal theory had created a closed system of legal rules, one that enshrined ephemeral anachronisms as fundamental principles, in conscious disregard of the society that law served. Although he was not yet prepared to suggest a comprehensive theoretical alternative, the ringing indictment he framed in Chicago served as a prelude to sociological jurisprudence. In identifying the central problems of law, he also charted the course for his developing legal philosophy.

Pound defined the basic problem in contemporary American law as "mechanical jurisprudence" or the "jurisprudence of conceptions." Mechanical jurisprudence, he declared, was "the rigorous logical deduction from predetermined conceptions in disregard of and often in the teeth of the actual facts."[1] It was artificial as well as analytical and abstract. The mechanical jurist reduced all legal problems to a series of unalterable assumptions and applied them in accordance with the internal logic of the assumptions. Hence the premise was not an aid to conclusion but rather contained the conclusion within itself. The entire American legal system was burdened with such sterile deductive thinking.

Advocates of mechanical jurisprudence insisted that their methods were scientific, but Pound regarded the process as the degeneration of scientific law. Science for the sake of science, he argued in tones reminiscent of George E. Howard, Edward A. Ross, and Albion Small, was hardly a proper standard for legal analysis. Lawyers should be scientific, but their science was a means to an end rather than an end in itself. Because science was only the method of law, a legal conception "must be judged by the results it achieves, not by the niceties of its internal structure." He condemned mechanical jurists for judging law "by the beauty of its logical processes or the strictness with which its rules proceed from the dogmas it takes for its foundation."[2]

This type of legal conceptualization was essentially a matter of mental gymnastics; mechanical jurists were not comfortable with hard facts. Loath to test their theoretical propositions by the evidence, they preferred to absorb the evidence into artificial categories of thought. In other words, they allowed theoretical questions to answer themselves. One of the most striking examples was a late-nineteenth-century doctrine in the American law of labor relations, liberty of contract.

Liberty of contract was a tortured extrapolation from widely accepted legal principles. Few Americans disagreed with the doctrine that all men were equal before the law, and few disputed the idea that the law of labor relations must respect both employers and employees as persons, protecting the rights of each as parties to a contract. From these premises courts concluded that wage and hour regulations were violations of the right of employees to contract at will for the terms of their labor. Liberty of contract was part of the "liberty" of which no person could be deprived without due process of law.[3]

It was the failure to test deductions that Pound condemned so bitterly. The courts, he wrote, did "not conceive any examination necessary in order to ascertain whether there is not *in fact* a difference."[4] In the new industrial state, employer and employee no longer confronted one another on a basis of equality. Perhaps the most absurd judicial offering at the altar of liberty of contract was an Illinois Supreme Court ruling in the mid-1890s. *Ritchie v. People* struck down a law regulating hours of women employed in the manufacture of clothing on the ground that it deprived women of the right to bargain freely for their labor while allowing men to retain such rights. The statute thus established an unconstitutional classification, denying to women what was granted to men. The opinion struck Pound as the emptiest legalism, and he suggested another mechanical deduction to show the bankruptcy of the general approach. At the time the Constitution was adopted, he noted, married women could not make any contracts. From this assumption, would it not follow that legislation could regulate the wages and labor of married women but not those of unmarried women? Perhaps, he mused, a court would not find such a deduction satisfying.[5]

Pound realized that the elimination of mechanical jurisprudence was a particularly formidable task, because mechanical jurisprudence was central to conventional legal theory. He disagreed with contemporaries who charged that lawyers and judges were not genuinely committed to a jurisprudence of conceptions but were simply using the method to rationalize non-legal beliefs. It was the lawyer's sincerity, declared Pound, rather than his cynicism that made change so difficult. He traced the sources of doctrines such as liberty of contract to the lawyer-as-lawyer rather than the lawyer-as-social-theorist. He did not discount the role of social, political, and economic influences, but he felt that mechanical jurisprudence was more a product of the contemporary lawyer's peculiar professional mystique. It had become a neutral principle of legal reasoning, and as such its presence was more pervasive and its influence more pernicious than any contrived rationalization. Mechanical jurisprudence was not a convenient device; it was an article of faith.[6]

Mechanical jurisprudence affected many branches of the law. Pound had labored diligently to demonstrate its operation in legal procedure and the administration of justice. Although the granting of new trials and appellate review was based on the doctrine that courts should be open to all, the practice enabled the wealthy litigant to exhaust his less fortunate rival. "If all men are equal," noted Pound, "their pocketbooks are not,—giving certain litigants a conspicuous advantage in reality through a theoretical equality." Like liberty of contract, the doctrine that trials were contests between equals was twisted by the jurisprudence of conceptions into a tortured conclusion.[7]

Mechanical jurisprudence was particularly ill-equipped

to handle the problems of a society being transformed through technological innovation, industrialism, and urban growth. A system of law in which all conclusions were contained within the rules was hardly appropriate for a society in which many of the rules were no longer relevant. Deductions marched onward to inevitable conclusions in spite of the changing contexts in which they must be applied. Such attitudes frequently paralyzed the bench; judges seemed helpless, for example, to meet the challenge that the modern press posed for fair trial. Pound was appalled at both the scurrilous newspaper comment on pending litigation and the frequent reluctance of courts to do anything about it. If an editor were to tell a juror to decide an issue a particular way, he would be punished for contempt. Yet if he put the same thing in his newspaper for the juror to read, he could not be restrained. Contempt became "freedom of the press" as the physical distance between editor and juror widened. "It is a singular illustration of the mechanical character of our jurisprudence," Pound complained, "that we deal severely with crude and ineffective methods of interference with the due course of justice which belong to a past age and suffer efficient and up-to-date methods capable of the greatest mischief to operate without check."[8]

Many legal concepts that were developed in a preindustrial era presumed a degree of community and an equality of status that no longer existed. Technology, industrialism, and metropolitan growth conquered physical distances but heightened social distances. Technological innovation introduced a new impersonality into public communication; urban development undermined an earlier sense of community; and preindustrial bonds between employers and employees could not survive the fragmented division of labor, anonymous factory organization, and separation of ownership and management. These new forces made the mechanical application of existing legal doctrine singularly ludicrous. Rules defining contempt in Chancellor Kent's courtroom were not adequate for an era of mass-circulation dailies; the shopkeeper's obligations to his clerks were anachronistic standards for labor relations in a steel mill; and equal access to the courts took on new meaning as individuals began to challenge corporations rather than other individuals.

In addition to undermining particular legal doctrines, modern industrial society also made certain larger theoretical approaches anachronistic. Pound was acutely aware that particular legal philosophies encouraged mechanical jurisprudence. "While lawyers affect to despise philosophy in law," he observed, "much of their legal thought is dominated by an obsolete philosophy."[9] Although he was not ready to announce a comprehensive philosophical alternative, Pound offered an inventory of obsolete theories, and the criticism provided a basis for his rapidly maturing sociological jurisprudence. The three modes of thought with the widest appeal among contemporary American lawyers—analytical jurisprudence, historical jurisprudence, and natural law—were particularly vulnerable to fossilization, and Pound argued that their persistence defined a major area of weakness in American law.

Natural law theory was the most common of the three. It had become part of the intellectual baggage of most American lawyers at the beginning of our national history, and nineteenth-century text writers and judges institutionalized it.[10] Natural law provided the foundation for analysis in the expanding field of private law and was virtually the sole factor in determining debate about public law. "Constitutional law," wrote Pound, "is full of natural law notions."[11] Perhaps he used the term "notions" to indicate his contempt for bankrupt doctrines parading under the banner of eternal truth. Pound refused to dignify much of the content of the natural law with the status of "ideas," and he was fundamentally opposed to the methods of conceptualization that gave natural law theory its peculiar character. It was the natural law as a mode of thought that Pound considered a serious barrier to modernity in law.

Despite the variety of the natural law tradition, and the constant requirement to adjust to changing conceptions of nature, certain common elements provided cohesiveness to centuries of philosophical inquiry.[12] The fundamental theme running throughout the tradition was a dualistic system whereby one would contrast positive law with a higher law, and then judge the doctrines of the former by the dictates of the latter. Natural laws were *a priori* standards, discoverable through reason for the secular theorist and through revelation for the religious, but always establishing absolute and immutable principles of universal validity. Natural law strove for unity as it proclaimed its universality, exhibiting a cosmopolitanism that provided a striking contrast to the particularism of the positive law. Pound applauded its cosmopolitanism and its traditional association with the quest for justice, but he was extremely hostile to natural law as a mode of thought. It reveled in universals, whereas Pound insisted on standards relative to time and place. It proclaimed the immutability of law, whereas Pound argued for evolutionary adjustment. It sought first principles through a deductive method; Pound stood firm for an inductive method. Natural law, he said, was a static system for a static society, and an appropriate ground for decision only "when all men are agreed in their moral and economic views and look to a single authority to fix them."[13]

Another legal philosophy that Pound considered detrimental to the proper development of law was analytical jurisprudence. Certain aspects of the analytical approach, such as its imperative features, had their origins in the rise of the modern nation-state. Yet the classic and most influential formulation of analytical jurisprudence came when John Austin first delivered his lectures at London University in 1832. Although Austin's lectures were not popular, his legal theory eventually caught the imagination of Britons and is still dominant in England, Canada, Australia, and New Zealand. Analytical jurisprudence enjoyed widespread popularity for a time in the United States, where it supplemented natural law as a dominant mode of legal thought.[14]

Unlike natural law theorists, analytical jurists established no dualism between existing law and higher law. Analytical jurisprudence was concerned only with the enacted positive law. Natural law was for theologians and metaphysicians; it had no place in the lawyer's learning. Analytical jurisprudence had no concern with morality or justice. "The philosophy of positive law," Austin insisted, "is concerned with law as it necessarily *is*, rather than law as it *ought* to be; with law as it must be, *be it good or bad*, rather than law as it must be, *if it be good*." The doctrine was echoed in Justice Holmes's "bad man" test; a bad man cared nothing for ethical rules, but he did "care a good deal to avoid being made to pay money, and will want to keep out of jail if he can." Urging this attitude as a working principle for lawyers, Holmes hoped it would encourage a concern with law as it is rather than as it ought to be.[15]

Whereas the natural law theorist looked to a higher law to test the validity of the positive law, analytical jurists accepted a temporal source. Law was the command dictated by a political superior to a political inferior. Law was, in

Thomas Hobbes's phrase, "the word of him, that by right hath command over others." Thomas E. Holland, an influential nineteenth-century legal writer, defined law as "a general rule of external human action enforced by a sovereign political authority." A similar attitude moved Holmes to state that the "prophecies of what the courts will do in fact, and nothing more pretentious, are what I mean by the law." The imperative element was one dimension of the insular focus that characterized analytical jurisprudence.[16]

In spite of these differences between natural law and analytical jurisprudence, the two shared an important feature that made both systems subject to mechanical operations. Both were self-contained bodies of thought. In the spirit of the natural lawyer, the analytical jurist isolated certain basic principles inherent in the existing law and spun out an entire system from those principles. There was no need to refer to nonlegal influences; the existing body of law contained all answers within itself.

The closed character of the analytical school was, for Pound, its most dangerous feature. It produced judges who dismissed causes for want of a legal remedy because they could not find an applicable statute or judicial decision. Pound treated the system with absolute contempt. "The process and the result," he complained, "are conceived of as something purely logical and scientific. If the result chances to be just, so much the better. But justice in the cause in hand is not the chief end. The facts of concrete causes are to be thrown into the judicial sausage-mill and are to be ground into uniformity; and the resulting sausage is to be labeled justice."[17]

A third tradition in legal philosophy, historical jurisprudence, posed another threat to progress. Historical jurisprudence reached its fullest flowering in the nineteenth century as part of the general reaction against the rationalism and natural rights philosophy of the Enlightenment. Its greatest popularity was in Germany, where Friedrich Karl von Savigny developed the doctrine for a generation of jurists. Historical jurisprudence entered English legal thought through the writings of Sir Henry Maine. Burkean in its basic spirit, it proclaimed a doctrine of organic growth, prescriptive usage, and extreme caution in all ventures to reform the status quo. But Rudolf von Jhering, Pound's predecessor in sociological jurisprudence, framed a powerful challenge in a debate with Savigny that anticipated Pound's attack on James Coolidge Carter.

Carter was one of the leading American advocates of historical jurisprudence. He had an impressive career in private practice and public service, founded the Association of the Bar of the City of New York, and served as its president five times. Having become president of the American Bar Association in 1895, he used the position to further a dramatic campaign to prevent the adoption of a civil code.[18]

It was fitting that one whose conception of law, in Pound's phrase, came "from Savigny through Sir Henry Maine" would reject natural law as vague and idealistic, condemn Austin's positivism for its force theory and lack of dignity, and build his own legal theory on the familiar foundation of custom.[19] Custom was not merely a source of law; custom was law, and law was custom. Law was simply the jural expression of organic folkways and mores, and like custom it was "self-existing and irrepealable." Law was "the unconscious creation of society, or, in other words, a growth." Carter revealed the dominant mood of historical jurisprudence in his conclusion that there was a "gradual, insensible and unconscious progress in the law," even though no mortal could perceive the movement.[20]

Because he believed law was the product of slow organic growth, Carter was understandably hostile to legislation. Statutes had a tendency to interrupt the normal development of legal doctrine. Judges were more able to understand the legal process than legislators, but they too had an extremely restricted function. "That the judge cannot *make* the law," he declared, "is accepted from the start. That there is already existing a rule by which the case must be determined is not doubted." A judge merely discovered rules that the mysterious process of time had created.[21]

To illustrate his theory of law, custom, and the role of government, Carter frequently used examples from the world of sports. In athletic events, he wrote, a referee was appointed to supervise the play. Games were not regulated by the commands of sovereign referees to subject athletes. The rules were derived from the habits and usages of time, habits that produced a set of standards to guide both players and officials.[22] But as a sports fan himself, Pound knew the weakness of the analogy. As a matter of fact, he observed, Austin's conception of law was a more accurate description of athletics. Commissions, committees, and congresses made the rules for every game from whist to baseball. Pound knew that legislation was "the source, the form and the formulating agency, to the exclusion of habits, usages or the standard of justice founded thereon."[23]

Pound did not deny that the habits of legal thought and practice were stubborn and difficult to change, but he rejected them as a standard for the profession or principle of legal science. Although Carter's fundamental position differed from that of most American lawyers, his conclusions tended to reinforce the conventional wisdom. "While he claims to be an historical jurist," noted Pound, "his philosophical position is that of natural law, with individualism and the principles of Anglo-American common law standing for nature." With this judgment on Carter, Pound caught the spirit of the entire body of American legal theory at the turn of the century. Although they began with a variety of theoretical premises, most American lawyers and jurists came to similar conclusions.[24]

American legal theory, over which the common law exerted a brooding dominance, exhibited an excessive fondness for individualism, a suspicion of legislation and administration, and a belief that judges discovered rather than created law. These principles had become basic tenets of a legal philosophy that grew increasingly difficult to square with reality and the requirements of modern life. Along with the habits of thought that characterized mechanical jurisprudence and the philosophical traditions that sustained them, these additional dogmas were a barrier to almost all reform campaigns that threatened existing relationships.

Although the prophets of laissez-faire had given individualism a new significance, it was nevertheless an integral part of the common law tradition. "If Coke were to come among us," Pound ventured, "he would be thoroughly at home in our constitutional law. There he would see the development and the fruition of his Second Institute." The liberties of the individual assumed a central position in the common law during the seventeenth-century struggles between the lawyers and the Stuarts, and the tradition in the following century passed to Sir William Blackstone, whose *Commentaries* became a bible for generations of American lawyers. American courts made a mystique of Blackstone's maxim that "the public good is in nothing more essentially interested than in the protection of every individual's private rights."[25]

The individualist conception of justice encouraged judicial hostility to legislation giving protection to laborers or aiding them in their relations with employers. The Illinois Supreme Court in the late nineteenth century, a bench peculiarly in tune with the status quo, invalidated a statute prohibiting company stores and requiring mine operators to pay a weekly wage. "Theoretically," held the court, "there is among our citizens no inferior class." In other cases the court held similar laws unconstitutional because they put laborers under guardianship, or degraded their manhood, or stamped them as imbeciles, or created a class of statutory laborers.[26] But to Pound and other sensitive observers of industrial America, it was becoming obvious that these criticisms were anachronistic. Industrialism was altering the nature of American life and redefining the impact of American law. The old formulas still persisted, but profound social and economic changes had given them new meaning. In the law, observed Pound, individualism "reached its complete logical development after the doctrine itself had lost its vitality."[27]

Another bankrupt doctrine was the maxim that statutes in derogation of the common law must be strictly construed. Legislation, Carter protested, "must limit itself to the office of aiding and supplementing the unconscious development of unwritten law."[28] The unwritten law was the product of common law courts; statutes, although politically superior, were spiritually secondary. The proper role of legislation was to clarify the common law, but when a statute altered common law practice or principles, the judge must interpret it in a rigorously strict manner, exercising great care that its application remain within the express letter of its language. Pound feared that this doctrine made creative legislation impossible. "No statute of any consequence," he observed, "can be anything but in derogation of the common law." As a result, the future was rather ominous, for "the social reformer and the legal reformer . . .

must always face the situation that the legislative . . . fruit of their labors will find no sympathy in those who apply it." Courts were so hostile to advanced social legislation that it became standard practice in drafting statutes to insert a preamble stating broadly the purpose of the act and to close with a provision declaring that the statute should be liberally construed.[29]

American lawyers, Pound complained, had fallen into the habit of equating the common law with the natural law, and in the realm of constitutional interpretation, the habit "lead judges to try statutes by the measure of common law doctrines rather then [*sic*] by the Constitution." He regarded the Ives case as a particularly dramatic example of this unfortunate practice. In the Ives case, decided in 1911, the New York Court of Appeals struck down a workman's compensation statute because it undermined the common law defenses of contributory negligence, assumption of risk, and the fellow-servant rule. The defenses allowed an employer to avoid a judgment for industrial accidents if the employee contributed to his injury through his own negligence or if another employee were responsible. If the accident were a common hazard of a particular job, the doctrine that the employee had assumed the risk by accepting the position frequently barred recovery. Regardless of the theoretical reasonableness of these defenses, the old law of master and servant had become as obsolete as its label, for the common law depended on a significant degree of intercourse, even intimacy, between employer and employee, and modern corporations did not provide it.[30]

The shattered social legislation that filled nineteenth-century judicial reports showed the toll that the doctrine of strict construction exacted. Judges frequently sacrificed statutes on the altar of the common law even in the face of clear expressions to the contrary by an admittedly superior legislature. The legislature could change the common law, ran the argument, but it was always to be assumed that it had not done so. A typical example was the Pennsylvania Supreme Court's interpretation of the Federal Safety Appliance Act in 1903. The statute, passed ten years earlier, required all railroad cars used in interstate commerce to have automatic couplings, and it provided that workmen injured on a car without the required couplings would not be considered to have assumed the risk of such employment. In the Schlemmer case a Pennsylvania trainman was ordered to couple manually a stationary car to one slowly moving toward him. It was nearly nine o'clock in the evening, and to perform the operation, difficult enough in full daylight, the workman crouched beneath the stationary car, holding an eighty-pound drawbar he was to guide into a small slot on the approaching car. As he moved into position to secure the coupling, he raised his head about an inch too high, and the moving car crushed the top of his skull. The man's widow brought suit for damages against the employer under the federal statute. The Pennsylvania Supreme Court upheld the validity of the statute; a legislature could eliminate the assumption-of-risk doctrine. Nevertheless, the court observed, "it would not be seriously contended that such an employee might recover for an injury to which his own negligence had contributed." In its faithfulness to the common law the court emasculated the statute and destroyed the prohibition against imputing assumption of risk to the worker by permitting the same defense under another label.[31]

Judicial suspicion of statutes was not limited to a dislike of legislation as an institutional force; judges were also suspicious of the legal abilities of legislators. This was particularly ironic since nineteenth-century requirements for judicial office were similar to those for election to a legislature.

In both cases political abilities were the supreme assets. Pound agreed that legislatures had passed some abominable statutes, but he also noted that failure had not been confined to one branch of government. "Freaks of judicial law-making," he wrote, "are abundant." The reports were filled with the folly of the bench, and judges themselves had admitted it. "Lists of overruled cases," he observed wryly, "are quite as long and quite as formidable as schedules of repealed statutes."[32]

One could no longer object that all statutes were ill-considered and hastily adopted. No judicial opinion was more carefully framed than the draft acts written by the Conference of Commissioners on Uniform State Laws or the National Congress on Uniform Divorce Legislation. "What court that passes upon industrial legislation," he asked, "is able or pretends to investigate conditions of manufacture, to visit factories and workshops and see them in operation, and to take the testimony of employers, employees, physicians, social workers, and economists as to the needs of workmen and of the public, as a legislative committee may and often does?" In addition to the advantages of legislative investigations, new agencies such as the Legislative Reference Library in Wisconsin, under the able directorship of Charles McCarthy, provided legislators with unprecedented opportunities for framing excellent statutes.[33]

What was needed in many fields of law, Pound maintained, was a new beginning that legislation alone could provide. Although he was an enthusiastic defender of the judiciary, he believed that courts were simply unequipped to perform the detailed investigations necessary for certain areas of legal reform. The demand for new initiatives by the legislature showed how markedly Pound differed from reigning professional opinion. Few lawyers felt that modern society required new organizing principles, or that the existing law could not provide all necessary remedies. "In my judgment," Pound confided to Ross with an uncharacteristic sense of urgency, "our only hope of any permanent improvement in the administration of justice is in legislation." He thought that no efforts should be spared in encouraging improvement in legislation and legislative techniques. The suspicion of statutes would merely intensify the anarchy of existing law, and he deplored the continued encouragement that eminent lawyers gave to the doctrine of strict construction. "The fact is," he said, "we are getting an immense amount of 'cloud-cuckoo-town' common law. We can only be delivered from this by a legislative new start, and I think such institutions as Doctor McCarthy's will prove to be our chief hope."[34]

The conflict between the common law and legislation was an impediment to modernity in law, and the conflict between the courts and administrative agencies represented a similar problem. Pound was no great friend of executive justice; it was an attempt to secure justice without law, and few lawyers could approve of that. Yet Pound deplored the blind hostility of the bench and bar toward administration. There was an unwholesome tendency for courts to hamper executive action and assume staggering and inappropriate administrative burdens. Pound applied a pragmatic test to the judge as an administrator and found him wanting. The judiciary simply could not perform the vital administrative functions that the proper conduct of modern affairs required. He pointed to the obvious bankruptcy of the Supreme Court's self-appointed role as a rate-setting agency for interstate carriers, a function it had usurped from the Interstate Commerce Commission. Pound suggested that the judicial version of the administrative regulation of business had also been a failure. Actions for deceit and suits for mismanagement did not attack the basic problems of stock manipulation. Similarly, the delay attendant upon putting a bank into receivership or reorganizing a public service company was a disgrace.[35]

The judiciary's attempt to perform administrative functions was demoralizing as well as clumsy and wasteful. Pound was particularly concerned about the insult that one coordinate branch of government heaped on another. He simply refused to believe that the governance of man must be restricted to the courts alone. "Surely the energies of government ought not to be dissipated in internal conflict," he reflected, "when there is more than enough to be done in the protection of society. Surely it is folly to pay one set of magistrates to do what another is paid to undo."[36]

Most jurists would have responded that it was folly to give administrative agencies anything to do in the first place. Law was not made, it was discovered, and any compromise with that wisdom did irreparable harm. American lawyers agreed with Blackstone that judges did not exercise a law-making function even when they overruled earlier decisions. "In such cases," Blackstone taught, "the subsequent judges do not pretend to make a new law, but to vindicate the old one from misrepresentation. For if it be found that the former decision is manifestly absurd or unjust, it is declared, not that such a sentence was *bad law*, but that it was *not law*." The old law had never been valid; the judges who announced it had simply erred by failing to discover the correct principle. Calvin Coolidge, with his characteristic attachment to the obsolete, summed up the larger aspects of this attitude. "Men do not make laws," he announced to what must have been a bewildered Massachusetts Senate. "They do but discover them. . . . That state is most fortunate in its form of government which has the aptest instruments for the discovery of laws."[37]

Pound condemned this narrow theory as unsound, fictitious, and even dishonest. Judicial lawmaking was a fact of life, and one must be blind to miss the creative aspects of the judge's art. Progressive theorists in Germany admitted and debated judicial discretion, but American lawyers refused to acknowledge its existence. "With us," wrote Pound, "the process is concealed. Ostensibly there is no such power. . . . But we have a great deal of *freie Rechtsfindung* in America, while disclaiming it in theory."[38]

It was necessary to understand the character of judicial legislation in order to appreciate the real complexity of a legal system. Pound borrowed two Austinian concepts —genuine interpretation and spurious interpretation—to illustrate alternative methods of statutory construction. Genuine interpretation was an effort to discover the intention of the lawmaker; spurious interpretation was an effort "to make, unmake, or remake, and not merely to discover." The latter technique, he insisted, was completely legislative, acceptable during a period of growth through juristic interpretation and legislative quiescence, but an anachronism in a period of active legislation.[39]

Pound did not mean that judges should refuse a creative part; he supported no version of mechanical jurisprudence. There would be room enough for judicial maneuver after legislatures established new standards. But judicial lawmaking was not adequate for the major tasks; by its very nature, it was incapable of achieving the far-reaching changes that modern society required. What judges needed more than anything else was a proper respect for legislation. Spurious interpretation of statutes was no less demoralizing than repeated injunctions to administrative agencies. He pleaded, in the tradition of Thayer and Holmes, for judicial restraint and reminded judges that judicial review rested on no express text, and "if contemplated at all, it was contemplated that the power would be exercised with shamefacedness and sobriety."[40]

Judicial restraint was only part of a larger warning of caution. Just as the judiciary had attempted too much, law itself assumed inappropriate burdens. Laymen as well as lawyers expected law to do too much. "Experience has shown abundantly," at least to Pound, "that law is not adapted to be a teacher of morals. Enactments which may not be enforced are but parodies of laws." There were limits to effective legal action, and beyond those limits law proceeded at its peril. Law was powerless to establish relationships, rights, and duties that the public would not support.[41]

The weaknesses in American law had their origins in diverse sources—the common law tradition, obsolete legal philosophies, and nineteenth-century laissez-faire conceptions. But these were not the only sources. In one of his most original insights Pound located many of the weaknesses in the influence of Puritanism. His sophisticated treatment of Puritanism and the law, which he first developed in 1910, came at a time when most American scholars either dismissed the Puritans as bigots or glorified them as architects of American democracy.

The first major growing period of the common law was the early seventeenth century, but the century of Coke was also the century of Cotton. Pound pointed to the Puritan doctrines of individualism and contract as major influences on English legal thought in its formative years. Anticipating the work of later scholars, he described the unique conjunction of the concept of man as a free moral agent and the concept of contract that permeated Puritan thought. The two ideas operating in tandem affected virtually every field of law.[42]

According to Pound, Puritan notions were immediately apparent in such doctrines as liberty of contract, assumption of risk, and contributory negligence. All were based on the concept of the employee as a free agent who, having freely chosen his occupation and bargained for the terms of his employment, chose to assume the risks of that employment. In the criminal law Puritanism prevented the individualization of justice. Because all men were equally free, all must be treated equally; one thief was like any other.[43]

Institutions in the administration of justice did not escape the influence of Puritanism. It encouraged an elaborate procedure to hem in the trial judge and frowned on equity because it elevated the judge above others. The Puritan hoped to eliminate the unfortunate consequences of depraved man in a position of power by narrowing the magistrate's personal freedom of maneuver. Administration was paralyzed for similar reasons. The Puritan, Pound argued, hated control by the magistrate but loved to lay down rules. "Accordingly we have an abundance of rules and no adequate provision for carrying them out."[44]

Above all, the Puritan loved to use law as a device for implementing his brand of morality and thus failed to recognize the limits of effective legal action. The Puritan feared power because he distrusted man; and he encouraged the erection of enervating checks and balances. All of these things—individualism, depraved humanity, love of rules, and fear of power—contributed to the growth of the judicial laissez-faire that permeated late-nineteenth-century constitutional law.[45]

Pound's strictures against the Puritans did not diminish his increasing attractiveness to the most successful Puritan institution. Ezra Ripley Thayer, dean-elect of the Harvard Law School, was impressed with Pound's scholarship and suggested his appointment to the recently vacated Story

Professorship. In February 1910 President A. Lawrence Lowell sent a discreet inquiry about Pound to Dean Wigmore, who recommended him as a congenial and rewarding colleague, a man of unsurpassed ability, and the most eligible candidate for the position.[46]

When the offer from Harvard came, Pound had to weigh it against an opportunity to return to active practice with a Chicago attorney. He missed the routine of a busy law office, but the Harvard position, which included the responsibility for developing a fourth-year graduate program as well as the Story Professorship, was a compelling one. The charming Thayer was extremely persuasive with both Pound and his wife, and Pound's friends were unanimous in urging him to accept the appointment. Emory R. Buckner, just beginning a lively career in New York, reminded him that Harvard graduates "scatter over the whole country and your influence at once becomes national instead of parochial." Omer F. Hershey believed that since "most of our Eastern radicals go west it is fitting that good Western stuff should take their place and tone up our effeteness."[47]

As he prepared to return to Harvard after an absence of twenty years, Pound had completed an impressive survey of the fundamental weaknesses in American legal thought. The diagnosis had been finished; the prescription came next. The Pound prescription was maturing rapidly, and many glimmers of it were already apparent, but the systematic articulation of his philosophy was still incomplete at the conclusion of the Chicago years. Sociological jurisprudence, the philosophy that became synonymous with the name of Roscoe Pound, would unfold at the Harvard Law School.

8

Pragmatism in
Legal Theory

Sociological jurisprudence made its appearance during an exciting period in the history of the American mind. The Progressive era was a time of feverish reassessment, and although many disparate soundings were taken, the revolt against formalism became a dominant theme of the age. In every field of intellectual activity, American thinkers began to challenge modes of analysis based on the internal logic of timeless, *a priori* systems. Classical economic theory, natural law, and scientific history were but a few of the great systems toppled by the critical relativism of Thorstein Veblen, Oliver Wendell Holmes, Jr., and James Harvey Robinson. Antiformalists called on social scientists in all fields to launch a united attack on closed systems, fixed principles, and deductive analysis. William James spoke for a new generation of thinkers when he demanded a new *"attitude of looking away from first things, principles, 'categories,' supposed necessities; and of looking towards last things, fruits, consequences, facts."*[1]

Pragmatism provided a philosophical framework for the revolt against formalism, and James, as a founder of prag-

matism, was a leader of the revolt. James gave his generation new meanings for experience, truth, and knowledge.
Experience was a "booming, buzzing confusion" of a world
in flux. Truth was not a static property; it was something
that "*happens* to an idea. [An idea] *becomes* true, is *made* true
by events." Knowledge was acquired through an active participation in the construction of reality rather than through
a passive observation of a completed reality. Pragmatism
placed a heavy burden on the knower, for he had constantly
to test hypotheses against the data of his experience.[2]

Because individuals had to undertake an active quest for
limited truths in an open, incomplete, and pluralistic universe, James called for a new habit of thought that "means
the open air and possibilities of nature, as against dogma,
artificiality, and the pretense of finality in truth." He implored his generation to reject "the monistic superstition
under which I had grown up," and he dismissed all "block
universes" that tried to make a metaphysics of a metaphor.
"Our laws are only approximations," he concluded; "no
theory is absolutely a transcript of reality."[3]

James's philosophy was a guide for the individual life. He
was primarily interested in the psyche and the soul, and he
gave little time to questions of social philosophy. In the
hands of John Dewey, however, pragmatism was refashioned for public problems. Ideas became instruments
and, as such, could be used in reshaping the environment.
Dewey implored philosophers to forswear "inquiry after
absolute origins and absolute finalities in order to explore
specific values and the specific conditions that generate
them." He condemned the quest for certainty for "its
paralyzing effect on human action" and argued for experimentation in solving social and political problems.
Philosophers should shift their attention from lifeless ab-

stractions to public questions of politics, morality, and education.[4]

Pound was excited about this new movement in American philosophy, and he told a bar association audience that "pragmatism must be the philosophy of the lawyer." The cadence of his address quickened as he chronicled the impact of pragmatism on current American thought. "This movement," he explained, "is remaking the natural and physical sciences, is rewriting history, is recasting political theories, is making over economic theory, and, under the name of sociology, is changing our attitude toward all problems of social life." Jurisprudence, he confessed, was one of the last fields to respond to the new intellectual ferment, but it could not escape the trends that were shattering nineteenth-century modes of analysis.[5]

The revolt against formalism that Pound described had its origin in Darwinism, which he had absorbed as a young botanist. Pound helped translate the relativistic, evolutionary, and experimental features of the new science into a modern theory of law, as other social theorists had pursued similar themes in history, political science, economics, and sociology. James Harvey Robinson, who would one day invite Pound to lecture at the New School, urged historians to seek the developmental patterns in history that explained contemporary social life. History must be more than a static reconstruction of the past, more than a rediscovery of "recipes for the making of statesmen and warriors"; it must call on the social sciences to explain the social, intellectual, and economic life of the people and must pay less attention to the comings and goings of kings.[6] In political theory, Arthur Bentley, with whom Pound expressed an intellectual kinship, argued that politics was a fluid, indeterminate process of group interaction, and he defined the state as an instrument for mediating among competing interests rather than an abstraction that possessed some mysterious quantity called sovereignty.[7] Charles Beard, who acknowledged Pound as an inspiration in his *Economic Interpretation of the Constitution*, studied politics as "the whole man participating in the work of government" and sought to explain the social dynamics of political decisions. "Man as a political animal," he concluded, "acting upon political, as distinguished from more vital and powerful motives, is the most unsubstantial of all abstractions." In a similar spirit, Thorstein Veblen called on economists to reject the "invisible hand" and "economic man" of classical economic theory; economic behavior could not be deduced from sterile, self-contained models of pure competition, but much could be learned from an anthropological study of predatory capitalists and the status-seeking consumers whom they bilked. Sociologists like Lester Ward, Edward A. Ross, and Albion Small declared that man need not be a passive victim of impersonal forces; he could exercise a measure of control over the volatile social environment that surrounded him, and could redefine progress in terms of social welfare rather than private gain.[8]

Pound had already developed a view of law that rejected formalism and finality, and within months after his return to Harvard in 1910 he began to mold the gropings of a decade into a comprehensive legal philosophy. His scholarship and teaching, combined with a flair for administration and public activity, had established him as an important figure in the legal profession. In Chicago he had offered his audience a diagnosis of the law's weaknesses, and now he was prepared to suggest a more complete prescription. Furthermore, he could locate his most advanced proposals within the "general movement in all departments of mental activity away from the purely formal, away from hard and fast notions, away from traditional categories which our fathers supposed were impressed upon the nature of things for all time." He expressed a strong kinship with the pragmatists and defined his position in unmistakably Deweyesque terms. "The sociological movement in jurisprudence," he announced, "is a movement for pragmatism as a philosophy of law; for the adjustment of principles and doctrines to the human conditions they are to govern rather than to assumed first principles; for putting the human factor in the central place and relegating logic to its true position as an instrument."[9]

The problems of social change and legal reform were, for Pound, fundamentally intellectual problems. The opponents of change were not bad men dominated by sinister interests; they were simply motivated by a different set of assumptions and a different social strategy. The conflict between reformer and reactionary was "an intellectual conflict, . . . a war of ideas not of men," and Pound refused to engage in speculation about the economic interests of his opponents. He felt that it was far more important to accept their integrity and to attempt to shatter their theoretical defenses. By keeping the debate at a high level and maintaining a spirit of generosity, he also minimized the danger of alienating large elements of his profession.[10]

The fundamental weakness of conventional legal theory was its attempt to erect a closed system of immutable principles. Mechanical jurisprudence, the bane of pragmatic reformers, treated legal principles as automatic conclusions rather than tentative premises. With regard to questions of public policy, Americans had long used " 'unconstitutional' as . . . a solving word which could dispose of every inconvenient problem." Legal conceptions, divorced from life, became empty phrases. "Like Habib in the Arabian Nights," Pound observed, "we wave aloft our scimitar and pronounce the talismatic word."[11]

If lawyers were to play a meaningful role in modern society, they would have to abandon the tyranny of labels and "think of legal principles as instruments rather than as eternal pigeonholes into which all human relations must be made to fit." As instruments, legal ideas must be judged by the goals they achieved and the purposes for which they were framed, for they had no intrinsic worth. Meaning and value were a function of their ends rather than their essences. "The futility of a self-sufficing, self-centered science of law," he wrote, was becoming apparent to lawyers everywhere.[12]

Legal ideas, as instruments, were not self-defining concepts. The attitudes and aims of those who wielded ideas contributed to the instrumental character of the ideas. A lawyer's psychological makeup affected his conception of due process, contributory negligence, and culpable action. As a pragmatist, Pound rejected the spectator theory of knowledge. Earlier empirical traditions insisted that the individual was a passive agent in the learning process, that the mind was a *tabula rasa* on which experience traced itself. Pound insisted that the individual was an active agent who brought his interests, plans, and purposes to the process of learning and applying law, and as an active agent he interpreted the data as he received and used them. Thus the purpose of the law was inextricably bound to the purpose of the lawyer.[13]

The process of social inquiry was not merely a matter of individual psychology, and Pound called for the constant testing of legal doctrine by a community of dedicated investigators. He deplored the tendency of many legal scholars to disguise intellectually unsound work as practical work.[14]

The task of evaluating law and adapting it to pressing social requirements called "for more science and more research than has ever been demanded in the past." Much of the work was so complex that government action would be required, and Pound hoped for widespread government-sponsored research in criminology and punitive justice. A ministry of justice, similar to the new legislative reference bureaus, should be created to study the law and its administration in functional terms and to make recommendations to meet the legal needs of the community. His passion for research was part of the larger intellectual pattern of the Progressive era, a period in which the rise of social research accompanied the rise of social reform. Promoters of change were no longer willing to rely on righteous slogans. Pragmatism had encouraged painstaking verification rather than comfortable expediency.[15]

Sociological jurisprudence dealt with facts rather than fictions, a focus that Pound considered liberating for American lawyers. It introduced a particularly healthy note of realism into theories of the judicial process, which had long labored under the delusion that judges never made law, but always discovered it. When Morris Cohen outlined the lawmaking functions of the bench, several prominent law school deans wrote him that the slot-machine theory of justice should be maintained even though judicial legislation was a fact of life. Cohen, dissenting, expressed "an abiding conviction that to recognize the truth and adjust one's self to it, is in the end the easiest and most advisable course."[16]

Pound agreed with Cohen's analysis and insisted that as a prelude to decision, "judicial law-making must know itself; it must know what it is." Finding, interpreting, and applying the law were often inseparable from making it, and judicial legislation was "a necessary element in the determination of all but the simplest controversies." In refusing to recognize the fact that judges must make law, the slot-machine theory placed severe intellectual limitations on judicial performance and gave judicial opinions a ring of hypocrisy.[17]

As a supplement to the larger fiction of judicial passivity, conventional theory also maintained a sharp division between law and fact, and held that judges dealt only with questions of law. But Pound argued that questions of law were intimately connected with questions of fact and that the failure to recognize their interrelatedness was a hazard to proper judicial decision. When viewed as a matter of law, liberty of contract seemed a reasonable legal doctrine. When viewed as a matter of fact, it appeared much less reasonable.[18]

Pound was not hostile to judicial legislation, but he objected bitterly to uniformed judicial legislation. Judges must be aware of the realities of the judicial process if they were to judge well. They must acknowledge the creativity of their station, accept the wide limits within which they were free to deal with individual cases, and think of legal rules as guides for decision rather than inevitable injunctions.[19] Above all, they must understand "that legal systems do and must grow, that legal principles are not absolute, but are relative to time and place."[20]

The idea of a passive judge applying a closed system of law was an image contrived for the appellate courts, where the issues for decision were often highly refined. Unlike most of his contemporaries, Pound recognized that the myth revealed a singular lack of concern for the trial courts, where the issues were less abstract, and where life loomed larger in the form of jurors, witnesses, and parties. Even the names given to courts of first instance were unattractive. They were "inferior" courts, "lower" courts, courts for the administration of "petty" justice. Pound deplored the fact that few people realized the importance of trial judges. He told a Texas audience that appellate judges should be required to sit in trial courts occasionally so that the issues would seem less abstract on appeal. Indeed, he felt that the problems of the lower courts should be the primary concern for legal reformers; these were "the only courts with which the mass of the people habitually come in contact, and courts which, therefore, should be the very best which the Commonwealth can afford."[21] Petty litigation should be quick, inexpensive, and just, for it was easy to wear down a poor man. Yet although the state should make justice cheap, it should not cheapen it by staffing its inferior courts with inferior judges.[22]

At the trial level, life made its presence felt in many forms, but the community's sense of justice was institutionalized in its representative at court, the jury. Pound had mixed emotions about the jury. Its methods of decision were frequently unsound, and it introduced an element of chaos into law. Pound liked his law a little neater, but he decided that juries atoned for their conspicuous defects by "tempering the administration of justice with common-sense and preserving a due connection of the rules governing every-day relations with every-day needs of ordinary men." If the law were too concerned with the abstract integrity of its principles rather than the social effects of their application, the jury would infuse a sense of justice into the administration of justice.[23]

Jury trials helped establish the limits of effective legal action, for they restricted the scope of unpopular law. In suits involving industrial accidents, juries often refused to apply rigid legal conceptions like contributory negligence, assumption of risk, and the fellow-servant rule, doctrines that, Pound agreed, were intolerable in modern industrial

societies.[24] "Laws are not self-enforcing," he observed, "and
. . . enforcement depends upon the general will." Law could
not be effective if it ran counter to existing standards of
justice, and Pound was certain that the end of law was
justice.[25]

A legal system designed for "an American farming community of the first half of the nineteenth century" simply
could not "administer justice to great urban communities"
of the twentieth century. A new kind of justice, "social
justice," was required for modern life. The state and law
were fundamentally social institutions that existed for social
ends. Individual interests, long the major concern of law
and government, should be treated only as a means of
securing larger social ends. As social ends changed, law
must change its conception of individual interests.[26] "It has
not proved enough," Pound argued, "to give to everyone a
free road, relieved of physical interference by the strong
and protected against fraud and deception."[27]

It was to the standard of social justice that juries repaired
when they sought to modify anachronisms in law; Pound
saw that social science techniques provided a better way of
infusing law with ideas from the outside. Lawyers and
judges must turn to the social sciences if the administration
of justice were to remain vital. In common with other advanced social thinkers in the Progressive era, Pound advocated an interdisciplinary assault on social problems. The
separation of jurisprudence from other social sciences had
created a "gulf between legal thought and popular thought
on matters of social reform," and one result was a misinformed bar. "Let us look the facts of human conduct in the
face," Pound implored. "Let us look to economics and
sociology and philosophy, and cease to assume that jurisprudence is self-sufficient. . . . Let us not become legal
monks."[28]

The social sciences offered many suggestive devices for improving judicial performance. Pound challenged lawyers to create a rational method for advising courts about the facts of a case and the consequences of a ruling.[29] Intelligent judges agreed that they needed more assistance with many of the complex problems coming before them for decision. "How long we shall continue to blunder along," said Judge Learned Hand of the federal bench, "without the aid of unpartisan and authoritative scientific assistance in the administration of justice, no one knows; but all fair persons not conventionalized by provincial legal habits of mind ought, I should think, unite to effect some such advance."[30] Pound thought that one solution for this problem was the Brandeis brief, a technique pioneered by Louis Brandeis in *Muller v. Oregon*. Brandeis persuaded the Supreme Court that an Oregon statute limiting the hours of working women was a reasonable police regulation; his unconventional brief contained a few pages of law and over one hundred pages of material from physicians, social workers, factory inspectors, and other nonjudicial authorities.[31]

Pound had known Brandeis before he came to Harvard, but his respect for the social justice views of the People's Attorney increased through more frequent contact.[32] Brandeis kept in touch with developments at the law school as a representative of the Harvard Board of Overseers, and Pound saw him often in the years between 1910 and 1916. In 1916, when Brandeis was appointed to the Supreme Court, Pound joined the Brandeis forces in the bitter confirmation struggle that followed. He gave a glowing tribute to Brandeis that appeared in the Boston *Post* at a time when his own appointment as dean of the law school hung in the balance. President Lowell, several leaders of the Boston bar, and sundry prominent friends of Harvard bitterly opposed Brandeis's nomination.[33] To his sister Olivia, Pound wrote that the opposition was "all prejudice." He condemned "the mighty of the bar" for their blindness, which he likened to the "arrant nonsense" of Populists who opposed the appointment of good lawyers to the bench simply because they had taken cases for corporations.[34]

In a bold and professionally dangerous move, Pound sent a thoughtful letter of endorsement to Senator William E. Chilton, chairman of the subcommittee conducting hearings on the nomination. He noted Brandeis's public service and social wisdom, pointed to his remarkable brief in the Muller case, and mentioned his path-breaking article on the right of privacy, published twenty-six years earlier. In addition to the well-known features of his career, Brandeis was one of the finest attorneys in the country. "So far as sheer legal ability is concerned, he will rank with the best who have sat upon the bench of the Supreme Court." Pound dismissed the charge that Brandeis was lacking in judicial temperament and observed that good advocates often made good judges. With regard to the charges of professional misconduct, which leading State Street attorneys had circulated, he mentioned, with subtle irony, that the Harvard Board of Overseers had chosen Brandeis for long service on the Committee to Visit the Law School, and Pound refused to believe "that these gentlemen would have appointed him . . . had they believed him deficient in professional honor." It was unnecessary for Pound to add that the Harvard Board of Overseers was a State Street institution.[35]

Brandeis' uncommon abilities as a lawyer appealed to Pound's standards of professional expertise, but he also admired the nominee's concept of social justice. A devotion to social justice rather than laissez-faire constitutionalism moved Pound to offer his services to the friends of child labor regulation, and on 30 August 1917 he presented the government's opening argument in a test of the national Child Labor Act of 1916.[36] A few months earlier he had written that society must "insist on social conduct on the part of owners and employers," and now he had an opportunity to act on his ideas.[37]

The reformers were delighted with Pound's offer of assistance, and Felix Frankfurter, a Harvard colleague on leave for wartime service in Washington, urged that Pound be put in complete charge of *Hammer v. Dagenhart*, the child labor test case. He told Attorney General Thomas W. Gregory that no one else could do the job as well, and Florence Kelley, general secretary of the National Consumers' League, agreed with Frankfurter. Felix Adler, chairman of the National Child Labor Committee, made every effort to secure the leading position for Pound, but Thomas I. Parkinson, a Columbia law professor who aided in drafting the statute, retained formal control of the case in spite of these entreaties.[38] Parkinson's position as principal attorney of record, however, did not prevent Pound from becoming the dominant figure as soon as he entered the case, and Florence Kelley reported that "having Roscoe Pound to defend the new Child Labor Law is as fine as our having had Mr. Brandeis for our [hours and wages] suits."[39]

The case was tried before Judge James E. Boyd in a federal district court at Greensboro, North Carolina, and able attorneys appeared for both sides. Pound delivered the opening argument for the government. His opposite number, Junius Parker, the general counsel for the American Tobacco Company, was joined by some of the leaders of the North Carolina bar in the attack on the statute.[40] The opposition argued that the law was an improper use of the commerce power. In forbidding the products of child labor access to interstate channels, Congress had invaded the police power of state governments. Parker contended that the Constitution gave no direct police power to the federal government, and it could not regulate such matters under the guise of regulating commerce. His colleague, William P. Bynum, presented a familiar interpretation, limiting regulation to products that were inherently harmful to health, safety, and morals.

Bynum and Parker offered arguments that had long been associated with laissez-faire constitutionalism. During the late nineteenth century, lawyers had fashioned an extremely limited definition of federal control over interstate commerce, a definition that became a major barrier to legislative regulation of economic behavior. The restricted version of the commerce power rested on a set of assumptions that extolled passive government and unrestrained economic acquisitiveness. Apologists for business enterprise, appropriating the language of the Enlightenment, transformed the natural rights of man into a manifesto for pure competition. The Enlightenment suspicion of arbitrary political power became an injunction against all government activity beyond the preservation of order; government could only disturb the equilibrium of natural economic forces. Social Darwinists like William Graham Sumner added a new dimension to the jungle ethic of the Gilded Age, for the analogy of natural selection suggested that the struggle for existence guaranteed the survival of the fittest in society as well as in nature. There was, in short, no justification for social welfare measures such as child labor laws, and laissez-faire constitutionalists implored the courts to protect individual rights and fundamental social processes from government interference.

Pound's forceful argument presented a different interpretation of federal power that made social justice the goal of legal action. He declared that the commerce power was extremely broad, so that Congress could regulate the interstate movement of virtually any article of commerce. The commerce power could not be exercised in an arbitrary or unreasonable manner, but it was not limited to purely "commercial" articles that were inherently evil. Congress had forbidden the interstate shipment of lottery tickets, the issuance of interstate railroad passes, and the interstate transportation of women for immoral purposes. The Child Labor Law was a similar regulation. It was designed to protect children and to encourage those enlightened states that had passed child labor laws. Although Congress had no police power, it could regulate such matters in the lawful exercise of the commerce power.[41]

The setting was not favorable for advanced views of social justice and federal power. Judge Boyd was a Confederate veteran who opened court with the singing of "Dixie" and held court in a similar spirit. He dismissed as chimerical the idea that people felt they were supporting an institution by buying the products of that institution. Pound objected to this reasoning, recalled that his abolitionist grandfather would not use sugar because it had been produced by slaves, and argued that Congress could have prohibited the interstate shipment of slave-produced sugar.[42] The judge was horrified by Pound's bold assertion. Did the present law, he asked, also extend to the products of children who worked in the healthy sunshine of cotton and tobacco fields? "Massachusetts, ye gods, and slaves," declared a local newspaper, "and a Harvard professor in the wilds of the south on another emancipatory pilgrimage!" Predictably, Judge Boyd ruled that the statute violated due process of law.[43]

Everyone involved in the case praised Pound's role in it. "I cannot say too much of Mr. Pound's generous modest and invaluable help," wrote Julia Lathrop, who as director of the Children's Bureau was charged with enforcing the statute. Grace Abbott, who headed the bureau's child labor division, felt that Pound had made an able argument. Even the hostile *Greensboro Daily Record* admitted that he "was clear and profound in his argument." Edward S. Corwin, a young political scientist, accepted Pound's analysis and condemned the decision as a "displaced fossil from a bygone epoch of constitutionalism."[44]

After the trial, Pound continued to maintain an interest in the case, and he gave Julia Lathrop advice on the appeal to the Supreme Court.[45] His role in the defense of child labor legislation revealed his passion for translating ideas into action. He was almost a literalist in the pragmatic acceptance of action as the primary context for the definition of meaning and value. Ideas must be tested in the crucible of experience, and, as a man of ideas, Pound felt it was his duty to see that the test was conducted.

The idea that the intellectual was the last best hope for social development was a familiar theme during the Progressive era. Lester Ward, a prophet of the new social science, argued that man could organize the chaos of nature through the use of intelligence. "All progress," he said flatly, "is due to intellectual activity." He looked forward to a time when "sociological laboratories" took precedence over legislatures in the formation of public policy and when legislation would be the product of "exhaustive experiments on the part of true scientific sociologists and sociological inventors." Other men proclaimed the creative social role of the expert. Robert A. Woods, a pioneer settlement-house worker, noted that social science, unlike other sciences, "includes within its data the constructive and reconstructive energy of the conscious mind." The economist Richard T. Ely pledged allegiance to a "natural aristocracy . . . which lives for the fulfilment of special service." Ely's

New England counterpart, Frank Parsons, had a dramatic conception of the potential of the expert. "Life can be molded," he asserted, "into any conceivable form. Draw up your specifications for man . . . and if you will give me control of the environment and time enough, I will clothe your dreams in flesh and blood." The theoretician of the New Nationalism, Herbert Croly, summed up a generation of thought when he called for "the selection of peculiarly competent, energetic, and responsible individuals to perform the peculiarly difficult and exacting parts in a socially constructive drama."[46]

In this spirit, Pound demanded a science of "social engineering" and he apotheosized "the instinct of the experienced workman." He was not plagued, like Croly, with the agonizing task of maintaining the democratic character and integrity of the elite. He put little faith in the wisdom of the masses, and he specifically rejected Felix Frankfurter's suggestion that the expert must be on tap rather than on top. "The wail of the unfit," he confided to Dean Ezra Thayer, "is very apt to be made in the name of Demos." The frontier experience, a vital determinant of the American character, had done much to make democracy "a synonym of vulgarity and provincialism." The "exaltation of incompetency and distrust of special competency . . . seems to be an unhappy by-product of democracy."[47]

Since he was not troubled by the antidemocratic implications of social engineering, Pound could advocate the need for expertise without any hesitation. "We must rely on the common sense of the common man as to common things and the common sense of the expert as to uncommon things," he declared. "And this common sense cannot be put in the form of a syllogism."[48] The social role of the intellectual was a complex and demanding one, but men of knowledge must not shirk their duty. Through the "efficacy of effort," a phrase of Lester Ward's that Pound constantly employed, intelligent men could order their environment anew.

Although Pound was distressed that, as a professional type, "the lawyer stands alone today in his lack of faith in the efficacy of organized human effort," he was confident that the bar was changing for the better. The current fatalism, a product of analytical, historical, and natural law theories, ran counter to the finest traditions of the law. Great lawyers had played a creative role throughout legal history. "If Coke and Marshall and Savigny were children of their times," he said, "they were children who knew how to get their own way!" Lawyers could again introduce new dynamism into law. The new legislative reference services and the hoped-for ministry of justice were institutional devices for modernity in jurisprudence. But the most encouraging preview of a new social engineering in law was the emergence of the professional law teacher. "As efficacy of effort, already part of the social and political creed, becomes part of the juristic creed," Pound ventured, "the law teacher and law writer—and I take it they will be one—must be our chief reliance." As the most expert of lawyers, the law professor would produce a new generation of legal experts.[49]

As dean of the Nebraska College of Law, Pound had argued for the centrality of professional education in improving the bar, and he continued to press those views as a Harvard professor. He taught some undergraduate law courses, but most of his time was devoted to supervising the graduate program in which he offered two courses, jurisprudence and Roman law. He thought the graduate program was especially important, for it would provide future law professors with an unprecedented expertise. Pound was bitterly critical of some older teachers who claimed to be more "human" than their more skillful young counterparts.[50] The older men had been responsible for much of the rigidity in legal thought, and although Pound opposed the recall of judicial opinions, he was not adverse to the "recall of law teachers, or at least recall of a great deal of law teaching."[51]

Pound discovered that Harvard offered attractive conditions for his teaching as well as his scholarship. He liked many things about the law school, but he was particularly impressed with the quality of its students. He enjoyed his classes, and he sensed that he was "having even more than my usual luck with them."[52] Zechariah Chafee, Jr., later a colleague, remarked that Pound's course in jurisprudence "entirely changed my views of law and I believe the results of it will stay with me through life." Other men at Harvard felt a new spirit at work in the law school. "What is it that you do," inquired Albert B. Hart of the history department, "that so arouses hard-thinking young minds? . . . You take the responsibility of upsetting people's cherished formulas." It was the presence of Pound that brought Felix Frankfurter to the law faculty. Frankfurter, who left a promising career in private practice and public service, had some misgivings about the quiet life of a university professor. "But, with Pound there," he wrote, "I see this as an opportunity for somebody to help fashion a jurisprudence adequate to our industrial and economic needs."[53]

Pound's reputation thrived in circles outside the Harvard ambit. Julian Mack, a leader in the juvenile court movement, thought him "as broad a man as I know in the law. . . . If there is one man whom we need on our side," he wrote Paul Kellogg, reform-minded editor of *The Survey*, "it is Pound." Another crusader, journalist William Hard, wrote, "I am now a kind of circulation agent for you." Albion Small, a leader of the first generation of American sociologists, confessed that "it is heartening to find that other voices in the wilderness are beginning to try to get within chiming distance and to form a chorus that is likely to give some concert before it quits."[54]

Others, however, raised their voices in more strident tones. Nicholas Murray Butler, president of Columbia University, dismissed sociological jurisprudence as a fad, part of the temporary academic flirtation with social science. "Just now law is under attack," pontificated President Butler, "from a curious mixture of sentiment and lore that calls itself sociological jurisprudence, and which I understand to be a sort of legal osteopathy." Edward A. Harriman, a Connecticut attorney, respected Pound as a thinker but felt that his intellectual abilities made his message more ominous. "His philosophical radicalism," Harriman shuddered, "seems to me so dangerous for our conglomerate American democracy."[55]

The most vicious attack came from men who equated sociology with socialism. Judge Robert Ludlow Fowler combined xenophobia and anti-intellectualism with laissez-faire in a major assault on the new jurisprudence. Judge Fowler detected an alien influence at work. "What is it," he asked, "that the lovers of German philosophies propose to substitute for the admirable philosophies of the .common law?" He was certain that "the new legal philosophies of law are the philosophies of socialism."[56] The real culprits, according to Fowler, were law professors. "The so-called 'jurists,' pure and simple," he declared, "are not well trained to fight in the arena of common life." He doubted their abilities in less recondite but more important fields like cross-examining witnesses. The jurists, in short, were guilty of the professional equivalent of never having met a payroll.[57]

Although this senseless attack must have infuriated

Pound, his reply was a model of restrained understatement. He asked if an idea should "be dubbed socialism because it is a bit unfamiliar." The common law was not endangered by contact with ideas from outside the law, and American lawyers since the era of John Adams and James Wilson had looked to Continental jurisprudence for inspiration. Friends of Pound and modern legal theory joined in the rebuttal. Morris Cohen doubted that reputable American geologists refused to read the studies of European scientists. "Of all works of vanity," he complained, "the erection of a dead Chinese wall around the American legal intellect is the vainest." Joseph H. Drake, a witty advocate of the new learning, suggested that Judge Fowler had been "frightened by the likeness of the term sociological to socialistic" and recommended a less frightening name for sociological jurisprudence. Albert Kocourek, Pound's colleague at Northwestern, remarked that Judge Fowler had found that legal philosophy was more dangerous for him than for his country.[58]

When Dean Thayer died, in September 1915, Pound, as the most prominent law professor, immediately came under consideration for the vacant deanship. The *New Republic*, observing the national significance of the position, expressed hope that Harvard would overcome "the spirit of the Brahmin caste" in making an appointment. Felix Frankfurter threw himself into the task of overcoming that spirit with tireless efforts in Pound's behalf. Other friends, however, hoped Pound would refuse the deanship. "Don't let them make you dean," wrote Henry M. Bates, dean of the Michigan Law School. "We can't afford to have your energies diverted from teaching[,] scholarship—and thinking." Similar advice came from Morris Cohen, and at Chicago philosopher James H. Tufts wondered if Pound would "fit in well to administrative work."[59]

Pound also had some doubts about the deanship, and he twice refused the position.[60] But the Harvard Corporation made certain adjustments in administrative obligations, and he finally accepted the offer.[61] He realized that the deanship was a strategic position in the world of American law, and he sensed a chance to do important work. "Things are more or less in transition in law everywhere," he wrote, "and this school has a great opportunity if we can rise to it."[62]

The corporation named Pound to the deanship in January 1916, and he began his duties the following month. Although he had feared that "the combination of a non-Harvard man, pro-German . . . and pro-Brandeis man is more than the traffic will bear," Harvard rose to the occasion. The New Republic predicted that Pound would "create a new and vital tradition" to supplement and subtly alter the revolution wrought by Langdell. The Christian Science Monitor commended Harvard for its choice and praised Pound's "radicalism as a citizen and as a thinker." Exercising the wisdom of hindsight, the Monitor proclaimed that it had been "a forbidding day for a reactionary, legally intrenched individualism when he got a professorial fulcrum in Cambridge."[63]

Friends and admirers sent their congratulations to the new dean. "Many of us," wrote Learned Hand, "look to you as the natural leader of legal education in the country today, both in equipment and in foresight." Emory Buckner, a friend from Nebraska days, was ecstatic about the appointment. "Now that the common peepul have established you and Felix within the walls of Troy as stool pigeons," wrote Buckner, "I tremble for the future of the codfish." Louis Brandeis told a Chicago audience that Harvard had secured the services of a leader in the movement for a living law. Orrin Kip McMurray, dean of the California Law School, predicted that Pound's deanship would eclipse the Langdell era.[64]

Most observers characterized the new dean as an advanced reformer, likely to set new revolutions in motion at Harvard, but one man, Lawrence B. Evans, had a different insight, one that was hauntingly prophetic. Evans, aware that many of his colleagues at the Boston bar thought Pound's views "savor of a dangerous radicalism," tried to quell their fears. The new dean, argued Evans, was an able lawyer and part of the profession's advanced guard, but he was not a radical. There would be no revolutions at Harvard, for Pound had a passion for the common law and a distaste for hasty changes.[65]

Evans was an obscure Boston lawyer, but he understood Pound's message more clearly than most of his famous contemporaries. As an instrumentalist and a critic of closed systems, Pound gave expression to some of the most advanced elements of contemporary social theory. But other intellectual loyalties served as a check on the reform potential of his instrumentalist impulses. His thought, like his personality, was a blend of boldness and caution. The instrumentalist features often seemed like grace notes in a larger chorus of traditionalism, professionalism, and organicism.

9

Organicism Versus Instrumentalism: An Unresolved Dualism

James Coolidge Carter must have turned in his grave when Pound was named Carter Professor of General Jurisprudence in 1913. Carter had been one of the leading disciples of historical jurisprudence, and his posthumous paean to the status quo, *Law: Its Origin, Growth and Function*, delighted in the imperceptible gradualism of legal development. In addition to that parting shot at progress, which Pound attacked without reservation, Carter endowed a chair at the Harvard Law School with the instructions that its occupant should expose the pernicious effects of legislation.[1]

Pound was not the sort of professor that Carter had in mind. His dynamic personality and self-assured ability to mobilize professional opinion suggested an agitator, and sociological jurisprudence suggested heresy. "The influence of the Harvard Law School through Frankfurter and Pound," wrote William Howard Taft in 1922, "is to break down that fundamental instrument [the Constitution] and make it go for nothing." Time has softened that judgment, but thoughtful students of American legal theory continue to give it some credence. Pound's historical reputation retains the aura of radicalism that a backward bar imputed to him early in the century. Henry Steele Commager has written that Pound united Progressivism with jurisprudence in order "to make law an efficient instrument for social reconstruction." Judge Charles E. Wyzanski recently called attention to "the social engineering doctrines as enunciated by Pound and practiced by the welfare state."[2]

Such interpretations obscure elements in Pound's thought that made it impossible for him to demand social reconstruction or serve as a prophet of the welfare state. The idea that law should be based on social realities rather than timeless abstractions, a major theme in Pound's message, represented a fundamental change in jurisprudence, but Pound did not intend to underwrite a program of widespread reform. Although others used sociological jurisprudence as a justification for social reconstruction, Pound's intentions were much more limited. The nature of his sociology, for example, restricted the range of law as an instrument of reform. When Pound demanded that law respond to the rhythms of life, he had in mind a life that was harmonious and directional rather than discordant and improvisational. Sociological jurisprudence established new rules for debate, but the new rules did not guarantee radical conclusions.

In spite of his demands for new directions in jurisprudence, there was no question about his ultimate loyalties. William Hard, a perceptive journalist, offered a far better interpretation than those of Commager and Wyzanski, when in 1908 he characterized Pound's philosophy as "the words of a cautious, conscientious man, of a man who loves the common law, of a man who wishes to see the common law revived to the needs and restored to the affections of the common people."[3] Throughout the Progressive era, the period when Pound reached his peak of creativity, there were always themes of caution that limited his boldest proposals. He demanded an alliance of law and social science, but law was to be the senior partner. He joined with other intellectuals in a plea for a unified social science, but law was to absorb the other disciplines.[4] He was relentless in his campaign to expose anachronisms in law, but his principal objection to bad law was its effect on the legal system rather than on society. The evil of anachronisms in law, he wrote, "will live . . . in impaired authority of the courts long after the decisions themselves are forgotten."[5]

The common law tradition was the central fact of Pound's intellectual life, and it forced him to compromise the instrumentalist features of his thought. That tradition encouraged loyalties to organicism, traditionalism, and professionalism, loyalties that conditioned his espousal of law as a mechanism for change. Pound wanted to implement only those reforms that promoted one of his larger loyalties. He was enthusiastic about procedural reform because it released the creative capacity of the judiciary, and thus increased the professional character of a traditional institution designed to preserve an organic connection among past, present, and future. But some reforms, such as the recall of judicial decisions, challenged Pound's most cherished values, and he was bitterly critical of those ventures.

Organicism, traditionalism, and professionalism affected all the advanced elements in sociological jurisprudence. Pound's fascination with organic social theory was succinctly captured in his frequent assertion that "the law will *absorb* the new economics and the new social science [italics added]."[6] When dominant modes of thought absorbed lesser modes, the latter were refashioned for the larger purposes of the former. Pound's thought was also steeped in traditionalism, and he urged the judiciary, as the central agency of the common law, to translate the new learning in the spirit of the common law.[7] Finally, professional consolidation and growth would give new vitality to law and enable the bar to regain its traditional position of social leadership. Law professors, Pound insisted, must "give to their teaching the color which will lift new generations of lawyers to lead the people as they should, instead of giving up their legitimate hegemony in legislation and politics to engineers and naturalists and economists."[8]

Organicism, a major theme of caution in Pound's thought, was a complex body of ideas to which social scientists with widely differing viewpoints had repaired. It was capable of endless nuance, but certain elements gave it peculiar unity as a mode of thought. All organicists considered society a compound of factors in mutual interaction, giving interrelatedness and internal dynamism to a social life that contained the seeds of its own development. Society, as Edward A. Ross put it, did not fall apart into segments like a peeled orange. Particulars were only meaningful in connection with the whole; the former received their character from the latter. Biological analogies and metaphors became familiar devices in the literature of organic social theory, devices that served as both abstractions and abstractions reified. "Society," Richard T. Ely argued, "is . . . a living, growing organism," and Ross marveled at "the consensus that unites facts the most diverse in character."[9]

Organicism came easily to Pound, for he extracted it from the common law tradition to which he was so passionately devoted. He insisted that the medieval idea of relation, the most creative feature of the common law, was also the most fruitful conception for modern jurisprudence. The idea of relation, intimately connected with the notion of status, was a legitimate child of organicism. It was more meaningful to interpret rights, duties, and liabilities as incidents of a relation rather than as terms of a transaction or a culpable action. Thus the rights and responsibilities of employer and employee received their legal definition in terms of the relationship of the parties rather than the will of the parties. Pound reversed Sir Henry Maine's famous generalization that the history of progress was written in the transition from status to contract. Maine considered the allied concepts of status and relation anachronistic, but Pound saw them as the only rational alternatives to the individualism of nineteenth-century Anglo-American law, and he interpreted the most modern legal doctrines in terms of these medieval common law conceptions. Workmen's compensation statutes replaced the triad of will, contract, and individualism with a new understanding of industrial labor in an impersonal economy. A similar theme appeared in the law of public service companies, where the obligations of the company proceeded from its relation to the public rather than from the terms of a contract. Pound based his theory of progress on doctrines found in the yearbooks.[10]

The common law tradition offered Pound a familiar channel to organicism, but it was not the only route traveled by this eclectic intellectual. There was a clear conjunction here of his law and his sociology. Sociologists had a fascination with medievalism in the formative era of the discipline, and organicism was a useful legacy for theorists bent on undoing the atomistic and antitraditional elements of Enlightenment thought. Ely claimed that all great thinkers accepted "the conception of the state as an organism," and certainly many in his generation did. The brilliant but eccentric Charles S. Peirce, whose subterranean influence affected many young intellectuals, demonstrated the appeal of organic analogies when he asked, "Now you and I—what are we? Mere cells of the social organism." "*Not merely in sociology*," concluded Albion Small, "*but in every department of knowledge, the organic concept is the most distinctive modern note.*"[11]

By the end of the nineteenth century, organicism had made major inroads in each of the developing social sciences, and most theorists accepted fundamental social coherence as an axiom of their disciplines. "If we take society to include the whole of human life," Charles Horton Cooley announced for a generation of American intellectuals, "this may truly be said to be organic, in the sense that influences may be and are transmitted from one part to any other part, so that all parts are bound together into an interdependent whole." The variables of social life had no separate existence but were joined in a continuous process of simultaneous interaction, "giving rise to an endless system of reciprocal growth."[12]

Cooley's definition of society gave a continuing significance to the unity and interdependence of the social process. Internal regulating principles allowed society to enjoy a dynamic equilibrium through successive stages of growth. In addition to ensuring an integrated balance at each level of society's progressive development, the inner dynamism gave cultural evolution a predictable direction as well. But in spite of the apparent openness that the analogies drawn from life suggested, organic social theories had a self-fulfilling character that made them closed systems. The internal monitors, the well-defined stages of growth, and the tendency toward equilibrium, even a dynamic one, placed severe restrictions on human agency as an instrument of social change and limited the range of social development itself. It was one of the modern mind's greatest ironies that a social theory drawing its inspiration from Darwinism left so little room for the play of the contingent and the unforeseen.

Pound's theory of social interests, the product of this important sociological tradition, reinforced the organicism of the common law. He had first encountered the conception in the jurisprudence of Rudolf von Jhering, but he was directly influenced by Albion Small, who defined "*the whole life-process* [as] *the process of developing, adjusting, and satisfying interests.*" Pound hoped that this theory would replace the conventional preoccupation with "rights" as the basis of law. Legal doctrines and claims seeking legal recognition, he argued, should be interpreted only in terms of the social interests that they secured.[13]

Pound defined six classes of social interests. The social interest in the general security included public health, protection against crime and foreign aggression, and security of contracts and property. The social interest in the security of social institutions required protection of religion, domestic relations, political freedoms, and the economy. The social interest in general morals included the problems of obscenity and other violations of community moral standards. A collection of concerns dear to many Progressives, the social interest in the conservation of social resources, included both physical and human resources. Finally, there were social interests in general progress and in the individual life.[14]

This comprehensive scheme was designed to promote thorough and systematic analysis of legal problems, but Pound did not consider his catalogue of interests complete or unchanging. He framed expansive categories that would accommodate new demands such as the emerging right of privacy.[15] Privacy was an elusive concept, still in search of a definition, and by including it as a legitimate demand, Pound served notice that his catalogue of social interests had room for novelty. In addition to their flexibility, the primary interests were social rather than individual and suggested clusters of interrelated problems. Furthermore, they were not *a priori* values. Social interests were constructs that emerged from the operation of society itself, and the balancing of those interests gave society its basic character and unity.[16] Like the organic notions of status and relation, the focal point of the theory was at the intersection of interests. This distinguished Pound from earlier organicists who, like Herbert Spencer, focused on the functions performed by the parts rather than the relationships among them.[17]

Pound acknowledged the contradictory impulses of social forces, but his theory of social development emphasized accommodation and consensus. His competing social interests represented a different orientation from earlier organic theories, whose laws of society made no provision for conflict, but Pound's conflicts were neither enduring nor irreconcilable. His social interests challenged one another as parts of a larger whole rather than as self-contained entities struggling within a vacuum, and their interaction, although occasionally violent, was fundamentally meliorative. There was conflict between interests, but the results were balanced ones rather than victories and defeats.[18]

Although law and sociology were the primary contributors to his organicism, Pound also received an assist from botany. Ideas derived from science provided subtle reinforcement for his mature social theory. "The analogies of modern thought," he declared, "are to be found not in geometry but in biology."[19] Pound made frequent use of such analogies. He used the idea of polyphylesis to explain the diverse origins of particular legal doctrines. Poly-phylesis, the converging development of many species into a single species, implied a complex harmonizing of diverse but interrelated factors. The phylogenetic image of a great branching tree of life informed his ideas of law as well as botany.[20]

Law, like the floral covering, developed by stages toward a final end. Pound's description of five stages on a teleological continuum of legal growth was a familiar conception, and it complemented the climax theory introduced in the *Phytogeography of Nebraska*. Teleological organicism had a pervasive impact on American thought at the turn of the century, and it encouraged the search for progressive levels of development in society as well as in nature. Pound's evolutionary scheme, which explained the growth of all legal systems, suggested that law had an internal dynamism impelling it toward an ultimate goal. The first stage, archaic law, was designed to keep peace by preventing private justice. The second stage, strict law, accompanied the rise of the state, and its goal was certainty and uniformity. The succeeding stage was equity, which modified the rigors of strict law through ideas of ethics, morality, and justice. The fourth stage, maturity of law, provided the certainty of strict law but extended equality and security to all men. By the late nineteenth century, society was entering the final stage, the socialization of law.[21]

The socialization of law required four steps. As with the larger stages, Pound's language suggested a process rather than a mere scheme of classification. In the beginning this final stage utilized the mechanical mode of Comte, but Spencer introduced biological conceptions that smacked of jungle ethics. Fortunately, jurisprudence hurried on to a psychological stage, where Lester Ward transformed social forces into psychic factors. The final step, representing the culmination of centuries, was the stage of unification, a fitting conclusion for an organic process.[22]

Pound pursued two unities, both of which were part of the larger unity of society. He wanted to unite the study of law with the other social sciences. "The legal problem," he said, agreeing with Ross, "is only part of a larger one—he who tries to separate it 'tears a seamless web.' "[23] In addition, he also spoke often of the "unity of our law from Coke to the present,"[24] and he predicted the coming of a "universal sentiment of justice."[25] Judge Hand did not fully understand the nature of this unity, but he hoped Pound would continue to seek it. "I am glad that Pound keeps insisting upon the essential unity of all law," he wrote. "If it turns out there isn't any, at least the time is not wasted."[26] Pound's quest for unity in law was never clearly defined, but the impulse clearly defined the nature of his quest.

This organic sense of unity made him suspicious of "special legislation," statutes designed to protect a particular class or interest. Broker-state grants to special groups threatened the larger unity by dividing it. With a few exceptions, notably laws affecting women and children, he insisted that statutes bestowing favors or exacting restrictions must be applicable to all relevant groups and persons. He deplored the fact that many jurisdictions denied railroads the use of contributory negligence as a defense in damage suits while allowing all other defendants to use it. Pound was not a partisan of the railroads; he objected to similar distinctions among other litigants. Several courts had held that a father was liable for his son's negligent operation of the family automobile, even if he had driven it without permission. Yet no court would hold a father liable for a son's mishandling of the family horse. Pound could see no legitimate reason for such distinctions, but they were "coming to be legion," he complained, "and they run counter to the very idea of law."[27] Law eliminated divisions; it must not introduce new ones.

Organicism rejected disunity, but it abhorred discontinuity. No gaps existed in the seamless web that described the natural state. Traditionalism was a frequent ingredient of organic social theory, and Pound had a profound attachment to received wisdom and institutions. "In law especially," he declared, "nothing is made at once, as it were, out of whole cloth." There were two elements at work in law, the traditional and the imperative, elements that corresponded to the organic and instrumental features of his own thought. It was to society's great benefit that the traditional element "usually swallows up the [imperative element], and incorporates its results in the body of tradition."[28] As in his own thought, where themes of caution established the limits of social engineering, tradition defined the ground rules for the operation of conscious manipulative change.

Although Pound recognized that tradition sometimes held too fast, and that it often created friction when forced to answer new problems, he argued that the traditional element was also "the surest means of deliverance" from the problems of modern life and "our great safeguard against the shaping of the law by class interests."[29] It was the internal dynamic in law, providing a much-needed stability as well as the potential for growth. In mature legal systems, he insisted, "growth takes place chiefly . . . by working out the results of principles which are found in the traditional materials."[30]

He never tired of advancing this proposition as an operational principle, and he berated his academic colleagues in political science and sociology for failing to pay closer attention to the legal wisdom of the ages. "Don't you think," he inquired of Morris Cohen, the reform-minded philosopher, "that one who endeavors to be scientific may be orthodox once in a while? Really, insurgency ought not to be practiced for its own sake and after all many of the orthodox ideas in jurisprudence represent a deal of experience which, off-hand, insurgents are sometimes likely to throw over on quite insufficient *a priori* grounds."[31]

This hostility to *a priori* reasoning did not prevent Pound from raising the traditional element in law to the realm of first principles. He was so devoted to the common law tradition that he considered it to be completely adequate for modern society. At a time when many thoughtful men questioned the utility of traditional responses to industrialism, Pound insisted that industrialism created no insurmountable problems for the common law. "It is not too much to say," he ventured, "that 'the common law is adequate to deal with all real industrial wrongs,' provided we address ourselves vigorously and intelligently to the difficult problem of enforcement."[32]

Pound was always eager to defend the common law tradition against the criticism that it was anachronistic. Some legal doctrines, of course, represented serious barriers to progress, but Pound insisted that they were usually not integral parts of the common law. The doctrine that statutes in derogation of the common law must be strictly construed was merely a product of American courts in the late nineteenth century, and not an enduring principle of Anglo-American law.[33] Similarly, liberty of contract was "simply wrong, not only in constitutional law, but from the standpoint of the common law." Another problem of deep concern to Pound, the inflated importance of an over-refined procedure, was also "quite a departure from the common law."[34]

A variety of self-adjusting features enabled the common law to discard obstructionist doctrines, and one of the most attractive of those features, for Pound, was the system's ability to contradict itself. Even when committed to a fatal course of action, the common law always seemed to harbor alternatives. When a body of law was based on an unsound principle, it "was gradually surrounded by a mass of exceptions, distinctions and limitations" that allowed "the current of judicial decisions to flow normally." In this manner the common law drew success from its failure. That Pound was able to put his faith in "exceptions, distinctions and limitations" was a mark of his deep commitment to the common law. He could take hope in its halting half-steps and asides even if the major thrust were objectionable. This gave him an optimism about the future development of law that was not always shared by other sensitive contemporaries. "What, then, is the hope for future labor legislation?" he asked in 1909, when courts were making the Sherman Act and the due process clause major hurdles for the labor movement. "On the whole one must say it is bright."[35]

Pound apotheosized the institution that had erected those barriers, the judiciary, for it was the agency that preserved the traditional materials of the common law. One of the points of controversy separating friends of the common law from friends of reform was the question of the courts. The judiciary often frustrated the efforts of reformers, whereas stalwarts saw it as a bulwark of sanity in a world gone mad. Pound tried to appeal to both groups by combining a defense of the judiciary with a program of reform. "On the whole," he assured the skeptical, "our courts have the best constructive record of any of our institutions." Because the judiciary was really the most creative element in American life, reformers should make every effort to secure those changes that would release the creative capacities of judges. The future, like the past, was in the hands of the courts, "the living oracles of the law."[36]

Background and belief drove Pound to pledge himself to

this most characteristic institution of the common law. His insistence on the centrality of the judiciary shaped the character of his reform efforts. "The most real grievance of the mass of the people against American law," he argued, "is not with respect to the substantive law." While other reformers agitated for wage and hour laws, antitrust laws, juvenile codes, and other substantive measures, Pound campaigned strongest for the reform of judicial procedure and the reorganization of courts. "You invite zealous social reformers everywhere," he complained to Paul Kellogg, the crusading editor, "to agitate for more legislation when it is better administration which is required."[37] Many problems could be solved if unnecessary restraints were removed from trial judges, if courts were allowed to devise their own practice rules, and if a unified judicial system were established to halt the dispersal of judicial energy. These reforms would enable judges, men who "see more and know more of life than almost any other class of men,"[38] to apply their uniquely creative talents to the task of modernizing the law.

In spite of innovations in law and government, the judiciary continued to be the indispensable agency in the administration of justice. Legislation was becoming increasingly important in the development of law, but Pound did not see it as a challenge to the common law. Statutes could often provide a fresh start for the solution of certain problems, but the ultimate direction of that change was in the opinions of judges. "The living law," Pound insisted, "is not the principle in the books, the dictum in the reports, the section of the code, but the rule which results from judicial treatment of controversies."[39]

The rise of administrative agencies gave him greater cause for alarm, and he condemned an excessive use of the administrative process as a "reversion to the methods of the

Orient, this recrudescence of Harun al Raschid and Baldwin of the Hatchet." Still he had faith that the common law
would triumph. "Time has always imposed a legal yoke
upon executive justice," he observed, "and has turned administrative tribunals into ordinary courts."[40] A different
problem arose with the necessity for innovations in juvenile
courts, domestic relations courts, and small claims courts.
There were dangers inherent in these deviations from traditional judicial practice, but they could be neutralized by
staffing the new courts with capable judges. Even bad
judges, he concluded, were superior to administrative officers. In matters involving the role of legislation, administrative agencies, and unconventional tribunals, he warned
fellow lawyers to exercise vigilance.[41]

Pound's devotion to the judiciary was so deep that it
enabled him to sustain the most contradictory and ironic
apologies. Although judges were the most creative men of
law, they could not be held responsible for any backward-
ness of the law. Courts, he insisted, "must go with the main
body, not with the advance guard, and with the main body
only when it has attained reasonably fixed and settled conceptions." His position thus protected the courts from criticism on virtually all counts. Courts should be esteemed for
their creative potential, but they should not be criticized for
a refusal to lead. Pound's high regard for the judiciary led
him to the ironic conclusion that an experienced judge
could arrive at just decisions "without consciousness of the
census of interests and the weighing and valuing of interests," without consciousness, in other words, of Pound's
most original contribution to jurisprudence—the theory of
social interests.[42]

The movement for the recall of judicial decisions reached
its height after 1911, when Theodore Roosevelt lent his
support to the reform. Pound regarded both the advocate

and the proposal as distasteful. As a student at Harvard in 1889, he had characterized a Roosevelt address as "considerable rot," and his opinion of the colonel's latest crusade was equally unkind. "I can't help feeling," he wrote, "that Roosevelt only half understands the point in what he writes about courts. Certainly the recall is not going to improve them."[43] He was critical of attempts to make judges "mouth-pieces of the will of the majority for the time being." "King Demos" mistrusted courts because he hated all restraint. "We see something of the same feeling," he complained, "in lynchings, in those irregular, arbitrary, ill-considered executions of what the mob thinks right at the crisis of action."[44]

Judicial recall was thus an attack on the very existence of judicial power, and Pound's identification of that attack with lynch law revealed another dimension of his enthusiasm for the courts. Judges were experts, uniquely equipped by training, tradition, and temperament to direct the administration of justice. Most Americans, unfortunately, minimized the importance of expertise and assumed that all men were competent to legislate and judge. Pound saw this unhappy attitude as a popular phase of the recurring seventeenth-century conflict between the Stuarts and the common law courts, and he frequently invoked Lord Coke's dictum that legal questions must be judged, not by ordinary reason, but by the "artificial reason and judgment of law."[45]

Coke supplied a link with the past, but Pound also drew on a contemporary stream of thought to develop the conception of judges as experts in the law. He was able to combine the classical wisdom of Coke with the modern wisdom of Ward in the comfortable amalgam of professionalism. Professionalism offered the promise of an improved bar and renewed public esteem for lawyers and judges. This vision had encouraged Pound to take a leading part in the creation of the modern Nebraska State Bar Association, it sustained him in his continuous effort to use bar associations as levers of reform, and it produced his lifelong concern with education, the most sensitive point in the creation and nurture of professions. Throughout his life, he saw professionalism as a means of giving institutional strength to expertise in law.[46]

Thus the "organization, training, and professional feeling of the bar" became a major goal in Pound's program for progress. It had a profound impact on his thought and operated as a brake on his intellectual range. His professional identification was a source of conventions and restraints, and it ensured that his vision would be channeled and limited. It led ultimately to an unhealthy parochialism, which emasculated his more familiar demand that lawyers must also be social scientists.

The parochialism was at once apparent in his conception of legal education. Although a lawyer should be familiar with the social sciences, it was not the duty of the law school to provide such training. The law school, in presiding over the rites of passage, must transmit only the special and peculiar wisdom of the profession. "The great variety offered by the college today," he insisted, "is thoroughly out of place in the professional school which should instead aim to do with complete thoroughness a given bit of work carefully selected for the purpose." He urged Coke's maxim—*non multa sed multum* (not quantity but quality)—as the guiding principle for professional schools. "For a season," he told Thomas Reed Powell, "law school men must stand together firmly against any attempt to dilute our curricula."[47] The profession should define itself and the world it served in its own terms.

In order to produce a generation of experts, Pound put

special emphasis on graduate education. The graduate program would enable students to become professors, professors to become jurists, and Harvard to become imperial. It would also have a liberating effect on the undergraduate work, for graduate professors would offer courses in the undergraduate division.[48] In addition to the familiar staples of legal education, Pound warned that lawyers should also have more training in legislation, or "it will scarcely be possible to check the movement away from law toward administrative absolutism."[49] But the Harvard Law School required no revolution to accomplish these goals. During the twenty years of his deanship, there was virtually no change in the curriculum. Perhaps the lone exception was a short-lived experiment in criminal law launched in 1929, and it was organized as a special program separate from the principal courses of study. One of Pound's successors, Erwin N. Griswold, who served as dean from 1946 to 1967, remarked that Pound did not "undertake to develop the ways in which law teaching might well be modified in order to give adequate recognition to the sociological approach."[50]

Although Pound's contribution to legal education was substantial, its significance rested in the relationship that he encouraged between the law school and the legal profession. Law schools with faculties of full-time scholars, utilizing the case method of instruction, enabled legal education to serve as a focal point for professional development. Pound was active in curriculum reform at Nebraska, but the reforms that he instituted were already well developed at Harvard when he returned in 1910.

Pound hoped that Harvard would train lawyers "who shall be useful socially as well as successful professionally."[51] Although he did not intend to train them for schemes of social reconstruction, he insisted that the idea of service was primary in defining the spirit of the profession. That professional men should use their knowledge unselfishly was a fundamental part of Pound's conception of the lawyer as an expert, a practitioner of an esoteric and difficult art. Unselfish application of the art would keep it pure. The disinterested quality of practice would protect the profession from charges of being dangerous to the public and shield it from investigations launched by laymen.[52]

The legal profession, in short, was a community within a community. It differed fundamentally from the larger community, which exalted incompetency and distrusted expertise. But the division was not merely between the wise and the foolish. There was also a division among the wise, and Pound felt keenly that the lawyer was being challenged by other experts. All professions, he argued, were jealous of the predominant position of the bar. Doctors, engineers, journalists, and especially academicians, following the traditions of the medieval clergy, were engaged in an attack on the legal profession. In his extreme defensiveness about criticism from other experts, Pound even hesitated to trust their competence within their special fields. While admitting that courts "have been groping somewhat" and that their "advance has been irregular and halting," he was quick to add that "American economists, sociologists, students of politics and philosophers have not been out of Egypt so very long themselves."[53] These nonlegal experts were "wont to speak *ex cathedra*." They needed "the constant check of a keen-witted opponent," and lawyers must assume the role that other professionals simply could not play.[54]

Pound had a low tolerance for criticism of the law from outsiders. When *The Survey*, a journal run by reform-minded social workers, published a typically sentimental article in 1913 decrying the law's failure to punish a man who had committed adultery, driven his wife insane, and forced his daughter to submit to an abortion,[55] Pound reacted with excessive indignation. He saw the mild moralism as an example "of reckless misstatement,"[56] and he deplored "the rashness with which certain well-meaning critics . . . set up some proposition outrageous on its face . . . to criticize our legal system."[57] When editor Paul Kellogg tried to assuage his ruffled sensibilities with an invitation to contribute an article, he refused, complaining that the magazine's "attitude of persistent misrepresentation . . . makes it an impossible organ for one who wishes to accomplish anything effective with courts and lawyers."[58]

Julian Mack gradually engineered a reconciliation between Pound and *The Survey*, and Pound continued to send an annual contribution of ten dollars. He liked the magazine, appreciated its goals, and felt that it helped him keep in touch with the law in action.[59] But an element of bitterness remained. He insisted that the dogmatic attacks of ignorant critics in the nineteenth century had been responsible, in part, for the rise of mechanical jurisprudence, and there was more than a hint in his language and behavior that the same problem remained. He recommended Mary Richmond's *Social Diagnosis* (1917) as a book that would "convince judge and lawyer that the social worker can give him something he can tie to and to dispel the not wholly unfounded suspicions by which he has been troubled in the past."[60] Pound appreciated her message, for Miss Richmond, a Baltimore social worker, advocated patient, persistent, and individualized casework rather than dramatic schemes of social reform.[61] The bond of understanding between them revealed a joint commitment to professionalism. Pound probably thought this was one social worker who knew her place. The social scientist, Miss

Richmond agreed, "is often the worst of sinners in the matter of interpreting life in terms of his own specialty." She thanked Pound for a review that would "be the greatest help . . . in making social workers and social reformers think straighter."[62]

Pound transformed the lawyer into an expert supreme among all others. He preferred attorneys to "King Rex or King Demos," arbitrary sovereigns that he characteristically linked together, but the professional ideal forced him to be suspicious of all nonlawyers, experts as well as common men. Lawyers possessed the mental habits "to hear and to ponder both sides"; others were not so gifted.[63] Not content with advising the bar to perform only such tasks that others could not do, he felt that lawyers alone should set the terms in which people think about social as well as legal problems. Although experts must be restricted to their field of expertise, the American tendency to "rely chiefly on the law to express social progress and to further legal progress" made the lawyer's sphere of operation a wide one.[64] For that reason, society must look to the men of law as the primary movers and shakers, and Pound implored the legal profession to accept its natural duties of leadership.[65]

Organicism, traditionalism, and professionalism had combined to make lawyers the natural leaders of society, but the combination also placed severe limits on their freedom of action. In a revealing passage, Pound admitted that

the great stream of society . . . went on before us and will go on after us, and if some of us are able to do something to shape some part of its course, yet how much more will it have shaped us, molding our thoughts by fixing the conditions under which and words by which we think, controlling our actions by bonds of convention, fashion, general opinion, of

which we are hardly conscious, which we can resist only
here and there, and then often but feebly.[66]

This powerful organicism operated as a major restraint
on his general conceptualization of social change and introduced a strong element of caution into his specific proposals for reform. He had never been enthusiastic about
widespread social reform. "Change in the substantive law,"
he advised, "must proceed slowly and cautiously."[67] But
even in fields where he waged his strongest campaigns for
change, Pound, a man with great confidence in himself and
his ideas, always shrouded his proposals in warnings against
precipitous action. He was the leading figure in the movement for procedural reform, but he advanced his comprehensive scheme in a spirit of gradualism. "What must be
urged now for a season," he said, "is, not reform, but
careful planning, study of methods and deliberate selection
of the best."[68] Although he demanded major reforms in the
organization of courts, he felt that the changes should be
effected with "conservative radicalism."[69] And the man
who stood at Armageddon in 1903 as dean of the Nebraska
College of Law explained nine years later, as president of
the Association of American Law Schools, that he did "not
urge that we overhaul our law-school curricula over
night."[70] Even admitted anachronisms in law must not be
pruned too hastily; they should be retained and modified to
preserve continuity.[71] In matters of legal reform, social
science could be of great assistance, but Pound again coun-
seled restraint. "The social science of to-day," he warned,
"is largely unlearning that of yesterday. We must not bring
our law so thoroughly up to date to-day that it will be out of
date to-morrow."[72]

This caution, buttressed by an acceptance of the law's
customs and usages, extended to matters of technique as

well as matters of substance. Although he praised the Brandeis brief as a brilliant innovation, he felt that it should not be used in judicial opinions and asked Harold Laski to pass the suggestion to Justice Holmes. Apparently Brandeis had failed to maintain proper judicial form.[73] Pound's sense of conventionality also prevented him from using the technique himself. In 1913 the New York Life Insurance Company retained him to argue a case it was appealing to the Supreme Court. Large insurance companies had long hoped to eliminate state regulation with a ruling that the business of insurance was interstate commerce.[74] Pound's brief was thorough and persuasive, but he made virtually no use of readily available extra-legal materials to prove that insurance was interstate commerce requiring uniform national regulation. His argument was clear but unimaginative; it was an argument from law rather than life.[75]

Although some of Pound's intellectual moods were decidedly Burkean, his view of the state was not a reverent one. He did not think of the state fondly as a partnership among those who are living, those who are dead, and those who are to be born. For Pound, the state was simply "an instrumentality . . . the chiefest of human agencies by which human society achieves its tasks of social engineering."[76] His was a coldly pragmatic conception of government, but it was not a prelude to a theory of the state as an instrument for social reconstruction. The primary function of government was still the administration of justice, and the principal agencies were law and the judiciary.[77] Pound had a deep suspicion of politics. Although he admitted that government could accomplish a great deal, he warned that "the great central machine may attempt too much. Friction and waste are not necessarily eliminated by setting this machine to do what may be done better by spontaneous individual initiative."[78]

Yet Pound spoke constantly of "social engineering," a phrase that suggested a kinship with an advanced Progressivism. Social engineering was a misleading phrase; for Pound, it was descriptive of a neutral process rather than prescriptive of pragmatic reform. It meant only that law was shaped in accordance with social ends; it did not define particular ends or particular means of attaining them. In the nineteenth century "the ideal of social engineering was a maximum of individual self-assertion." The ideal had changed, but law was still framed in terms of social ends,—a fact that Pound urged lawyers to recognize as a continuous theme in legal history.[79] Any suggestion of progressive reform was unintended, for Pound had little sympathy with reform politics. He identified "the progressive courtiers who sought to give the king [James I] . . . arbitrary power" with "the progressive courtiers who have the ear of King Demos" and were trying to destroy all impediments, real or imagined, to his will.[80]

Pound frequently stressed "the limits of effective legal action" and warned that society should not attempt too many changes through law. Law was "the skeleton of social order," a delicate mechanism of social control for adjusting relations and ordering conduct.[81] "Over-ambitious plans to regulate every phase of human action" would impair that delicate mechanism, destroy the basic element in the ordering of society, and invite social disorganization.[82]

Themes of caution, important and controlling themes in Pound's thought, coexisted in his legal philosophy with bolder themes, and a curious dualism emerged. Organicism competed with instrumentalism in a relentless intellectual tug-of-war. When dealing with particular legal problems, he called on instrumentalism for a solution. Much of his writing was devoted to the analysis of particulars, a concern that obscured the larger framework of organicism.

But this framework, if often obscured, was always present, and it established the boundaries within which instrumentalism could operate.

This dualism had serious consequences for Pound's intellectual development. It introduced an ambivalence into his thought that prevented him from erecting the system he longed to complete. He loved the common law, but he felt it lacked an adequate systematic approach, and his quest for unity demanded thorough integration of the disparate compartments of contracts, torts, property, and other divisions of Anglo-American law.[83] His dream would always remain unfulfilled, and although he added details during the succeeding decades, no great system ever emerged. He was, perhaps, too much a creature of the common law, for its strengths, by and large, were his strengths, and its weaknesses, his weaknesses. Both accepted much that was traditional, displayed an inability to erect an overarching system, innovated on an *ad hoc* basis, and then only when the need was great.[84]

On another level, the common law tradition lent a certain resolution, although an uneasy one, to the dualism between instrumentalism and organicism. The central feature of the tradition was a method that allowed courts to solve legal problems through the application of judge-made precedents on a case-by-case basis. Pound adopted a judge-centered view as the touchstone of his jurisprudence, and his ability to interpret the judicial process as either organic or instrumental, as the need for different philosophical positions arose, prevented the dualism from becoming too uncomfortable. In spite of his dislike for its unsystematic character, he praised the case-by-case approach as an inductive method that subjected legal doctrine to continual testing against the facts of life. At the same time, he considered judge-made precedent to be an internal dynamic in a continuous process of legal growth. Although he could see pragmatic principles at work within law, he also understood the law in organic terms.

His commitment to the common law enabled Pound to sublimate the contradictory tendencies of his thought, but he was vaguely aware of their presence. In 1914 he remarked that the "movement for liberalization, an infusion into the law of ideas developed in the social sciences, has led to a tendency away from courts and law and a reversion to justice without law . . . and reliance upon arbitrary governmental power."[85] Perhaps this glimpse of the reform potential within sociological jurisprudence encouraged him to keep it in check by means of traditional devices and attitudes. At any rate, he made no effort to resolve the internal contradictions in his legal philosophy. He continued to develop the organic and instrumental elements of his thought in completely separate channels. Both lines of development yielded deep insights; yet one tended to neutralize the other. The skill and sophistication with which he developed each of the two currents of thought made sociological jurisprudence as a whole all the more unsatisfactory. A corrosive organicism enveloped the instrumentalist promise of this new direction in legal philosophy.

10

Variations on
Familiar Themes

By 1920 Pound had completed nearly twenty years of his long academic career. His reputation as a legal theorist was secure, and contemporaries increasingly acknowledged the growing influence of his work. "Thoughts that seem fairly obvious today," wrote Benjamin Cardozo in 1920, "have become part of the common stock of ideas for American lawyers and judges as a result, in large measure, of your efforts."[1] Pound had become the best-known law school dean in the country, and his public activities, which supplemented the deanship, enhanced his stature as one of America's leading men of law.

Pound's reputation continued to grow after 1920, but the creative period in his intellectual development had ended. For the next decade and a half, his contributions to legal philosophy and public policy were limited to elaborations of familiar Pound principles. He continued to apply his ideas widely, but he ceased to pursue them more deeply. A series of lectureships in the early 1920s set the tone for the coming years. The lectures were summaries of past work; Pound neither explored new problems nor offered the larger synthesis that he had long promised.[2]

This failure to make new advances in legal theory resulted from Pound's competing philosophical loyalties, his success in promoting sociological jurisprudence, and his deep conviction that legal education must be strengthened. The tension in his thought between organicism and instrumentalism prevented Pound from integrating his ideas into a coherent system. By 1920 he had exhausted his original contribution to legal philosophy. Unable to move beyond the vulnerable compromises that held his insights in an uneasy resolution, he simply echoed earlier answers in the remaining torrent of scholarship. In addition to the internal conflicts that paralyzed his intellectual development, Pound's jurisprudence changed little because it was challenged little. As the catch phrases of sociological jurisprudence replaced those of mechanical jurisprudence, Pound could relax his efforts to rid legal philosophy of its anachronisms. His sociological jurisprudence was, in spite of its unresolved weaknesses, easily the most vital contemporary legal theory. But widespread acceptance of his ideas did not make Pound complacent, for he was eager to accept new challenges and there were many uncompleted tasks for a dynamic law professor and dean. Professional legal education was still in its infancy, and Pound was deeply committed to making law schools the center of the profession. The stalemate in his intellectual development caused him to redirect rather than reduce his amazing capacity for work. As his magnum opus became more elusive, his plunge into administration and public affairs allowed him to satisfy his enthusiasm for the "efficacy of effort" and to fulfill his deep personal need to play a public role.

World War I made great demands on college administrators. The mad drama being staged in the French mud brought severe dislocation to American university life, and the very existence of the Harvard Law School for a time seemed threatened. Enrollment at the school plummeted from 850 students in September 1916 to 70 students two years later. Members of the faculty were also tapped for wartime service, and those who remained on campus had to assume new burdens. When the Armistice was declared, Harvard was immediately flooded with hundreds of returning veterans, and the law faculty held a special session from February through August 1919 to accommodate them. Keeping the school in operation under these conditions was an enormous burden and Pound shouldered the responsibility with admirable poise and skill.[3] But still the task was onerous, and it left him vulnerable to other disturbing circumstances.

Pound was able to cope with the administrative chaos at Harvard, but he felt powerless against the intolerance of the war and the Red Scare. It corrupted American life and threatened the integrity of American education. As an intellectual and educator, he felt isolated, embattled, and, worst of all, ineffective. Life seemed to be "governed by $14 a week reporters" intent on inventing sensational headlines. He deplored the easy misunderstanding of the era and complained to Justice Holmes that "many zealous alumni think that all of my writing is a cover for socialism—and they are exceedingly clamorous." When James Harvey Robinson, the controversial historian, invited him to deliver a series of lectures at the New School for Social Research, Pound suggested "The Socialization of Law," hoping that it would not be "too shocking a title for a course."[4]

The wartime hysteria was so pervasive, and the university seemed so vulnerable to it, that Pound felt compelled to resign both the deanship and the Carter chair. "I doubt if an intellectually honest man," he wrote, "can justify himself in teaching in this country in the next decade." Universities, he complained, were being reduced to the status of nineteenth-century mills, where owners completely controlled the lives and thoughts of the community. Pound was not wilting before the onslaught of the irrational; events would show that he was prepared to be bold. But the pressure of the superpatriot was so formidable that the game no longer seemed worth the candle. When rumors of his possible resignation began to circulate widely, innumerable admirers expressed shock and disappointment. Holmes was very upset when he learned that Pound might leave Harvard, and Brandeis urged the wavering dean to reconsider. "To lose you as teacher of law and of lawyers," wrote Brandeis, "would be a calamity." Albion Small chided Pound for his misgivings, insisting that his influence as a law professor and dean was so great that he should "have no excuse for a moment's depression."[5]

Pound's despair began to lighten considerably in May 1920, when he participated in a successful attack on the Palmer Raids. A. Mitchell Palmer, the Attorney General, had fed postwar passions for half a year with a violent and frequently lawless effort to collect alien "Reds" for deportation. In response to this ugly episode, Pound joined Zechariah Chafee, Felix Frankfurter, Ernst Freund, and eight other distinguished lawyers in a report, *To The American People*, which reviewed some of the most shocking excesses of the Palmer Raids. The report was a sensation, and Lucille Milner, secretary of the American Civil Liberties Union, thought it was "the principal blow to Palmerism."[6]

Chafee engineered the attack on Palmer, and Pound, who had joined him in an earlier assault on the Espionage Act, quickly became an enthusiastic ally. He was indignant at the Attorney General's wholesale violation of traditional

American liberties and offered his support without a moment's hesitation. It was a courageous act at a time when most American lawyers were indifferent, and Pound thought it "nothing short of scandalous that the bar should remain quiescent." Perhaps he thought he was upholding the traditions of the profession as well as the traditional rights of Americans.[7]

The successful attack on Palmer must have been deeply satisfying to Pound, but it was merely a prelude to a much more personal triumph. At the Harvard commencement exercises of 1920, he was awarded an LL.D. Several admirers, realizing his spirits were low, had hoped an honorary degree would convince him that his labors had not gone unnoticed. Both Brandeis and Holmes lent their great prestige to the movement, and the latter wrote President A. Lawrence Lowell that Pound helped "impart the ferment which is more valuable than an endowment, and makes of a Law School a focus of life."[8]

His personal and public successes gave Pound a sense of security that was invaluable in the spring of 1921, when the Red Scare came to Harvard and threatened the law school with an inquisition of its own. Austen G. Fox, a prominent New York attorney and Harvard alumnus, submitted a petition to the Board of Overseers condemning certain members of the law faculty, and thus set in motion the great "Heresy Trial" at Harvard. Fox had been a leading tactician for the opponents of the Brandeis nomination, and now he sought to eliminate an equally disquieting development. Many leading attorneys, like Fox, feared that the practicing lawyer, formerly the spokesman for the bar, was taking a back seat to dreamy radicals in the law schools. The rise of an aggressive professoriat threatened their professional position as well as their political philosophy.[9]

The Fox petition assailed Chafee's vigorous criticism of

the Espionage Act in the *Harvard Law Review* as an example of intentional falsehood or reckless indifference to the truth. Furthermore, Chafee had not only ignored Fox's earlier complaints about the article, but added insolence to injury when he repeated the offending statements in his book, *Freedom of Speech* (1920). The petitioners also condemned Pound, Frankfurter, Francis Sayre, and Edward B. Adams for joining Chafee in a petition for the pardon of the Espionage Act defendants. Such men, they fumed, were not fit to be entrusted with the training of youth.

The Harvard Overseers referred the petition to the Committee to Visit the Law School, a group whose fourteen members included Benjamin Cardozo, Augustus N. Hand, Julian W. Mack, John H. Wigmore, and Henry L. Stimson. On Sunday, May 22, eleven members of the committee met at the Harvard Club of Boston to try the professors. Fox assumed the role of prosecutor, and President Lowell took charge of the defense. The case against Pound, Frankfurter, Adams, and Sayre crumbled rather quickly, but Chafee had a more difficult time. He was acquitted by the narrowest of margins, six to five, with Judge Cardozo casting the tie-breaking vote for sanity and scholarship.[10]

"With Lowell's energetic support," wrote a buoyant Chafee, "we threw the Wall St. invaders back with heavy losses." The closeness of their acquittal did not dampen the enthusiasm of the defendants, who saw the outcome as a personal victory and a victory over the Red Scare. It gave Pound renewed strength and softened some of the bitterness of the preceding years. He continued to press the cause of academic freedom, made several public appearances in behalf of free speech, and protested the refusal of a visa to Tom Mann, an English labor leader who was invited to a peace congress in the United States. Judge Charles Letton received his unstinting praise for a dissent from the Nebraska Supreme Court's decision upholding a ban on the teaching of foreign languages. He was an early supporter of Senator Burton K. Wheeler, whose investigations of the Ohio Gang won him the enmity of the Justice Department and a vindictive indictment for conflict of interest. For his services in behalf of free speech and fair play, the Daughters of the American Revolution rewarded Pound with a prominent place on their blacklist.[11]

The DAR was not the only institution that noticed Pound's challenge to the darker side of American life. In April 1923 Edward A. Ross advised him that the University of Wisconsin was looking for a new president and asked if he would be available for the position. "The Progressives," he remarked, "are in power in Wisconsin now and desire, for [the] successor of President Birge, a man of popular sympathies, a forward-looking man" who could provide the leadership that the university had enjoyed when it was a laboratory of liberal reform. Pound responded eagerly to these overtures. He was reluctant to give up legal education and scholarship, but he considered Wisconsin "the hope of education in this country," and its presidency was a very attractive prospect. Almost two years later, in January 1925, a committee of the Board of Regents offered Pound the presidency. Unfortunately, the Madison *Capital-Times* announced the offer before it had been made, and in a few days, newspapers across the country reported his acceptance. In Montana *The Daily Missoulian* lost no time in advising him on the conduct of his administration and suggested that the first order of business should be a vigorous crusade against campus drinking parties.[12]

The newspaper pressure increased the difficulty of Pound's decision. The pressure from friends at Harvard was enormous, and petitions imploring him to stay poured in from all over the country. Some bore the names of leaders of the law like Charles Evans Hughes, the Secretary of State; others bore the names of leaders-to-be like Arthur E. Sutherland, Jr., a young editor of the *Harvard Law Review*. Judge Cardozo made a personal appeal, arguing that Pound's departure "from the Harvard Law School threatens an immeasurable calamity to the cause of jurisprudence." But one of the most telling objections came from Calvert Magruder, then a colleague at the law school, who warned him against "frittering away your energies in state and legislative politics."[13]

Pound's rejection of the Wisconsin offer stunned the university and created some temporary embarrassment. Everyone had expected him to be the new president. When John R. Commons learned of the decision at a dinner party in New York, he turned pale and complained of a sudden illness. But all respected Pound's decision "to go on with law teaching and endeavor to improve the administration of justice." The law had been his life's work, and it was best that he continue it. Furthermore, Mrs. Pound was not well, and he feared she could not discharge the responsibilities of a president's wife.[14]

Although his public statements emphasized a concern for legal science and the health of his wife, he privately suspected that the presidency might become a political football. There was widespread speculation that the selection committee was merely an extension of Robert LaFollette's personality. The committee was dominated by Progressives, and Pound had the blessing of LaFollette himself.[15] Pound worried that he would "be regarded as the choice of a party, and should have to expect political difficulties in the near future." When he expressed this fear to Zona Gale, a member of the selection committee, she simply replied that the present Board of Regents would remain intact for six years, but she did not deny the university's sensitivity to state politics. Messages from admirers in Wisconsin also gave him pause. "The Progressive movement," ran an urgent telegram from Professor M. G. Glaeser, "regardless of party labels in state needs your leadership."[16] Pound had already been through one distasteful example of a university's vulnerability to politics in the Heresy Trial at the Harvard Club, and he balked at entering a more uncertain situation in Wisconsin. In addition, he had no desire to be identified with LaFollette Progressivism, far too exotic a program for one who had faithfully voted the Republican ticket since 1892.

Pound's insistence that he wished to continue his work in the law was, of course, completely sincere, and one of the problems he explored throughout the 1920s was the administration of criminal justice. He had first given the matter serious attention in 1909, when he organized the National Conference on Criminal Law and Criminology, but his concern mounted as the "crime wave" that followed in the wake of Prohibition gained momentum and headlines. Criminal law was a vital part of the common law, and Pound thought it tragic that serious students had long neglected it. The administration of criminal justice lacked professionalism, and it perennially suffered at the hands of incompetent zealots. It was too closely associated with politics and too appealing to laymen, a combination that encouraged persecution of unpopular ideas and minorities, publicity-seeking by prosecutors, and an exaggerated reliance on criminal sanctions to implement novel statutes. Most of the excesses of criminal law were inevitable in a democracy, for the criminal aroused the wrath of the people, and no man or institution, Pound sighed, "should stand between the all powerful people and its doing what it thought best." Fortunately, the judiciary had been able to put justice into criminal justice, but executive bureaus were gradually absorbing its jurisdiction. The growth of executive influence was an unfortunate turn of events, for although there was a role for bureaus and social scientists, the most important agents of reform were judges and lawyers, "who alone have command of that body of continuous and long continued experience of the legal handling of concrete cases which is an indispensable quarry of materials for the reformer of law." His concern for the future of the criminal law was merely a feature of his larger concern for the future of the common law.[17]

An opportunity to act on his insights came to Pound in 1920, when a citizens' committee in Cleveland invited him to direct a survey of criminal justice in the city. Cleveland had long suffered a corrupt and inadequate system, but a sensational murder trial generated overwhelming public support for reform. In May the chief judge of the Municipal Court, William McGannon, was charged with conspiracy in the murder of his favorite bootlegger; the principal witness was the judge's mistress. After two trials in which McGannon was acquitted, it was revealed that he had bribed a prosecution witness. Reeling from the scandal, the Cleveland Foundation hired Professor Raymond Moley, a young political scientist at Western Reserve, to organize a thorough study of criminal justice in Cleveland.[18]

The foundation, which had already sponsored social surveys of public education and recreational facilities, provided a generous budget of almost $40,000 to finance an investigation similar to the classic Pittsburgh Survey. Moley was extremely anxious to secure Pound as the director, and he made every concession that Pound requested, including the appointment of Felix Frankfurter as co-director. The principal investigators, all experts in their fields, were drawn from all parts of the country in order to keep the report free of local prejudices. The highly qualified survey staff worked closely with a local advisory committee and city officials, but it was not subject to restrictions or censorship. The city was so disgusted with recent events that it gave the survey team every encouragement. Encouragement also came from outside Cleveland. "Are you going to blow up the whole administration of petty justice," inquired Learned Hand. "It would be a good work. It would be a good work to include major justice as well."[19]

Although each area the survey explored—police, prosecution, courts, correctional treatment, medical science, legal education, and newspapers—was assigned to a specialist, there was no doubt that Pound was first among equals. Judge Florence Allen, who presided at the McGannon trial, remembered him as the most dynamic member of the survey team. It was Pound who insisted that the survey report be an integrated volume rather than a series of separate reports, and he demanded a scientific investigation shorn of the emotionalism that surrounded most discussions of crime.[20] Justice Brandeis hoped for dramatic exposés of the Ku Klux Klan and the American Legion; Newton D. Baker, former Secretary of War and president of the Cleveland Foundation, felt that a concern with embarrassing specifics was sadly inevitable; the Cleveland *Press* feared that the report would not be specific enough where names and organizations were involved.[21] To prevent the survey from degenerating into "a matter of foam and froth," Pound continually urged objectivity on his weekly visits to Cleveland during the four months of field work. At the conclusion of the staff's work, he closeted himself in a Cleveland hotel for several days of furious writing and produced a brilliant summary of the entire survey.[22]

A generous mood toward the social sciences, from which the methodology of the Cleveland Survey was drawn, permeated Pound's summary. "Perhaps," he confessed to a friend during the course of the fieldwork, "the lawyer can do no more than deal with the symptoms, and the ills which are beneath those symptoms must be left to the economist, the sociologist and the moralist." Accordingly, he urged a greater role for the nonlawyer in criminal investigation, the trial of issues, and correctional treatment. He was especially hopeful that psychologists could reduce the chaos of trial courts and increase the reliability of evidence in criminal prosecutions. The social sciences could produce no miracles, but Pound neither promised nor expected them, and he urged patience with the inevitable fumbling that accompanied new techniques.[23]

Pound gave little attention to the substantive law of crimes, but he was convinced that it should be rebuilt on a very different foundation.[24] "Psychopathology," he declared, "has overturned much that the criminal law of the past had built upon," and it had shattered the major premise that offenders were motivated by perverse wills, which retributive justice could discourage. The diverse causes of crime, sociological as well as psychological, made it impossible to explain motivation in terms of willful intent alone. Simplistic theories of criminality and its correction had to be discarded if criminal law were to be substantially improved.[25] The common law as well as modern psychology sustained his objections to the "will-intent" hypothesis and its corollary, the retributive theory of justice. Nineteenth-century enthusiasts of Roman law had introduced both concepts into criminal law theory; neither was part of the common law tradition.[26] If criminal justice were freed of the unwanted imports, the common law could realize its inherent genius.

The common law tradition furnished Pound with most of his inspiration, and he preferred to recast old tools for modern use and let others develop new social science techniques and theories of preventive justice. He considered the juvenile court and domestic relations court to be recent examples of the system's creativity and proof of its endless ability to restore itself from within. A commitment to received tradition as the fundamental standard of reform ensured that his principal recommendations for improving criminal justice would be familiar themes to those who had followed his career: unification of the court system, incorporation of the bar, professional law schools, and "above all . . . the taking of the bench out of politics and restoring the common-law independence of the judiciary." True to the common law's spirit of cautious, case-by-case advance, Pound warned that "these things must come slowly."[27]

The reaction to the Cleveland Survey was mixed. It was a threat to some, and a few Cleveland attorneys responded with predictable pique. "Conditions here are no worse than in Boston and elsewhere," declared Judge Willis Vickery. "I suggest the surveyors get back there at once and clean house at home." Some accused the survey team of conducting an unfair trial. "None of the highbrow, sweet smelling reformers came to see me," complained Judge Homer G. Powell.[28] But the negative reaction was definitely a minority view. The *New Republic* praised the survey as an investigation "of national interest and importance. . . , broadly and courageously planned." As the first modern attempt to describe the entire process of criminal justice, it was a path-breaking investigation, one that stimulated similar efforts throughout the country. Some students felt it was the best example of a social survey in any field, and its educational value was widely applauded. "No doubt," said Frankfurter from the perspective of eight years, "the survey only proved what some already knew. But the point is that the survey proved it."[29]

The Cleveland Survey was only one phase of Pound's

continuing involvement with the improvement of criminal justice. As a member of the American Law School Association's Committee on the Survey of Crime, he met regularly with counterparts in the American Bar Association and the Social Science Research Council. He also joined a wider group of interested laymen on the National Crime Commission, a private organization that appealed to men as different as Judge E. H. Gary and Franklin D. Roosevelt. Pound encouraged legal aid societies to assist indigent defendants, but he favored public defender systems, an extremely advanced position in the 1920s. He was a leader in the probation movement and served the National Probation Association and its successors from 1927 until his death in 1964. Everywhere he carried the message of the Cleveland Survey.[30]

As dean of the Harvard Law School, he missed no opportunity to encourage the systematic study of criminal justice. He was convinced that essential reform could only come from the law schools, and he continually bemoaned the fact that American legal scholars had "all but left the field to enthusiasts and cranks and charlatans." To remedy this neglect, he urged students and professors to develop an interest in criminal law; he secured fellowships for promising graduate students like Sheldon and Eleanor Glueck, and he encouraged Professor Francis B. Sayre in his efforts to restructure criminal law. In 1926 he organized the Harvard Crime Survey, a project that included students from a variety of disciplines and promised to eclipse the Cleveland Survey. Three years later the law school announced the creation of the Institute of Criminal Law, an ambitious enterprise to promote the study of crime and provide training in correctional administration. Unfortunately, the institute disappeared by 1935, a victim of the Depression. The Harvard Survey fared somewhat better; it produced a number of valuable studies, although it failed to live up to its original promise. Nevertheless, the appearance of the programs demonstrated the increasing concern that both Pound and Harvard lavished on the reform of criminal justice during the 1920s.[31]

The National Commission on Law Observance and Enforcement, established in 1929 as one of the first acts of the Hoover Administration, enabled Pound to explore criminal justice on a national scale. Hoover appointed Pound as one of eleven commissioners to investigate the enforcement of criminal law throughout the country, to make recommendations for improving it, and to devote particular attention to the problems of prohibition. Although George W. Wickersham was chairman of the commission, Pound was predictably the most active member throughout the two years of its existence. He was granted an academic leave for the first year, but during most of the second year he left Cambridge for Washington on Tuesday night, returned Saturday evening, and crammed six hours of teaching and the deanship into the remaining three days.[32] Shortly before his appointment to the commission, his wife died, leaving him a very lonely man after thirty years of marriage, and his total absorption in a new task may have been related to his great sense of loss. Fellow commissioners frequently noted his domination of the staff work, and in an after-dinner speech Newton Baker announced that he himself signed everything, Pound wrote everything, and Max Lowenthal objected to everything.[33]

The Wickersham commission resembled a much-expanded Cleveland Survey that ranged over the entire complex process of criminal justice, but the Prohibition hearings captured most of the headlines and congressional attention. "I hope they will be patient," wrote Chafee, with more fear than reassurance, "and realize that a scholarly

investigation takes at least as much time as a tariff bill."
Pound and the other commissioners tried to analyze the
problems objectively. They refused to allow the hearings to
degenerate into moralism, nativism, or misplaced defenses
of personal liberty, and Pound was particularly harsh with a
witness intent on ascribing innate criminality to various
immigrant groups. Although the majority report advised
against repeal of Prohibition, there were several separate
statements, all urging various compromises. Pound's position was typical: national abstinence was an impossible goal,
but the Eighteenth Amendment should be retained to ensure the elimination of saloons and guarantee federal control over the liquor traffic. The spirit of compromise, however, did not appeal to a nation polarized into Wets and
Drys. The Prohibition report was condemned by virtually
everyone, and the rest of the commission's very substantial
work on prosecution, police, correctional treatment, and a
host of other items was neglected and misunderstood. The
Prohibition controversy overwhelmed it, and the public,
observed Frankfurter, "leaped upon every pronouncement, ready to drag it and all the Commission stands for
into the maelstrom that surrounds that contentious
issue."[34]

Pound's public service was formidable, but it merely
punctuated the increasingly demanding duties of the deanship. The physical growth of the law school between 1916
and 1936, the years of his deanship, was impressive. Student enrollment doubled, the faculty quadrupled, and the
endowment, aided by a massive fund-raising campaign in
the mid-1920s, increased over six-fold. Much of the school
moved into a magnificent new home in 1929, when the
monumental additions to Langdell Hall were completed.
Such spectacular growth would have pleased any university
administrator, but Pound's view of legal education as the

determinative factor in society's most important profession heightened his sense of accomplishment.

As an academic entrepreneur, Pound was superb, but, unfortunately, the growth of the law school was not accompanied by the growth of its dean. What the school gained in numbers it lost in intimacy, and it became more difficult for a single man to dominate it. This was hard on Pound, for his natural impulse was to exercise complete control, and he rarely could be persuaded to delegate authority to a colleague. The measure of command that he exercised at Nebraska was not so easy to transfer to the more prestigious and strong-willed Harvard faculty. In addition, several challenges during the 1920s and 1930s in jurisprudence, legal education, and politics seemed to threaten him, making his urge to dominate more abrasive and authoritarian. W. Barton Leach, who joined the faculty in 1929, recalled that "Pound ran the Law School as if he had just bought 51 per cent of the stock. He neither sought nor tolerated opposition." He established an autonomous position during the last years of Lowell's reign and vigorously resisted the mild intervention of the next president, James B. Conant, who was alarmed at the divisions within the law faculty. Pound decided all questions with a minimum of consultation, and he once offered a research professorship of legislation to a Boston attorney in spite of the recommendation from a unanimous faculty that the position go to a young assistant professor, James M. Landis. The crisis was resolved when the attorney refused the appointment, but Pound complained bitterly about faculty dissent.[35]

There was a growing note of caution in his activities during the late 1920s. He refused to be drawn into the public debate over the Sacco-Vanzetti case, although he thought the defendants had been unfairly convicted, and he comforted Walter Lippmann with the illusion "that the dilatory revolution of the judicial machine may yet bring about a right result." He thought Frankfurter's case for the pair was fair and accurate, but he did not defend his colleague against a savage attack by Dean Wigmore, an attack that Pound himself considered "a disgrace to legal scholarship."[36] Perhaps he was less willing to criticize judges than attorney generals, and his campaign for an increased endowment may have made a public appeal inexpedient. Yet Pound's refusal to speak out against what many regarded as a new nadir in American law increased tensions within the faculty, and the rising clamor fed his growing sense of isolation. He had long claimed that many of his colleagues were suspicious of him because he was neither an easterner nor a Harvard man, and he often recalled more congenial times in Lincoln and Chicago.[37]

Political differences divided the faculty in a more dramatic fashion. Pound disapproved of both Franklin Roosevelt and the New Deal, and he became increasingly annoyed with Frankfurter's role as a New Deal insider. Apparently forgetting his own recent service with the Hoover Administration, Pound tried, unsuccessfully, to reduce Frankfurter's trips to Washington on the ground that they interfered with his classes.[38] Tempers also flared over some careless remarks Pound made about Nazi Germany. He was in Germany and Austria in June 1934, when Austrian Nazis assassinated Chancellor Engelbert Dollfuss, but his principal impressions were of domestic peace. He saw no soldiers, noticed no tension, and explained that Hitler was "a man who can bring them [the Central Europeans] freedom from agitating 'movements.' " He felt that the violence had been greatly exaggerated and blandly predicted the rise of a similar leader in France. The following September, Pound accepted an honorary degree from the University of Berlin, which the German ambassador presented at Harvard. President Conant refused to be photographed with the group, Charles Beard insisted that Pound was a dupe of the Nazis, and the *New Republic* criticized him for accepting an honor from a regime dedicated to destroying the life of the mind. Judge Julian Mack, one of his most fervent admirers, wondered why he had seemed to approve National Socialism, and Frankfurter complained that Langdell Hall was being "turned into a Nazi holiday."[39]

Frankfurter and Pound found themselves at odds over a wide range of issues, but nothing created more bitterness than Pound's uncharacteristic timidity in response to President Lowell's periodic acts of anti-Semitism. Others shared Frankfurter's disgust that Pound, the most powerful dean at Harvard, failed to wage a vigorous campaign when Lowell objected, on two occasions, to appointing Jewish scholars to the law faculty. Both incidents created enormous ill will and added to the mounting dissatisfaction with Pound's leadership. Joseph H. Beale declared that Pound was "growing nuttier and nuttier" and dreamed that a World Court appointment could be arranged. During a brief tenure as acting dean, Edmund M. Morgan complained that Pound constantly interfered with his administration of the school, and the experience reinforced his former hostility. Landis insisted that Pound was only happy when he was absorbed in intrigue: "Pound delights in putting artificial corns on peoples' toes and then stepping on them."[40]

Pound was also being challenged by new departures in legal education at Columbia, Johns Hopkins, and Yale. All three schools sought to institutionalize social science techniques in teaching and research, and Pound's negative reaction to the experiments revealed the limits of his jurisprudence. Columbia began a thorough study of its curriculum in 1926, and its searching examination provided a sense of direction for a decade of reform in legal education. Columbia added social scientists to a law faculty that already bristled with unconventional professors, and when the pace of change began to slow a bit, several reformers left for Yale and Johns Hopkins, where they could participate in more dramatic ventures. Yale reconstructed its curriculum, substituted a social science orientation in undergraduate classes for an exclusive reliance on casebooks of appellate opinions, and urged a consciously manipulative attitude toward law and social problems. Johns Hopkins established the Institute of Law in 1928, a frank rejection of the traditional limitations of a law school, and proposed a genuinely interdisciplinary approach to the problems of law and society. These were all extensions of Pound's ideas, but they were extensions he was unwilling to accept, for they extolled instrumentalism without a proper regard for organicism. The new departures in legal education demonstrated the incompatibility of Pound's conflicting intellectual commitments. Consequently, when Justin Miller, an advocate of the new mood, summarized the implementation of social science techniques in legal education during the 1920s, Harvard was scarcely mentioned.[41]

These new developments assumed a much more aggressive conception of social science and made legal research a prelude to social reconstruction. Pound advised against the new additions to law school curriculums, for educators "ought not to expect every graduate of a national law school to become a great law reformer." His use of the social sciences, however, had always been more descriptive than prescriptive, and although he occasionally spoke of them as tools of change, the change he desired was usually a matter of adjustment. His organic conception of society, with its regular rhythms and teleological development toward a final end, did not permit fundamental redirection in social life. Instrumentalism could operate interstitially, he believed, but men bent on change must realize the limits of legal action. Furthermore, law was not the only medium with a limited capacity to alter society, and Pound cautioned critics in other fields against exaggerating the reform potential of social science. His conception of social work revealed a general lack of sympathy with total schemes of reform; social workers should employ "retail" techniques that concentrated on the individual client rather than "wholesale" measures to change the environmental source of his problems. More comfortable with Mary Richmond than with Jane Addams, he had little enthusiasm for the social scientist as social reformer.[42]

As a young scholar, Pound had insisted that law schools could only function within a university community, but he grew fearful that the university was "an incubus on the law school rather than an asset," and he resisted "the pressure of the opinion and traditions and modes of thought of the arts faculty."[43] The new experiments in legal education brought the university into the law school, and Pound felt this would seriously compromise both the quality and character of American law. "If we are not careful," he warned, "all that has been gained in a generation may be lost." Legal education was facing a crisis, and he saw himself and stalwarts like Dean James Parker Hall of Chicago and Dean Henry Moore Bates of Michigan as defenders of the faith. Nothing must deter the law school from its historic mission, he declared, "to teach the technique of the common law and ability to handle common-law materials."[44]

During the two long decades of Pound's tenure as dean of the Harvard Law School, there was not a single significant revision of the curriculum. As the 1920s gave way to the 1930s, his emphasis shifted irrevocably from pursuing new glories to preserving old ones. "As the American law teachers of one hundred years ago assured the definite reception of the common law," he wrote, "so the law teachers of today and of tomorrow may assure its preservation."[45] Such a condition was hardly conducive to institutional self-examination, and when the law school faculty undertook such a course in 1933, Pound had few changes to suggest. A new curriculum was adopted in 1937, the year after Pound retired, but it could not have displeased him, for it did not radically alter the direction of the school.[46]

The denouement of Pound's deanship was not a happy one. During his final year he confided to Judge Robert Patterson that there was "little left of the old spirit which has come down from Langdell and Ames." The bitter conflicts over academic policies and personalities as well as corrosive political differences must have made it easier for him to resign his office on 28 September 1936, one month before his sixty-sixth birthday. He was to become the first University Professor, a position he held until 1947, and one that allowed him to teach in any of Harvard's colleges. But his new professorship did not demand a new role, and he continued to pursue goals that he had increasingly emphasized during the last years of his deanship. "When we train common-law lawyers," he had proclaimed, "we give soundness to judgment and stability to the state." The absence of administrative burdens gave him more time to attack the new jurisprudence and the new politics that questioned that soundness and challenged that stability.[47]

11

A Restless
Retirement

From the final years of his deanship to the period following
World War II, new developments in legal thought and
practice placed Pound's world in danger. Advocates of legal
realism, administrative law, and the New Deal used many of
his ideas in ways that were unacceptable to Pound, and he
responded by emphasizing the limited nature of his most
progressive insights. Although Pound argued for instrumentalism and social science in legal theory, his fervor
for organicism, traditionalism, and professionalism created
an intellectual straightjacket for the operation of instrumentalism. As long as instrumentalism could be kept
within proper bounds, as long as it could be made to serve
his larger common law loyalties, Pound could disregard the
dualism in his sociological jurisprudence. But reformers in
the 1930s demonstrated the potential for change within his
most pragmatic insights, and Pound was forced to deal with
the incompatibility of his intellectual commitments. The
crisis in American life during the 1930s created a crisis in
his intellectual life. Unable to live any longer with the competing elements of his thought, Pound discarded his re-

formist instrumentalism for a celebration of the common law tradition, organic modes of thought, and an insular professional spirit.

The most important challenge that Pound faced was legal realism, a new development in American jurisprudence that emerged after World War I, coalesced in the late 1920s, and raised questions that dominated legal thought until the 1940s. The rise of realism and Pound's response to it demonstrated the contradictions between his influence and his intentions. Although spawned by his own theory of sociological jurisprudence, realism was not a child that Pound wished to acknowledge, for its advocates, as Judge Cardozo observed, were "content with nothing less than revision to its very roots of the method of judicial decision which is part of the classical tradition." It was an aggressive new theme that appropriated Pound's instrumentalism, separated it from his organicism, and offered law reformers a broad mandate for dramatic change. Realism did not require allegiance to an elaborate creed, but it possessed an intellectual cohesiveness that Pound regarded as extremely dangerous. Less than a program but more than a point of view, it blended a contempt for tradition with a passion for reform that was always militant and often abrasive.[1]

Skepticism was a distinctive characteristic of the realist mood, which was suspicious of all quests for first principles. "Human experience discloses no ultimates," argued Underhill Moore, a prominent realist theoretician. "Ultimates are phantoms drifting upon the stream of day dream." Jerome Frank, influenced by Freudian insights, mocked the ideal of legal certainty as a father substitute. Rules of law were not self-fulfilling, added Karl Llewellyn, for even when a legal question seemed settled, "one lifts an eye canny and skeptical as to whether judicial behavior is in fact what the paper rule purports (implicitly) to state." Skeptical realists refused to accept the presumptive adequacy of traditional precepts as tools of decision. "It is quite possible," Llewellyn noted, "that the received categories as they already stand are perfect for the purpose. It is, however, altogether unlikely."[2]

The most commonly shared suspicion among legal realists was "rule-skepticism," an attitude that Llewellyn defined as the "distrust of the theory that traditional prescriptive rule-formulations are *the* heavily operative factor in producing court decisions." The rules of law were inadequate descriptions of the realities of law, and their prominence in published judicial opinions often obscured more basic determinants of judicial decision-making. Few realists suggested that lawyers and judges sought to deceive the public with empty verbalism; lawyer and layman alike overestimated the inevitability of legal doctrine as the primary source of legal decisions. The familiar phrases that ran through judicial opinions and bar association addresses, Felix Cohen insisted, were simply "poetical or mnemonic devices for formulating decisions reached on other grounds." Although legal rules occasionally described uniformities of judicial decision, they rarely determined those uniformities.[3]

Rule-skeptics advanced many reasons for the inherent uncertainty of law. The overwhelming abundance of legal rules contributed to their inadequacy. Centuries of common law accretions and decades of effective reporting provided judges with ample precedent for the most contradictory decisions. In addition to the plethora of precedents, there were also different methods of interpreting them. "Strict construction" and "loose construction" invariably produced different conclusions from the same source. The ambiguities of lawyerly language intensified the uncertain-

ties of precedent and precedent technique. The "reasonable and prudent man" who provided an "objective" standard for the woefully subjective law of torts became on
closer inspection "a mere figure of speech," said Leon
Green, "[and] does exactly what any good ritual is designed
to do. . . . It serves as a prophylaxis."[4]

Realists responded to rule-skepticism in a variety of ways.
Frank gloried in the indeterminate character of legal doctrine, urged its acceptance as a mature admission of life's
uncertainty, and argued that *"much of the uncertainty of law
. . . is of immense social value."* Other realists agreed that legal
certainty had been greatly exaggerated, but insisted that it
was a legitimate objective. "There is something," Felix
Cohen objected, "to which the judicial 'hunch' should conform; there are some patterns to which it does conform."[5]
Paper rules did not often determine patterns in law, but
certain patterns existed nonetheless, and it was the task of
jurists to seek them in judicial practices if they were absent
from judicial pronouncements.

The realist attack on traditional doctrine was not simply a
negative response to legal rules, legal reasoning, and legal
rhetoric; sociological and psychological ideas contributed
positive features to the critique. Sociology provided the
inspiration to study law in terms of its environment. Since
modern society was in a continual state of flux, Llewellyn
insisted, "and in flux typically faster than the law . . . the
probability is always given that any portion of law needs
reëxamination." Whereas modern sociology forced realists
to reinterpret legal doctrine, modern psychology encouraged a reevaluation of legal decision-making. Sigmund
Freud, Jean Piaget, and John Watson had varying effects
on different realists, but the competing psychological viewpoints united to minimize the role of *a priori* reasoning.
Armed with these insights, realists argued that legal think-

ing began with conclusions rather than premises, and that lawyers undertook the search for relevant principles only as a final ritualistic gesture. Joseph C. Hutcheson, a federal district judge, frankly admitted that "the judge really decides by feeling, and not by judgment; by 'hunching' and not by ratiocination."[6]

Modern science contained the promise of a new jurisprudence, empirical and inductive in spirit, which could replace the bankrupt legacy under which lawyers labored. Walter Wheeler Cook spoke for all realists when he argued that "the application of truly scientific methods to the study of legal phenomena . . . has never yet been tried." One of the prerequisites of scientific jurisprudence was the elimination of subjective value judgments from the initial legal analysis. Realists did not deny the need for ideals, but they thought normative judgments were fatal for a science of law and demanded a temporary divorce of Is and Ought to ensure objective analysis. Diagnosis was a necessary prelude to prescription.[7]

One of the most fruitful realist ventures was its examination of the judicial process, a venture in which imaginative lawyers employed social science in a comprehensive reassessment of the judge's art. They replaced the analysis of rules with the study of behavior and created a working hypothesis of Justice Holmes's contention that law was simply "what the courts will do in fact, and nothing more pretentious." By making behavior the focal point of legal analysis, realists hoped to achieve one of the movement's most cherished goals—the scientific prediction of judicial decisions. The vision of law as a predictive science was a compelling one; it inspired a number of imaginative models that anticipated the behavioral techniques in social science by a quarter-century.[8]

To supplement their models for predicting judicial behavior, realists developed techniques for judges that made rule-skepticism a fundamental principle of decision-making. They retained the doctrine of *stare decisis* but insisted that judges regard precedents as guides rather than injunctions. A high degree of flexibility existed within the received tradition in all branches of law. Indeed, there were frequently more limitations in a judge's personal frame of reference than in an impersonal rule of law, and realists urged judges to complement rule-skepticism with introspection. All realists advocated rigorous self-analysis; some, like Frank, even insisted on "something like psychoanalysis." Careful consideration of his own unspoken assumptions would enable a judge to produce more rational decisions; it would release him from the subconscious restraints of his psyche, just as rule-skepticism would release him from the limitations of conventional legal theory.[9]

Certain features of legal realism were borrowed from sociological jurisprudence, and Pound grumbled that the most meaningful ideas of the new movement "were anticipated by the sociological jurists of a generation ago." The realists, more generous, openly acknowledged their debts to Pound. "I think it is fair to say," wrote Felix Cohen, "that 'realistic' and 'sociological' jurisprudence are in part complementary and in part overlapping, but in no way antithetical." Yet as important as Pound's contributions had been, realists considered them inadequate. His "brilliant buddings," wrote Llewellyn, "have in the main not come to fruition." Part of the movement's mission, Oliphant insisted, was "to make 'sociological jurisprudence' a fact rather than a mere aspiration."[10]

Although the realists wished to convert Pound's incomplete prescription into a positive program, there were important parts of his legacy that they clearly rejected. They absorbed the instrumental features of his philosophy but dismissed his traditionalism as irrelevant. Furthermore, the organicism that played such a major role in Pound's jurisprudence was completely absent from legal realism. The realist world, one of concrete and disparate elements, had no organic unity; the relationships among the parts were not evidence of the innate associations that Pound saw as a metaphysical imperative. The idea of necessity did not appeal to a generation of thoroughgoing pragmatists. Indeed, the realists were so intellectually predisposed against organicism as a conceptual tool that they were incapable of responding to it as a controversial issue. They paid it the supreme insult of simply ignoring it.

That Pound's organicism failed to become an intellectual legacy or even to surface as an intellectual problem was due as much to peculiarities within his thought as to the realists' extremely pragmatic angle of vision. The uneasy alliance of organicism and instrumentalism that made his thought so distinctive was maintained at great cost to its permanence. Pound's organicism, in short, was scientific and empirical after the manner of Darwin rather than idealistic in the tradition of Hegel. In choosing empiricism as a method of uniting organicism and instrumentalism, he had unwittingly exposed his organicism to erosion. When subjected to the scrutiny of radically pragmatic relativists like Llewellyn and Frank his organicism, cloaked in the garb of empiricism, lost its identity as an independent factor in his thought and, for realists, became simply a misunderstood part of Pound's failure to live up to his instrumentalist promise.

By extracting the instrumentalism and ignoring the organicism of Pound's thought, the realists freed sociological jurisprudence from its internal restraints and increased its potential as an instrument of reform. "Social engineering," in their hands, became a manipulative policy science of enormous scope. Because they defined law as an act of official behavior, legal realists moved easily across the uncertain boundary separating law and politics, and many found congenial employment in the New Deal. In politics as in jurisprudence, they preferred experimentation rather than established formulas, functional analysis rather than speculative thinking, and a rhetoric of possibility rather than moral idealism.[11]

Pound, extremely hostile to legal realism, complained as early as 1924 about "the increasing group of those who seem to conceive of legal precepts as incapable of interdependence and logical connection." Although he claimed to have anticipated everything valuable in the movement, he objected to everything distinctive in it. As a creature of the common law tradition, he found skepticism intolerable. He insisted that attacks on legal certainty obscured the high degree of stability that existed in many branches of law, and he condemned suggestions of introspective judicial techniques as an insult to the bench. The definition of law as an act of official behavior and the quest for predictive techniques robbed law of its majesty. He dismissed the temporary divorce of Is and Ought as valueless positivism and insisted that "what-ought-to-be . . . has first place in the social sciences." Legal realism was misguided, misinformed, and a menace to the vital common law system.[12]

Pound responded to the challenge of realism with a powerful reaffirmation of traditional common law virtues. He admitted that the nineteenth-century conception of law as a closed system containing fixed principles of certain application was no more accurate than the realist emphasis on legal uncertainty. "Yet of the two," he declared, "the old-fashioned lawyer has the more warrant." The realists treated law as a mere collection of rules, but law included techniques and ideals as well as precepts. Legal reasoning was an "application of the received technique to the authoritative precepts so as to shape them to the exigencies of new states of fact," and he insisted that "the technique is likely to be the controlling factor in the result." Furthermore, he had long argued that different branches of law required various degrees of certainty. Some flexibility was desirable in tort law, but it was dangerous in property and commercial law, which must "provide assured constancy of the conditions under which property is held and business is carried on." His passion for certainty in property law combined two sets of verities, for his understanding of economic development was rigidly classical. Finally, he felt that the realists exaggerated the relevance of social science. "We have problems enough of our own in the science of law," he wrote, "without wasting our ammunition in broadsides at each other over our wrong choices of psychological parties." First things, insisted Pound, must come first.[13]

The disruptive effect of realism on the contradictions in Pound's jurisprudence shattered the restraint and balance with which he characteristically approached philosophical debate. Although he assured Llewellyn that the realists "were a group of thinkers with whom I have a great deal of sympathy," that sympathy vanished when his initial public overtures, designed to correct their errors and remind them of their debt to sociological jurisprudence, failed to gain converts.[14] Suspicious of their doctrine and stung by their occasional abrasiveness, Pound became increasingly vituperative, and the fantastic accusations that he hurled so effortlessly demonstrated his loss of proportion. His gloomy mood, fed by the realists, by his frustrations at Harvard, and by dissatisfaction with the New Deal, generated a rhetoric of mud-slinging.

As Pound's mood blackened, legal realists became both philosophical anarchists and economic determinists who glorified brute force and celebrated the unpleasant. His continual identification of realism with Marxism astonished Morris Cohen, himself a critic of the realists, who tried unsuccessfully to convince Pound that his analysis was faulty. "The Marxian or the skeptical realist of today," Pound argued, "might . . . have said what is attributed to Thrasymachus, that 'the just is nothing else than the interest of the stronger.' " He could detect no concern for justice among the realists. They were even hostile to the idea of law and hoped that law would disappear. As economic determinists and anarchists, they recaptured the juristic pessimism of the nineteenth century. In a passage that demonstrated his narrowness and hardening attitudes, he compared realism in art and jurisprudence. "It is essentially an art that cultivates the ugly," he observed, "and in jurisprudence it is the cult of what we always supposed abnormal." His complete loss of perspective came in an address to the Chicago Rotary Club, where he charged that the realists denied constitutionalism, the division of powers, the separation of powers, limited government, guarantees of individual freedom, and the supremacy of law.[15]

These strictures, which ranged from conscious exaggeration to complete misunderstanding, revealed Pound's sensitivity to attacks on traditional common law values. Llewellyn characterized Pound's fulminations as "queer blindness or wilful perversity," and he insisted repeatedly that "a realist's interest in fact . . . in no measure impairs interest on his part for better law." The idea that they were Marxists was equally mistaken. Frank was a vigorous critic of Marxism, and realists were adamant in their attack on all determinisms.[16] Their relativism did not make them soft on absolutism, nor did it impart any fatalism into their jurisprudence. Indeed, they were the least pessimistic of modern legal philosophers. Instrumentalism liberated them to restructure the law and to utilize it in a genuinely creative fashion.

Pound and the realists also clashed over legal institutions, and mutual agreement on institutional devices usually required radically different rationales. Fundamentally different attitudes appeared, for example, in a mutual acceptance of judicial councils and the Restatements of the American Law Institute. Judicial councils, which began as agencies for developing new rules of procedure, gradually assumed additional responsibilities, and by 1940 were operating in about half of the states. Realists thought they could be useful bodies for developing rules, collecting statistics, recommending legislation, and acting as administrative control centers for the judiciary. Similarly, the restatements could reduce the law to more manageable proportions by eliminating anachronisms and introducing flexible principles to accommodate the inherent volatility of law. Both restatements and judicial councils were understood as instruments to develop a better law. Pound agreed with this analysis, but his own justification for restatements and councils was not fundamentally instrumental. He saw them as agents of the common law and allies of the courts. Judicial councils would become bulwarks of judicial justice that would "stay the march of absolutism and make for freedom under law." The restatements would ensure the dominance of judicial experience in the development of law by relying on "traditional conceptions and traditional categories." The realists called for creative social engineering, whereas Pound labored to preserve the continuity of traditional legal forms.[17]

Competing theories of legal education also separated Pound and the realists. The latter were the most vocal advocates of those changes that had disturbed him since the mid-1920s. Their aggressive attempt to convert legal study into a policy science and their extensive use of nonlegal materials compromised what he considered the primary mission of legal education—preservation of the common law tradition. Pound regarded these efforts as "a corollary of the proposition that there really isn't any law and that what we have been calling law will disappear with the coming of an ideal society." Both Pound and the realists agreed that law students should have more contact with practicing attorneys, but even this mutual demand was based on strikingly different assumptions. Frank wanted students to observe trial courts and study their operations because the neglected law in action often differed from the law in books. Pound argued for a closer relationship between students and practicing attorneys to ensure "the handing down . . . of the traditional ideals and professional standards of the bar." Frank would introduce students to the realities of the present; Pound would initiate them into the heritage of the past.[18]

No controversy over legal institutions, however, was more bitter than the argument between Pound and the realists about administrative agencies. Administrative agencies enjoyed a phenomenal growth during the New Deal years, and realists applauded what Pound saw as a threat to the judiciary. Promoters of administrative law insisted that agencies and courts had complementary roles, but Pound knew that the realists were not particularly sensitive to judicial prerogatives. Because of the increasing importance of social research, wrote Felix Cohen, "courts that shut their doors to such nonlegal materials . . . will eventually learn that society has other organs—legislatures and legislative committees and administrative commissions of many sorts—that are willing to handle, in straightforward fashion, the materials, statistical and descriptive, that a too finicky judiciary disdains." Because they were not captives of the common law tradition, realists did not consider the growth of administrative agencies a chilling development. Indeed, they welcomed institutions that could circumvent a recalcitrant judiciary.[19]

The growth of administrative law, which accompanied the challenge of legal realism, reinforced Pound's increasing malaise. In the early years of his academic career, he had advocated a large role for administrative agencies and had criticized legal traditionalists for treating them with hostility. By 1933 he regarded their growth with greater suspicion, but he still insisted that they posed no immediate threat to the common law. At the end of the decade his attitudes had hardened, and he exclaimed that administrative law "will involve the common-law judges in a conflict quite analogous to that which they waged with the Stuart kings in the seventeenth century."[20]

New Deal advocates of the administrative process made such exaggerated claims for the technique that it has become fashionable to criticize them for naiveté, a charge that surviving advocates often accept meekly.[21] Pound exposed some weaknesses in their arguments, but he considered them nefarious rather than naive. His attack, sharpened by his fears of new follies, was an attempt to protect the past rather than permit the future. It was not designed to correct weaknesses in administrative justice; it was a demonstration that the entire system was unworkable.

Pound's quarrel with administrative justice was based on a point of view that made the common law a standard for all legal and political activity. The administrative process was a threat to that standard, and Pound decried "the tendency of administrative bureaus to extend the scope of their operations indefinitely even to the extent of supplanting our traditional judicial regime by an administrative regime." He was chairman of the American Bar Association's Special

Committee on Administrative Law, which in 1938 renewed its long battle against the agencies with a final version of the Walter-Logan bill. It was a measure designed to cripple the administrative process with exaggerated requirements of notice, judicial review, and an incredible one-year limitation on an agency's power to develop regulations. Pound wrote the special committee's report, an unsparing indictment of the administrative process, which reduced executive justice to ten characteristic tendencies: (1) to decide without hearing all parties, (2) to decide on the basis of hearsay evidence or on evidence and matters not before the agency, (3) to decide on the basis of prejudices, (4) to demand action at the expense of deliberation, (5) to disregard jurisdictional limits, (6) to be expedient and yield to political pressure, (7) to make rules in an arbitrary manner, (8) to fall into a perfunctory routine, (9) to delegate authority to incompetent subordinates, (10) to combine rule-making, investigating, and prosecuting functions. Unlike judges, administrators were not checked by professional habits and training, the criticism of a watchful bar, or the publication of decisions in public records. The partisanship and unprincipled expediency of an administrative agency made it necessary for the judiciary to examine the facts underlying its decisions as well as the fairness of its procedures.[22]

An elaborate scheme of judicial review was the principal device to throttle the burgeoning bureaucracy. Pound thought that a single court of appeals would have no trouble reviewing the decisions appealed from all administrative agencies. He favored this procedure over an earlier American Bar Association proposal to create a separate court to hear such appeals. A special court was not necessary, because the circuit judges were men "with large experience in every kind of legal question." They were fully as capable of supervising the development of contemporary agencies, he observed with unintentional irony, as nineteenth-century judges like Thomas Cooley, whose narrow views had crippled earlier regulatory agencies.[23]

The aim of the Walter-Logan bill was so transparent that Louis L. Jaffee, on the threshold of a distinguished career as a student of administrative law, called it "A Bill to Remove the Seat of Government to the Court of Appeals for the District of Columbia," and he declared that the 1938 report was "the most unfortunate event in the life of the Special Committee." James M. Landis, one of the most articulate defenders of the administrative process, complained that the bill made no real attempt to correct anachronistic practices but simply imposed a confusing superstructure on the existing system. Jerome Frank's convincing demonstration that the "ten tendencies" were not features of the Securities Exchange Commission made many of Pound's larger generalizations appear questionable. Pound's fulminations and the Walter-Logan bill were examples of what Justice Harlan Fiske Stone had condemned as "nostalgic yearnings for an era that has passed," and Stone was certain that they were "destined to share the fate of the obstacles which Coke and his colleagues sought to place in the way of . . . equity."[24]

The figure of Coke loomed large in Pound's mind, and he saw himself as another embattled spokesman for justice, lonely in his loyalty to a noble cause. This sense of isolation intensified his antagonism to administrative law, and he repeated many of the errors in Coke's attack on equity. Pound seemed to forget that administrative agencies were established features of the American legal system, just as Coke had miscast the prerogative courts as upstart intruders in English law. Like Coke, Pound's criticism was largely speculative, founded on little genuinely empirical evidence. Furthermore, neither defender of the common law hesitated to torture the evidence to substantiate his prejudices. Pound charged Frank with advocating methods that were slipshod and expedient when Frank merely argued for less artificiality in statutory construction. He accused Landis of admitting that administrators did not decide issues on the basis of fairness between the parties to a controversy, although Landis had simply defended an agency's power to make independent investigations as superior to deciding issues solely on a record prepared by contending parties. On another occasion, Pound cited three cases to prove that administrative agencies had an aversion to hearings. The sources themselves revealed that one agency dispensed with hearings at the request of the regulated defendants; a second proceeded with a hearing when the defendant refused to appear; and the third held hearings that everyone considered unnecessary. Kenneth Culp Davis, a student of administrative law, remarked that the distortions in Pound's use of evidence "always run in one direction; they always aid his strictures about the agencies."[25]

Most of Pound's impressions of the agencies came from judicial opinions and his service on the Wickersham commission—sources that confirmed his common law prejudices against the administrative process. His frame of reference prevented a comprehensive view of the process and encouraged an exaggerated emphasis on the problem of judicial review. He failed to see the diversity of administrative law, and he neglected his earlier insight that it would judicialize itself by adopting common law practices. The attack on the agencies complemented his previous crusade for procedural reform, a parallel that did not escape his attention, for both efforts reflected his desire to reinvigorate the judiciary. He was convinced that his proposals for change in procedure and judicial organization a generation earlier would have forestalled the current challenge, but there was still time for measures that would halt "the re-crudescence of absolutism."[26]

Although Pound's customary analysis of legal problems was coldly analytical, his criticism of executive justice was careless and emotional. He detected a conspiracy between legal realism and administrative law, considered both to be Marxist, and had no difficulty comparing the growth of the agencies with the rise of totalitarianism in Russia and Italy. He overreacted badly to an act that permitted the Securities Exchange Commission to enter certain corporate reorganization proceedings as a friend of the court, and he warned the Investment Bankers Association of America that the agencies would intervene in private disputes "like the man who intervenes in a brawl" and would subject all private property to unrestrained administrative control.[27] Corporate venality was a problem that should be controlled by means of long-dormant equity jurisdiction rather than administrative law. At any rate, administrative law should not be dignified as "law," for it was actually a means of eliminating law. As part of his general loss of balance, he also exaggerated his isolation and complained privately that the administrative absolutism dominating law schools made law reviews unsympathetic to his ideas, although none of his articles ever seems to have been rejected.[28]

In assuming the mantle of Coke and the legal myopia that it represented, Pound also inherited the tendency to introduce politics into jurisprudence. He mistrusted the growth of administrative agencies, but he was even more alarmed that they were administering the New Deal. Although the most serious abuses were found in older establishments such as the Post Office, War Department, and Veterans Administration, Pound focused his attack exclusively on those associated with the New Deal. Like his fellow drafters of the Walter-Logan bill, which exempted many pre-New

Deal agencies from its coverage, Pound was more concerned about the impact of the Tennessee Valley Authority
than inequities in the Bureau of Indian Affairs.[29]

The New Deal was a challenge to his lifelong Republicanism, and after he retired from the deanship he began
to accept minor assignments from the Republican National
Committee. The suspicions of political reform movements
that he developed as a McKinley booster persisted; he voted
for Taft in 1912 when Roosevelt stood at Armageddon and
Wilson promised a New Freedom, and he scorned the
Committee of Forty-Eight, a short-lived Progressive Republican group in the 1920s. He saw the New Deal as a
threat to the rights of property, and to John Marshall's
dictum that the power to tax involved the power to destroy,
Pound added the corollary "that regulation may easily run
into destruction."[30]

One of the recurring themes in Pound's jurisprudence
was the idea that law was divided into two spheres; one
required certainty and the other allowed flexibility. Many
legal problems had no automatic solution, but economic
activity required rigid certainty. This static aspect of his
thought reflected an allegiance to classical economic
theory, in which life responded to laws but never altered
them. In spite of his wide reading in the social sciences, his
economics never advanced beyond his youthful McKinleyism. "Civilized society," he continued to argue, "demands . . . that free individual initiative which is the basis of
economic progress." He was incapable of conceptualizing
alternative economic hypotheses, and although he quoted
Simon Patten with enthusiasm, the proto-Keynesianism of
the eccentric economist completely escaped him. Wedded
as he was to the conventional wisdom, he was extremely
uncomfortable with the occasional economic radicalism of
the New Deal.[31]

The New Deal also did violence to Pound's organic conception of social development. He sensed that it had interrupted the normal flow of history and had prevented the trend toward executive justice from running its natural course. If the Roosevelt Administration had not intervened, the cyclical resurgence of judicial justice would have been assured. The havoc of discontinuity was compounded by a novel chaos that the New Deal introduced into political life. Pound was deeply disturbed by the ardent experimentalism of the New Deal, which he correctly saw as a directionless instrumentalism. It advocated fundamental alterations without advocating fundamentals. The New Deal generation adopted a clinical attitude toward social problems that earlier generations found uncomfortable. "One cannot be so sure of what is held by Americans of today," he said sadly. Americans no longer saw society whole; they saw it as a collection of special groups and problems that were not necessarily related, and like the broker state they elected, they preferred to deal with different problems on different terms. This trend was anathema to a man who saw special legislation as a threat to larger social harmonies.[32]

"Liberty," he complained, "is becoming a legend, justice a superstition." The New Deal's administrative absolutism, he told the Bond Club of New Jersey, "is in exact accord with the political ideas of dictatorships." Abundant evidence revealed the growing division of a free people into tribute payers and bureaucrats led by "a Duce or Führer or superman head administrator." The government was trying to eliminate private enterprise, he informed the Investment Bankers Association, by holding business to strict codes of fair competition while allowing its own enterprises to violate those standards at will. The Supreme Court's effort to contain absolutism was greeted by the court-packing plan of 1937, a brutal attempt to destroy another obstacle to unlimited presidential power. "To reduce the judicial office to one of rubber stamping what is done or procured by the executive," wrote Pound during the crisis, "is to destroy constitutional government." Three years later, Roosevelt's angry veto of the Walter-Logan bill cut him to the quick; the President condemned the bill's sponsors for preferring "the stately ritual of the courts, in which lawyers play all the speaking parts, to the simple procedure of administrative hearings which a client can understand." The accusation that the bill elevated technical legalism over substantial justice wounded Pound, and he described the veto message as "thoroughly in keeping with the Marxian idea of the disappearance of law." If government were to proceed without regard to law, constitutionalism, and due process, he continued, "we may as well give up all pretence of being a constitutional democracy and set up an avowed dictatorship."[33]

The battles of the 1930s with legal realists, administrative absolutists, and New Dealers introduced new rigidities into Pound's thought, and he gradually abandoned most of the reform impulses of sociological jurisprudence. He began to flirt with once-rejected dogmas and argued that "absolute ideas of justice have made for free government. . . . If the idea is absolute, those who wield the force of politically organized society are not." He also began to doubt his former suggestions that legislation could provide new legal starting points, and in 1936, while the Supreme Court invalidated statutes with abandon, Pound declared that "judicial decision is showing a revived creative power" and legislatures were becoming sterile. He did not advocate the slot-machine theory of justice, but he treated it sympathetically. At least "the mechanical theory had the public good in view," which was more than he would admit for current legal theory.[34]

Throughout the 1940s and 1950s, Pound eliminated much of the sociology from his sociological jurisprudence. "The law," he said in a surprising statement, "cannot but morals may admit environment as an excuse." Once, he had labored against great odds to prove that law was intimately connected with morals and that both were inseparable from their environment; now he dismissed the social context without hesitation. Similarly, he cautioned an audience of lawyers and students against allowing "our faith in the efficacy of effort to blind us to the limitations upon the efficacy of conscious effort in shaping the law." He displayed less interest in the social sciences, frequently treating them with suspicion and contempt. "They do not impart wisdom," he said. "They are not foundation subjects."[35] By the late 1940s he decided to disregard new developments in social science in order to devote his full time to reading the reports of English and American courts. Looking back over sixty years of study, he told a friend in 1956 that the social sciences reminded him of this doggerel:

> The wise old men of Hindustan debated loud and long,
> For each in his opinion persistently was strong,
> And each of them was partly right,
> And all of them were wrong.[36]

The strangest development in Pound's thought, however, was the appearance of xenophobia. Throughout his life he had sought inspiration from European intellectuals, but he became increasingly critical of "refugee teachers from abroad who have not the smallest notion of our polity" and who were producing a generation of students "filled with what can only be called totalitarian ideas." He saw the values of decadent continental philosophies at work in legal realism and administrative law. In 1914, when Judge

Robert Ludlow Fowler had criticized sociological jurisprudence for its reliance on continental authors, Pound replied with a ringing defense of intellectual cosmopolitanism. Thirty years later he erected an equally parochial defense of the common law tradition and insisted that Americans "do not . . . need any advice on law or politics from continental Europe."[37]

His new emphasis on certainty in the common law was matched by a new sympathy for natural law, a tradition he had earlier rejected as bankrupt. "In jurisprudence," he wrote as late as 1921, "the whole doctrine of natural rights has been definitely abandoned." He considered the classical doctrines irrelevant for contemporary society, and he found Rudolf Stammler's modern conception—a natural law with changing content—particularly vacuous. By the 1940s he was calling for a revival of natural law, one "with a changing or growing content" rather than a fixed body of immutable principles. The content and boundaries of the new natural law were never clear, but his growing fascination with old certainties betrayed an increasing inflexibility in his jurisprudence.[38]

The chaotic developments of the New Deal years ended any urge for change that Pound once had. Professor Edmund Cahn, a man particularly sensitive to the law's moods, observed in 1946 that Pound appeared "well satisfied with the law as it now is." He no longer called bar associations to the banner of law reform; he was content to caution them about their enemies and urge them to keep the faith. Colleagues at the University of California at Los Angeles Law School, where Pound taught from 1949 to 1953, noted his increasing narrowness and insularity. He wanted a self-contained law school that would have little contact with the larger university community. He offered no encouragement to interdisciplinary activities, and his hostility to laymen within the law had grown so intense that he tried to dissuade the UCLA Law School from adding a political scientist to its faculty.[39] In his new mood, he preferred that law be made relevant to society through adjustments in the society rather than in the law. Since the changes must come in life rather than law, there was no need to tolerate outside influences in legal education.

In spite of his frustration with the course of events, Pound continued to maintain an interest in social and political developments. The future of China occupied much of his attention in the years after World War II, and he was a vocal critic of American policy in the Far East. He found Chiang Kai-shek an exceptional leader—wise, tenacious, and democratic. He insisted that there was little corruption and no censorship in China, and he compared the exclusion of liberal political parties to the fate of Republicanism during the New Deal. After a trip in 1947 he dismissed the threat of civil war, and as late as 1948 he refused to admit that a significant Communist element existed. He was on the fringes of the China Lobby and frequently offered his services to its leaders, echoing its constant refrain that the State Department was undermining the Nationalists, encouraging the Communists, and playing into the hands of the Soviets.[40]

Pound's interpretation of Far East politics, a product of his growing defensiveness and bitterness, obscured a brief return to neglected progressive themes. After World War II he spent many months in China advising the government on the reconstruction of its legal system, and his efforts recaptured the positive spirit of earlier ventures in legal reform. Inevitably, an enthusiastic American lawyer compared his work in China with Macaulay's codes for India, but Pound rejected Western traditions as a standard for Chinese law reform. Chinese jurists, he argued, must experiment with Chinese materials for solutions to Chinese problems, and the process would contribute to the cultural pluralism so badly needed in the emerging world order. The generous impulses in Pound's legal theory went, in these later years, into his study of Chinese law rather than American law, and enabled him to maintain a link with his former progressivism.[41]

Pound's experience in China left him particularly sensitive to the threat of Communism, and he frequently expressed himself in the most extreme Cold War rhetoric. He regretted being labeled a reactionary, he wrote his sister in 1946, but he was not prepared "to believe 100 per cent in Communism and in the benevolent intentions of Russia in the Orient in order to be liberal." While at UCLA, his anti-Communism grew more pronounced. He called *The Daily Bruin*, a student newspaper, "The Daily Communist," and he was an early advocate of the loyalty oaths that brought chaos to California campuses. Pound never wavered in his support of loyalty oaths for teachers; in 1957 he expressed his agreement with Louis Wyman, the witch-hunting attorney general of New Hampshire, that "teachers are certainly . . . not entitled to special privileges." His fears that "the country is being flooded with Communist propaganda" made him an enthusiastic supporter of the Council Against Communist Aggression.[42]

His sharpest barbs, however, were reserved for the "service state," his synonym for the welfare state. "The term welfare state," he insisted, "seems to me a boast." He was so disillusioned about its influence on American political life that he refused to support the Eisenhower movement in 1952, because "Eisenhower as president would give us four years more of what we have been having for the last twenty years." The service state abhorred individual initiative, because self-help interfered with government programs; it promoted totalitarianism by encouraging administrative absolutism; it made each citizen an "involuntary Good Samaritan" for his less capable fellows; it undermined the enforcement of contracts with the notion that the state could absorb everyone's losses. Proposals like "freedom from poverty," he wrote, were "mere preachments . . . [and] invitations to plundering." A state that guaranteed freedom from want and fear was a threat to democracy. By promising more than it could deliver, the service state enfeebled the whole society. "There is still," he insisted fervently, "in a world drifting to absolute government, something to be said for Blackstone's proposition that the public is in nothing more essentially interested than in securing to every one his individual rights."[43]

In spite of his fears that the service state had become a permanent feature of modern life, Pound was incapable of fatalism, and he continued to attack the service state in each of its many guises. He was critical of the United Nations, which he saw as a superservice state, and was relieved that world government was so ephemeral. He criticized American courts for leniency toward administrative agencies, hostility toward state and local government, and sympathy for expansions of federal power. The Federal Tort Claims Act of 1946, which permitted a vast range of new actions against the government, was a welcome exception to the steady growth of centralized power, and Pound applauded the measure in spite of its implicit "involuntary good Samaritanism." Far more satisfying, however, was the blow that he struck against Leviathan in the Tidelands Oil Controversy, when Texas, California, and Louisiana challenged the federal government's authority over oil exploration on the continental shelf. Pound contributed to the brief that Price Daniel, the Texas Attorney General, presented to the United States Supreme Court, and he won the gratitude of Congressman Sam Yorty, a spokesman of California oil interests, who used Pound's arguments in congressional debate. Pound felt that the federal government's claim "would do away with private ownership of land throughout the country," and he saw the states' victory in Congress as a major defeat for absolutism.[44]

The bitter controversies of the New Deal and postwar years gradually ceased to be all-consuming, and when Pound returned to Harvard in 1953, he chose to lead a quieter, less turbulent life, one that would ease his entry into a ninth decade. Although his life was less frantic, he continued to be remarkably active, writing articles and addressing bar associations by the score. A foundation grant allowed him to complete a project that he had announced half a century earlier, and in 1959 the long-awaited *Jurisprudence* appeared in five magnificent volumes. It was, regrettably, an anticlimax, for it summarized his work without synthesizing it. Yet if he failed to develop the system that he had sought, he could still take pride in producing the most comprehensive work of jurisprudence in the twentieth century.[45]

Throughout his final years Pound continued to live a full life. Honorary degrees, awards, and tributes came to him in increasing numbers and served as reminders that his work continued to thrive wherever law was discussed. Younger colleagues at Harvard gave him the respect and attention that he so richly deserved, and the Pound Law Club reappeared to contribute a student dimension to his audience. The law school provided an office for him to pursue his lifelong interests in pleasant, familiar surroundings.

But he was not, despite all appearances, indestructible, and when his second wife died in 1959, he grew older and lonelier. Still, he made the daily trip from the Commander Hotel to Langdell Hall, and he even took the initiative in organizing a festshcrift for Austin Wakeman Scott, who had been appointed to the faculty with Pound in 1910. Pound's ninety-third year was a difficult one, and his strength began to ebb alarmingly. His last months were spent in the Harvard infirmary, and his few remaining trips to Langdell Hall were made in a wheelchair. By July 1964 modern science and his pioneer constitution could do no more, and he died peacefully.

Three years after his death a fledgling law review published Pound's final article, "The Case for Law." It was a remarkably appropriate epitaph. Strengthening the law and ensuring its centrality in American life had defined his frame of reference as an intellectual and his social strategy as a reformer. His varied experience as an attorney, judge, teacher, scholar, administrator, and government adviser possessed a unifying leitmotiv, a tireless devotion to the case for law.[46]

Coda

"The work of Dean Pound," Samuel Williston, a Harvard colleague, remarked in 1930, "has made the proposition a familiar one that law should be treated as a social science. His emphasis on this idea is probably the greatest contribution that has been made in the twentieth century to American legal thought." At the same time, Karl Llewellyn, a critic of Pound, admitted that "Pound's work . . . is full to bursting of magnificent insight. . . . The more one learns, the more one studies, the more light and stimulus Pound's writings give."[1] These judgments were fair ones. Pound modified the ground rules for the discussion of law and introduced a new language of expansive phrases—"sociological jurisprudence," "social justice and legal justice," "law in books and law in action," "the socialization of the common law," and "social engineering."

Still, one must not confuse his legacy with his learning. The instrumentalist impulse in Pound's legal theory became the dominant feature of his influence: it made law less parochial by substituting a flexible, interdisciplinary analysis for an exegesis of timeless abstractions. But to interpret Pound solely as a pragmatist exaggerates a secondary element in his thought, and to characterize his jurisprudence as an ideology of social reconstruction mistakes his influence for his intentions.[2] "Social engineering"

283

has become a catchword for ambitious, manipulative policy science, but Pound did not develop sociological jurisprudence as a foundation for far-reaching social departures. The instrumentalist nature of his legacy has obscured the less venturesome character of his learning. His principal commitment was to the common law, and he buttressed that devotion with organicism, traditionalism, and professionalism, conceptions that held the innovative features of his thought in check and made the expansive phrases of his philosophy largely rhetorical.

The competition between instrumentalist and organic elements in Pound's thought created a crippling dualism, which undermined his attempt to erect a comprehensive theoretical system, and confined his mature jurisprudence to a collection of brilliant but inconclusive insights. The organic elements in his thought made it impossible for him to develop the implications of instrumentalism in a sustained fashion, and the expansive phrases of his progressive vocabulary obscured his fundamental caution, both for Pound and his contemporaries and for later readers.

Pound compensated for this debilitating dualism by finding nonintellectual outlets for his energies and by relying on certain theoretical expedients. His administrative responsibilities and occasional forays into public service were particularly important in the 1920s, for they allowed him to continue as a vital, creative person after his jurisprudence had lost its dynamism. The tension in his thought was also relaxed by the effect of two intellectual themes. The common law tradition gave Pound a judge-centered jurisprudence that was at once instrumental and organic. He could interpret the case-by-case development of law as an inductive approach that tested legal doctrine against the data of experience. In another mood, he could consider the judicial process an internal dynamic that lent the legal system an organic unity and continuity. Pound also drew on science to bridge the dualism in his thought. The Darwinian character of the "new botany" gave his organicism an empirical foundation, which provided an alternative to the idealistic organic schemes of thinkers like Hegel. In addition to sustaining a new organicism, the empirical tradition also generated instrumentalism. Although the two modes of thought were incompatible products of empiricism, the parent tradition did constitute a link of sorts, providing Pound with a momentary stay against the contradictions in his thought. But the common law and empirical resolutions were, at best, uneasy ones, and the dualism would not down. It continued to leave Pound vulnerable on both his instrumental and his organic flanks, and it checked his development as an intellectual.

As a scholar, Pound's voracious appetite for evidence also held his insight in check, and his learning became more ponderous as his career progressed. "I think he believes," complained Harold Laski, "in the natural right of every German to be quoted." Felix Frankfurter expressed fatigue with "the accumulated logomachy of centuries. . . . Pound is too damned scholarly for me." Justice Holmes, a great admirer of Pound, was impressed "more by the mass of his writing and the army of knowledge that he commands than by the poignancy of any particular insight." Laski's criticism was especially biting. If, in an essay on jurisprudence, "Pound found it necessary to say that the bathroom had made large developments in America he would put in references (a) to the *Sanitary News* (b) to the *Plumbers Journal* and (c) to the Commerce Department's report on the increased manufacture of lead-less glaze together with a note to the effect that there was a Czech thesis on the sociological significance of the American bathroom which he had not seen."[3]

Pound's wide-ranging scholarship, administrative duties, and conceptual expedients were inadequate defenses against the tensions in his jurisprudence. During the 1920s and 1930s a number of developments shattered the delicate accommodation between organicism and instrumentalism, and revealed the limited character of his reform objectives. As the dualism in his thought became untenable, he resolved the dilemma by discarding the instrumentalist foundation of his legal progressivism. When academic innovators advocated a larger role for social science in legal education, Pound defended the virtues of a traditional, parochial curriculum. When legal realists underscored the law's inherent uncertainty, Pound accused them of substituting anarchy for common law verities. When New Dealers demanded a wider use of administrative agencies, Pound responded with an apotheosis of the judiciary. It is ironic, however, that although Pound eventually sacrificed the manipulative features of his philosophy to its self-adjusting features, the residue of organicism lost its identity as an independent theoretical construct and disappeared as an element of his influence. The empiricism that linked the polarities in his thought did not adequately underscore his organicism. A later generation of American legal theorists, who were inclined to see empiricism in instrumental terms alone, misinterpreted his apology for the common law as a retreat from an earlier advanced position. He was simply restructuring the elements rather than the object of his defense.

Pound's thought revealed the limitations both of the common law tradition and organic social theory as instruments of change. Yet although his dualism, administrative responsibilities, and erudition absorbed his creativity, there was an ironic strength in these inner checks. His commitment to professionalism may have narrowed his intellectual range, but his professional associations provided institutional channels for communicating sociological jurisprudence, and his traditionalism made him appear safer to fellow lawyers. His erudition may have become tiresome, but it lent weight to his authority. The dualism undermined his efforts to develop a grand system, but his boundless energy made the attendant fragmentation a noble moment in legal thought, for the overwhelming flood of books, articles, and addresses enlarged Pound's audience and the influence of sociological jurisprudence. And in spite of his announced reservations about their zeal, he provided social scientists with a valuable ally in the law.

Pound was thus the perfect type to direct the transmission of new learning to an intellectually rigid profession, and American jurisprudence still stands in his shadow. His legal theory was marred by its contradictions and ambivalence, but there was nothing ambivalent about his influence. His work advanced the revolt against formalism and ensured the triumph of a pragmatic social science in law. A later generation failed to detect his treasured organicism, but it borrowed what it understood and reinforced the vitality that Pound infused into legal development.

"Diagnosis," declared Pound, "is the larger part of our task in dealing with any problem. Given a sound diagnosis, to find the treatment is largely a matter of time and persistence."[4] This was one of Pound's most common themes. One must understand a problem in order to solve it. In the last analysis, his most important legacy was in the questions he posed rather than the answers he provided. It was a legacy in which he could take pride, for in establishing the questions for legal thinkers to ponder, he set the fundamental tone and issues of debate throughout his long life and beyond.

Notes

Chapter 1. Nebraska Boyhood

[1]Cyrus Woodman to his brother, 15 December 1869, in C. L. Marquette (ed.), "The Plattsmouth Letters of Cyrus Woodman, 1869-1870," *Nebraska History* 32 (March 1951): 55.

[2]Andrew J. Sawyer (ed.), *Lincoln and Lancaster County, Nebraska*, 2 vols. (Chicago: S. J. Clarke, 1916), 1: 80-81; Neale Copple, *Tower on the Plains: Lincoln's Centennial History, 1859-1959* (Lincoln: Lincoln Centennial Commission Publishers, 1959), p. 46.

[3]J. R. Johnson, "Nebraska in the Seventies," *Nebraska History* 37 (June 1956): 81; Sawyer (ed.), *Lincoln*, 1:322, 144, 147; Roscoe Pound to Mary Catherine [?], 21 February 1938, Roscoe Pound Papers, Nebraska State Historical Society (NSHS); Everett Dick, "Problems of the Post-Frontier City as Portrayed by Lincoln, Nebraska, 1880-1890," *Nebraska History* 28 (April-June 1947): 132-143.

[4]Willa Cather, "Nebraska: The End of the First Cycle," in Ernest Gruening (ed.), *These United States* (New York: Boni and Liveright, 1924), p. 143.

[5]James C. Olson, *History of Nebraska* (Lincoln: University of Nebraska Press, 1955), pp. 156, 266-267; Sawyer (ed.), *Lincoln*, 1:219-221; Robert N. Manley, *Frontier University, 1869-1919* (Lincoln: University of Nebraska Press, 1969).

[6]A. B. Hayes and Sam D. Cox, *History of the City of Lincoln, Nebraska* (Lincoln: State Journal Co., 1889), p. 169.

[7]Sawyer (ed.), *Lincoln*, 1:118-119; Olivia Pound to Paul Sayre, 18 March 1946, Roscoe Pound Papers, NSHS.

[8]N. C. Abbott, "Lincoln: Name and Place," *Publications of the Nebraska State Historical Society* 21 (1930): 131.

[9]Olivia Pound, "Stephen Bosworth Pound," unpublished manuscript in Roscoe Pound Papers, NSHS; *National Cyclopedia of American Biography*, 30 vols. (New York: James T. White and Co., 1941), 29:310; Dixon Ryan Fox, *Union College, An Unfinished History* (Schenectady: Graduate Council, Union College, 1945), pp. 14, 16, 22; Frederick Rudolph, *The American College and University: A History* (New York: Knopf, 1962), pp. 107-108, 184.

[10]*Nebraska State Journal*, 16 May 1909.

[11]Everett Dick, *The Sod-House Frontier, 1854-1890* (New York: D. Appleton-Century, 1938), p. 451.

[12]Charles Wake, "Birth of Lincoln, Nebraska," *Collections of the Nebraska State Historical Society* 16 (1911): 221; Hayes and Cox, *History of Lincoln*, p. 148.

[13]Dick, *The Sod-House Frontier*, pp. 449-450; J. J. Ingalls to his father, 7 October 1860, "Ingalls Letters," *Collections of the Kansas State Historical Society, 1915-1918* 14 (1918): 119.

[14]Hartley B. Alexander, *The Pageant of Lincoln* (Lincoln: n.p., 1915); W. W. Cox, *History of Seward County, Nebraska* (Lincoln: State Journal Co., 1888), p. 38.

[15]Albert Watkins (ed.), "The Constitutional Convention of 1875," *Publications of the Nebraska State Historical Society* 13 (1913): 622; A. E. Sheldon, *Nebraska, The Land and the People*, 3 vols. (Chicago: Lewis Publishing Co., 1931), 2:230.

[16]Stephen B. Pound, "Legal Results of the Pioneer Session," *Proceedings of the Nebraska State Historical Society* 7 (1898): 157.

[17]*Nebraska State Journal*, 14 January 1912; Abbott, "Lincoln: Name and Place," p. 131.

[18]Olivia Pound, "Stephen Bosworth Pound," Roscoe Pound Papers, NSHS.

[19]Seth Robinson to Stephen B. Pound, 5 July 1875, *ibid.*; Charles Wake to Roscoe Pound, 15 May 1911, Roscoe Pound Papers, Harvard Law School Library (HLSL); see also Wake, "Birth of Lincoln, Nebraska," p. 222, for a public confession.

[20]N. Thompson to Roscoe Pound, 25 October 1909, Roscoe Pound Papers, HLSL.

[21]Stephen B. Pound to Laura Biddlecome, 12 January 1868, Stephen B. Pound scrapbook, Roscoe Pound Papers, NSHS.

[22]Marriage license, 21 January 1869, Laura B. Pound Papers, Nebraska State Historical Society; Daughters of the American Revolution information forms, Olivia Pound Papers, Nebraska State Historical Society.

[23]Earnest Elmo Calkins, *They Broke the Plains* (New York: Scribner's, 1937), p. 6.

[24]Carl Sandburg, *Always the Young Strangers* (New York: Harcourt, Brace, 1953), pp. 291-292.

[25]"Lombard-Lincoln Banner at Knox College," *Journal of the Illinois State Historical Society* 53 (Summer 1960): 184; Christian J. Eager-Young, "Ancestry and Recollections of Mrs. John Young, Rochelle, Ill.," *ibid.*, 6 (July 1913), 241; Olivia Pound, "Laura Biddlecome Pound," unpublished manuscript in Laura B. Pound Papers; letter of recommendation from H. R. Sanford, principal, Clyde, New York, High School, 2 November 1863; *ibid.*

[26]*Nebraska State Journal*, 15 April 1925.

[27]*Ibid.*, 19 April 1920; *ibid.*, 24 April 1896; *ibid.*, 17 May 1896; *Lincoln Star*, 11 December 1928.

[28]Laura B. Pound to her mother, 1881, quoted in "Living Memorial to Honor Roscoe Pound," *Sunday Journal and Star* [Lincoln], 5 December 1948; Olivia Pound, "Home Life of the Pound Family," unpublished manuscript in Roscoe Pound Papers, NSHS.

[29]*Nebraska State Journal*, 11 December 1928.

[30]Laura B. Pound to Mrs. E. L. Stout, 12 December 1919, Roscoe Pound Papers, NSHS.

[31]Olivia Pound to Grace Munson, 16 June 1937, *ibid.*

[32]Olivia Pound to Paul Sayre, 18 March 1946, *ibid.*

[33]Olivia Pound, "Roscoe Pound," unpublished manuscript, *ibid.*

[34]Cather, "Nebraska: The End of the First Cycle," p. 146; Hattie Plum Williams, *A Social Study of the Russian German* (Lincoln: University of Nebraska Press, 1916).

[35]Roscoe Pound to Olivia Pound, 30 March 1946, Roscoe Pound Papers, NSHS; Olivia Pound to Grace Munson, 16 June 1937, *ibid.*; Olivia Pound, "Roscoe Pound," *ibid.*

[36]Olivia Pound, "Stephen Bosworth Pound," *ibid.*; George E. Woodberry to Roscoe Pound, 13 November 1927, Olivia Pound Papers; George E. Howard, *An Introduction to the Local Constitutional History of the United States* (Baltimore: The Johns Hopkins Press, 1889), p. vii.

[37]Olivia Pound, "Home Life of the Pound Family," Roscoe Pound Papers, NSHS.

[38]John H. Randall III, *The Landscape and the Looking Glass: Willa Cather's Search for Value* (Boston and New York: Houghton Mifflin, 1960), p. 394; Lewis Atherton, *Main Street on the Middle Border* (Bloomington: Indiana University Press, 1954), pp. 122-127.

[39]*Lincoln Star*, 5 February 1922; *ibid.*, 11 December 1928.

[40]Olivia Pound, "Roscoe Pound," Roscoe Pound Papers, NSHS.

[41]Olson, *History of Nebraska*, p. 352; E. K. Brown, *Willa Cather, A Critical Biography* (New York: Knopf, 1953), p. 49.

[42]Roscoe Pound, "Ellen Smith," unpublished manuscript in Roscoe Pound Papers, NSHS.

[43]*The Sombrero*, 1883-1884, I (1884), 46-47; *The Hesperian Student*, vol. 12, 15 November 1883.

[44]*The Hesperian Student*, vol. 12, 15 April 1884.

[45]Grove E. Barber, "Chancellor J. Irving Manatt," *Semi-Centennial Anniversary Book, The University of Nebraska, 1869-1919* (Lincoln: University of Nebraska Press, 1919), p. 124.

[46]Olson, *History of Nebraska*, pp. 156, 352; Lowry Charles Wimberly, "Oscar Wilde Meets Woodberry," *The Prairie Schooner* 21 (Spring 1947): 111; Samuel Haber, *Efficiency and Uplift: Scientific Management in the Progressive Era, 1890-1920* (Chicago: University of Chicago Press, 1964), pp. 55-57.

[47]Quoted in Mari Sandoz, *Love Song to the Plains* (New York: Harper & Bros., 1961), p. 235.

[48]Edith Lewis, *Willa Cather Living: A Personal Record* (New York: Knopf, 1953), p. 29; Willa Cather, *My Antonia* (Boston and New York: Houghton Mifflin, 1918), p. 258; Will Owen Jones, "Un-

dergraduate Life in the Early Eighties," *Semi-Centennial Anniversary Book, The University of Nebraska*, pp. 42-47; Alvin Johnson, *Pioneer's Progress* (New York: Viking, 1952), p. 82.

[49]Louise Pound, "Hartley Alexander as an Undergraduate," *The Prairie Schooner*, 22 (Winter 1948), 373; Johnson, *Pioneer's Progress*, p. 99.

[50]Roscoe Pound to Olivia Pound, 17 December 1918, Roscoe Pound Papers, NSHS.

[51]Andrew Denny Rodgers III, *American Botany, 1873-1892* (Princeton: Princeton University Press, 1944), p. 200; Raymond J. Pool, "Charles Edwin Bessey," *Semi-Centennial Anniversary Book, The University of Nebraska*, p. 142.

[52]Charles E. Bessey, "Modern Botany and Mr. Darwin," *American Naturalist* 16 (June 1882): 507-508.

[53]Rodgers, *American Botany*, p. 229; Pool, "Charles Edwin Bessey," p. 140; Raymond J. Pool, "The Evolution and Differentiation of Laboratory Teaching in the Botanical Sciences," *Iowa State College Journal of Science* 9 (January 1935): 239.

[54]Ernst A. Bessey, "The Teaching of Botany Sixty-Five Years Ago," *Iowa State College Journal of Science* 9 (January 1935): 232; Andrew Denny Rodgers III, *John Merle Coulter* (Princeton: Princeton University Press, 1944), p. 51.

[55]"Editorial," *Botanical Gazette* 11 (March 1886): 65.

[56]Arthur E. Sutherland, Jr., *The Law at Harvard: A History of Ideas and Men, 1817-1967* (Cambridge: Harvard University Press, 1967), pp. 237, 239; Edwin W. Patterson, *Jurisprudence: Men and Ideas of the Law* (Brooklyn: Foundation Press, 1953), pp. 509-510.

[57]Charles E. Bessey to Roscoe Pound, 30 April 1909, Roscoe Pound Papers, HLSL; Roscoe Pound to William A. Nitze, 10 May 1918, *ibid.*; Roscoe Pound, "Ash Rust in 1888," *American Naturalist* 22 (December 1888): 1117.

[58]*The Hesperian*, vol. 16, 15 December 1887; Louise Pound, "Organizations," *Semi-Centennial Anniversary Book, The University of Nebraska*, p. 59; *Tenth Biennial Report of the Board of Regents of the University of Nebraska*, 1890, p. 29; Johnson, *Pioneer's Progress*, pp. 91-92.

[59]*The Hesperian*, vol. 17, 16 April 1888; *ibid.*, vol. 16, 15 De-

cember 1887; *ibid.*, vol. 15, 15 June 1887; Roscoe Pound to Paul Sayre, 14 October 1946, Roscoe Pound Papers, HLSL.

[60]Pound to Sayre, 5 December 1945, Olivia Pound Papers.

[61]Report cards, Roscoe Pound Papers, NSHS; *Year Book of the College of Law of the University of Nebraska*, 1904, p. 26; Albert Kokourek, "Roscoe Pound as a Former Colleague Knew Him," in Paul Sayre (ed.), *Interpretations of Modern Legal Philosophies; Essays in Honor of Roscoe Pound* (New York: Oxford, 1947), p. 430.

[62]Laura B. Pound to Mrs. E. L. Stout, 12 December 1919, Roscoe Pound Papers, NSHS.

[63]Roscoe Pound to Paul Sayre, 14 September 1945, Olivia Pound Papers.

[64]Austin Wakeman Scott, "Pound's Influence on Civil Procedure," *Harvard Law Review* 78 (June 1965): 1576.

[65]Laura B. Pound to Mrs. E. L. Stout, 12 December 1919, Roscoe Pound Papers, NSHS.

[66]Roscoe Pound, "Fifty Years' Growth of American Law," *Notre Dame Lawyer* 18 (March 1943): 174-175; quoted in Sutherland, *The Law at Harvard*, p. 200; Oliver Wendell Holmes, *Collected Legal Papers* (New York: Harcourt, Brace, 1921), p. 301.

[67]*The Hesperian*, vol. 18, 1 October 1888.

[68]H. L. Shantz, "Frederic Edward Clements," *Ecology* 26 (October 1945): 317; Roscoe Pound, "Frederic E. Clements As I Knew Him," *Ecology* 35 (April 1954): 112.

[69]*The Hesperian*, vol. 18, 1 June 1889.

[70]*Ibid.*, vol. 18, 15 April 1889.

Chapter 2. The Law at Harvard

[1]Arthur E. Sutherland, Jr., *The Law at Harvard: A History of Ideas and Men, 1817-1967* (Cambridge: Harvard University Press, 1967), pp. 199-200.

[2]Roscoe Pound to Stephen B. Pound, 24 September 1889, Olivia Pound Papers.

[3]Roscoe Pound to Laura B. Pound, 29 September 1889, *ibid.*

[4]Roscoe Pound to Laura B. Pound, 26 January 1890, *ibid.*

[5]Roscoe Pound to Laura B. Pound, 3 November 1889, *ibid.*; Roscoe Pound to Laura B. Pound, 27 April 1890, *ibid.*; Roscoe Pound to Laura B. Pound, 10 March 1890, *ibid.*; Pound interview conducted by Arthur Sutherland, 25 July 1962, copy in my possession.

[6]Roscoe Pound to Laura B. Pound, 3 November 1889, Olivia Pound Papers.

[7]Roscoe Pound to Stephen B. Pound, 10 November 1889, *ibid.*

[8]Roscoe Pound to Laura B. Pound, 16 March 1890, *ibid.*; Arthur Mann, *Yankee Reformers in the Urban Age* (Cambridge: Harvard University Press, 1954).

[9]Roscoe Pound to Laura B. Pound, 3 November 1889, Olivia Pound Papers.

[10]Roscoe Pound to Laura B. Pound, 16 March 1890, *ibid.*

[11]Roscoe Pound to Laura B. Pound, 29 September 1889, *ibid.*; Roscoe Pound to Stephen B. Pound, 22 December 1889, *ibid.*

[12]Sutherland, *The Law at Harvard*, p. 203.

[13]James Barr Ames, "Christopher Columbus Langdell," in Ames, *Lectures on Legal History and Miscellaneous Legal Essays* (Cambridge: Harvard University Press, 1913), p. 472.

[14]Christopher C. Langdell, "Teaching Law as a Science," *American Law Review* 21 (January-February 1887): 123; see also his *Selection of Cases on the Law of Contracts* (Boston: Little, Brown, 1871), p. vi.

[15]Oliver Wendell Holmes, Jr., to Sir Frederick Pollock, 10 April 1881, in Mark DeWolfe Howe (ed.), *Holmes-Pollock Letters; The Correspondence of Mr. Justice Holmes and Sir Frederick Pollock, 1874-1932*, 2 vols. (Cambridge: Harvard University Press, 1961), 1:17; Holmes to Pollock, 6 July 1908, *ibid.*, 1:140; James Willard Hurst, *The Growth of American Law; The Law Makers* (Boston: Little, Brown, 1950), p. 269.

[16]Roscoe Pound to Laura B. Pound, 29 September 1889, Olivia Pound Papers; Roscoe Pound to Stephen B. Pound, 22 December 1889, *ibid.*; Roscoe Pound to Laura B. Pound, 10 March 1890, *ibid.*

[17]Roscoe Pound to Morris Cohen, 20 March 1912, in Leonora Cohen Rosenfield, *Portrait of a Philosopher: Morris R. Cohen in Life and Letters* (New York: Harcourt, Brace, 1962), p. 229.

[18]James Barr Ames, "The Vocation of the Law Professor," in Ames, *Lectures on Legal History*, p. 363.

[19]Charles W. Eliot, "James Barr Ames," *Harvard Law Review* 23 (March 1910): 321; Joseph H. Beale, "The History of Legal Education," in *Law; A Century of Progress, 1835-1935*, 3 vols. (New York: New York University Press, 1937), 1:110; Harlan B. Phillips (ed.), *Felix Frankfurter Reminisces* (New York: Reynal, 1960), p. 22.

[20]Ames, "The Vocation of the Law Professor," p. 367.

[21]*Ibid.*, p. 364.

[22]Francis Biddle, *A Casual Past* (Garden City, N.Y.: Doubleday, 1961), p. 252; Morris Cohen, "A Critical Sketch of Legal Philosophy in America," in *Law*, 2:292.

[23]Roland Gray, "Memoir," in *John Chipman Gray* (Boston: priv. print., 1917), pp. 24-27.

[24]*The Centennial History of the Harvard Law School, 1817-1917* (n.p., 1918), p. 212.

[25]John Chipman Gray, "Methods of Legal Education," *Yale Law Journal* 1 (March 1892): 161.

[26]John Chipman Gray to Charles W. Eliot, 8 January 1883, in Mark DeWolfe Howe, *Justice Oliver Wendell Holmes; The Proving Years, 1870-1882* (Cambridge: Harvard University Press, 1963), 2:158; Oliver Wendell Holmes, Jr., *The Common Law* (Boston: Little, Brown, 1881), p. 1.

[27]John Chipman Gray, "Some Definitions and Questions in Jurisprudence," *Harvard Law Review* 6 (April 1892): 35.

[28]Gray, "Methods of Legal Education," p. 160.

[29]Roscoe Pound to Laura B. Pound, 10 March 1890, Olivia Pound Papers; Moorfield Storey, "John Chipman Gray," in M. A. DeWolfe Howe (ed.), *Later Years of the Saturday Club, 1870-1920* (Boston and New York: Houghton Mifflin, 1927), p. 225; Roscoe Pound to Stephen B. Pound, 10 November 1889, Olivia Pound Papers.

[30]John Chipman Gray, "Judicial Precedents—A Short Study in

Comparative Jurisprudence," *Harvard Law Review* 9 (April 1895): 27.

[31]John Chipman Gray, *The Nature and Sources of the Law* (New York: Columbia University Press, 1909), p. 82.

[32]Gray, "Some Definitions and Questions in Jurisprudence," p. 28.

[33]Gray, *Nature and Sources of Law*, p. 165, quoted in Roscoe Pound, *An Introduction to the Philosophy of Law* (New Haven: Yale University Press, 1959), p. 50.

[34]Gray, *Nature and Sources of Law*, p. 292.

[35]Gray, "Some Definitions and Questions in Jurisprudence," p. 28.

[36]Joseph H. Beale to Roscoe Pound, 15 August 1912, Roscoe Pound Papers, HLSL.

[37]Roscoe Pound to Laura B. Pound, 10 March 1890, Olivia Pound Papers; Horace Coon, *Columbia; Colossus on the Hudson* (New York: E. P. Dutton, 1947), p. 228; Julius Goebel, Jr., et al., *A History of the School of Law, Columbia University* (New York: Columbia University Press, 1955), pp. 138, 139.

[38]Roscoe Pound to Laura B. Pound, 10 March 1890, Olivia Pound Papers; Goebel, *A History of the School of Law*, pp. 141-142.

[39]James Parker Hall, "James Bradley Thayer," in William D. Lewis (ed.), *Great American Lawyers*, 8 vols. (Philadelphia: The J. C. Winston Co., 1909), 8:345.

[40]James Bradley Thayer, "The Origin and Scope of the American Doctrine of Constitutional Law," in Thayer, *Legal Essays* (Cambridge: Harvard University Press, 1927), p. 7.

[41]James Bradley Thayer, "Constitutionality of Legislation: The Precise Question for a Court," *The Nation* 38 (10 April 1884): 314.

[42]James Bradley Thayer, *John Marshall* (Boston and New York: Houghton Mifflin, 1901), p. 110.

[43]Thayer, "The Origin and Scope of the American Doctrine of Constitutional Law," p. 27.

[44]Thayer, "Constitutionality of Legislation," p. 315.

[45]Thayer, "The Origin and Scope of the American Doctrine of Constitutional Law," p. 39.

[46]Roscoe Pound, "The Common Law and Legislation," *Harvard Law Review* 21 (April 1908): 403.

[47]Roscoe Pound to Stephen B. Pound, 3 March 1890, Olivia Pound Papers; Laura B. Pound to Mrs. E. L. Stout, 12 December 1919, Roscoe Pound Papers, NSHS.

Chapter 3. The Lure of Botany

[1]*The Hesperian*, vol. 21, 15 February 1892.

[2]*Ibid.*, vol. 21, 1 November 1891; *ibid.*, vol. 21, 15 November 1891.

[3]*Ibid.*, vol. 21, 1 December 1891.

[4]Emory R. Buckner to Samuel Williston, 16 February 1910, Roscoe Pound Papers, HLSL.

[5]H. L. Shantz, "Frederic Edward Clements," *Ecology* 26 (October 1945): 317; Roscoe Pound, "Frederic E. Clements as I Knew Him," *ibid.*, 35 (April 1954): 112; Frederic E. Clements, "Roscoe Pound," manuscript in Olivia Pound Papers; *The Book of the Sem. Bot.* (Lincoln: Botanical Seminar, n.d.).

[6]Andrew Denny Rodgers III, *John Merle Coulter* (Princeton: Princeton University Press, 1944), pp. 119, 217, 117-118.

[7]Harry Baker Humphrey, *Makers of North American Botany* (New York: Ronald, 1961), pp. 159-160.

[8]Quoted in Shantz, "Frederic Edward Clements," p. 319; see also Humphrey, *Makers of North American Botany*, p. 52.

[9]Bernard S. Meyer, "Awards of Certificates of Merit at the Fiftieth Anniversary Meeting [of the Botanical Society of America]," in William C. Steere (ed.), *Fifty Years of Botany* (New York: McGraw-Hill, 1958), p. 15.

[10]Clements, "Roscoe Pound," Olivia Pound Papers.

[11]Paul Sayre, *The Life of Roscoe Pound* (Iowa City: College of Law Committee, 1948), p. 64.

[12]Pound, "Frederic E. Clements as I Knew Him," p. 113.

[13]Clements, "Roscoe Pound," Olivia Pound Papers; Olivia Pound, "Roscoe Pound," Roscoe Pound Papers, NSHS.

[14]Roscoe Pound, "Progress of the Botanical Survey of Nebraska," *Publications of the Nebraska Academy of Sciences, 1897-1900* 6 (1901): 138.

[15]A. Hunter Dupree, *Asa Gray, 1810-1888* (Cambridge: Harvard University Press, 1959), pp. 394-395.

[16]Roscoe Pound, "The Plant-Geography of Germany," *American Naturalist* 30 (June 1896): 465-468; Pound, "Frederic E. Clements as I Knew Him," p. 113.

[17]Paul B. Sears, "Plant Ecology," in Joseph Ewan (ed.), *A Short History of Botany in the United States* (New York: Hafner, 1969), p. 125. A second edition, much revised, was published in 1900 after a fire destroyed most of the first edition.

[18]Pound, "Frederic E. Clements as I Knew Him," p. 113; Clements, "Roscoe Pound," Olivia Pound Papers.

[19]Roscoe Pound and Frederic E. Clements, *Phytogeography of Nebraska*, 2nd ed. (Lincoln: Jacob North, 1900), pp. 13-14. All following references are to the second edition.

[20]*Ibid.*, pp. 60-61. This method was treated at greater length in Roscoe Pound and Frederic E. Clements, "A Method of Determining the Abundance of Secondary Species," *Minnesota Botanical Studies* 2 (15 June 1898): 19-24.

[21]Pound and Clements, *Phytogeography*, p. 161.

[22]*Ibid.*, p. 314.

[23]*Ibid.*

[24]Quoted in Erik Nordenskiöld, *The History of Biology: A Survey*, trans. Leonard B. Eyre (New York: Tudor, 1936), p. 516.

[25]Arthur O. Lovejoy, *The Great Chain of Being: A Study of the History of an Idea* (Cambridge: Harvard University Press, 1936); Loren Eiseley, *Darwin's Century: Evolution and the Men Who Discovered It* (Garden City: Doubleday, 1958), pp. 82, 118-119.

[26]Frederick J. Teggart, *Theory and Processes of History* (Berkeley and Los Angeles: University of California Press, 1962), p. 136.

[27]H. J. Muller, "The Views of Haeckel in the Light of Genetics," *Philosophy of Science* 1 (July 1934): 319.

[28]Bert James Loewenberg, "Darwinism Comes to America, 1859-1900," *Mississippi Valley Historical Review* 28 (December 1941): 363.

²⁹Sidney Ratner, "Evolution and the Rise of the Scientific Spirit in America," *Philosophy of Science* 3 (January 1936): 111.

³⁰Asa Gray, *Darwiniana: Essays and Reviews Pertaining to Darwinism* (New York: D. Appleton, 1876), p. 288.

³¹Charles Darwin to Asa Gray, 22 May 1860, in Francis Darwin (ed.), *The Life and Letters of Charles Darwin*, 2 vols. (New York: Basic Books, 1959), 2:105; Darwin to Gray, 5 June 1861, *ibid.*, 2: 165; Charles Darwin, *The Variation of Animals and Plants Under Domestication*, 2 vols. (London: John Murray, 1868), 2:432.

³²Francis Darwin (ed.), *Life and Letters of Charles Darwin*, 2:430.

³³Thomas H. Huxley, "On the Reception of 'Origin of Species,'" *ibid.*, 1:554-555.

³⁴Pound and Clements, *Phytogeography*, pp. 315, 316.

³⁵Robert Leo Smith, *Ecology and Field Biology* (New York and London: Harper, 1966), pp. 140-141.

³⁶Frederic E. Clements, "Development and Structure of Vegetation," *Reports of the Botanical Survey of Nebraska*, vol. 7, 1904; Frederic E. Clements, *Research Methods in Ecology* (Lincoln: The University Publishing Co., 1905); Frederic E. Clements, *Plant Succession: An Analysis of the Development of Vegetation* (Washington: Carnegie Institute, 1916).

³⁷E. V. Walter suggests that botany was determinative in freeing Pound from the analytical viewpoint. See Walter, "Legal Ecology of Roscoe Pound," *Miami Law Quarterly* 4 (February 1950): 184.

³⁸Roscoe Pound to Omer F. Hershey, 27 January 1895, quoted in Sayre, *Life of Roscoe Pound*, p. 11; Roscoe Pound, "Sociology of Law," in Georges Gurvitch and Wilbert E. Moore (eds.), *Twentieth Century Sociology* (New York: Philosophical Library, 1945), p. 335.

³⁹Rodgers, *John Merle Coulter*, pp. 134-135.

⁴⁰Pound and Clements, *Phytogeography*, p. 314.

⁴¹Roscoe Pound, "Some Recent Papers on Nomenclature," *Botanical Gazette* 22 (October 1896): 338-339.

⁴²Edward L. Rand and John H. Redfield, *Flora of Mount Desert Island, Maine* (Cambridge: J. Wilson & Son, 1894).

⁴³Quoted in Rodgers, *John Merle Coulter*, p. 136. Rodgers incorrectly attributes the review to Bessey.

⁴⁴Roscoe Pound, "Messrs. Rand and Redfield on Nomenclature," *American Naturalist* 28 (December 1894): 1037, 1039.

⁴⁵Roscoe Pound, "As Regards Some Botanical Latin," *American Naturalist* 23 (April 1889): 444-445.

⁴⁶Roscoe Pound, book review of Otto Kuntze, *Revisio Generum Plantarum, American Naturalist* 26 (February 1892): 154-155.

⁴⁷*Nebraska State Journal*, 23 October 1898.

⁴⁸*Fourteenth Biennial Report of the Board of Regents of the University of Nebraska*, 1899, p. 40.

⁴⁹*Publications of the Nebraska Academy of Sciences, 1897-1900* 7 (1901): 5; "News," *Botanical Gazette* 28 (October 1899): 286.

⁵⁰J. McKeen Cattell (ed.), *American Men of Science: A Biographical Directory* (New York: Science Press, 1906), p. 256.

⁵¹Raymond J. Pool, "Frederic Edward Clements," *Ecology* 35 (April 1954): 110.

⁵²Henry C. Cowles, book review of Pound and Clements, *Phytogeography* (1898), *Botanical Gazette* 25 (May 1898): 371; Colton Russell, book review of Pound and Clements, *Phytogeography* (1900), *American Naturalist* 35 (July 1901): 602.

⁵³H. A. Gleason to [?] Cohn, 15 November 1952, E. J. Palmer Papers, State Historical Society of Missouri.

Chapter 4. Years of Growth: Law and Politics in Nebraska

¹Charles G. Dawes, *A Journal of the McKinley Years*, ed. Bascom N. Timmons (Chicago: R. R. Donnelley, 1950), p. 5.

²Roscoe Pound, "The Bar Examinations in Retrospect," *American Law School Review* 8 (December 1935): 305-306; *Omaha Daily Bee*, 30 April 1911; Roscoe Pound to Joseph F. Francis, 10 July 1922, Roscoe Pound Papers, HLSL; George D. Ayers to G. W. Wickersham, 12 December 1911, *ibid*.

³Pound interview conducted by Arthur Sutherland, 25 July 1962; Roscoe Pound, "Judicial Organization," *Proceedings of the Texas Bar Association* 37 (1918): 87.

⁴Roscoe Pound to A. H. Kidd, 1 September 1900, A. H. Kidd Papers, Nebraska State Historical Society; Roscoe Pound to

Samuel M. Chapman, 7 January 1901, Samuel M. Chapman Papers, Nebraska State Historical Society.

[5]Roscoe Pound to A. H. Kidd, 14 September 1900, Kidd Papers; H. B. Waldron to Samuel M. Chapman, 26 July 1901, Chapman Papers.

[6]Roscoe Pound to Omer F. Hershey, 10 February 1895, quoted in Paul Sayre, *The Life of Roscoe Pound* (Iowa City: College of Law Committee, 1948), p. 85.

[7]Jerome Frank, *Courts on Trial* (Princeton: Princeton University Press, 1950), p. 255; Roscoe Pound, "Wig and Gown," *Nebraska Legal News*, 5 (31 July 1897); Arnold Paul, *Conservative Crisis and the Rule of Law* (Ithaca: Cornell University Press, 1960).

[8]Christopher G. Tiedeman, "The Doctrine of Natural Rights in Its Bearing upon American Constitutional Law," *Proceedings of the Seventh Annual Meeting of the Missouri Bar Association*, 1887, p. 117; John F. Dillon, "Address of the President," *Report of the American Bar Association* 15 (1892): 210-211; Pound, "Wig and Gown"; Paul, *Conservative Crisis*, pp. 19-38, 61-81.

[9]"Response by Professor Pound," *Proceedings of the Iowa State Bar Association* 20 (1914): 145; another example appears in an address quoted in Lewis C. Cassidy, "Dean Pound: The Scope of his Life and Work," *New York University Law Quarterly Review* 7 (June 1930): 908; Roscoe Pound to Olivia Pound, 9 February 1916, Olivia Pound Papers.

[10]Roscoe Pound, "The Price of Wheat," *Nebraska State Journal*, 2 August 1896.

[11]Gilbert C. Fite, "Republican Strategy and the Farm Vote in the Presidential Campaign of 1896," *American Historical Review* 65 (July 1960): 789-790.

[12]Pound, "The Price of Wheat."

[13]*Nebraska State Journal*, 2 August 1896; *ibid.*, 4 August 1896; *ibid.*, 4 September 1896; Lincoln *Evening News*, 3 August 1896; Omaha *Daily Bee*, 6 August 1896; Frank Irvine to Roscoe Pound, 25 August 1896, Roscoe Pound Papers, NSHS.

[14]*Nebraska State Journal* 29 September 1896; *ibid.*, 7 October 1896; *ibid.*, 5 August 1896; *ibid.*, 10 April 1901.

[15]*Ibid.*, 8 October 1896; *ibid.*, 21 October 1896.

¹⁶Roscoe Pound, *The Lawyer from Antiquity to Modern Times* (St. Paul: West, 1953), p. 316.

¹⁷*Proceedings of the Nebraska State Bar Association, 1900-1903* 1 (1903): 25, 27.

¹⁸Francis Brogan to Roscoe Pound, 24 September 1910, Roscoe Pound Papers, HLSL.

¹⁹*Proceedings of the Nebraska State Bar Association* 9 (1916): 128.

²⁰*Proceedings of the Nebraska State Bar Association, 1900-1903* 1 (1903): 10.

²¹*Ibid.*, p. 30.

²²Eleazer Wakely, "Address of the President at the First Annual Meeting," *ibid.*, p. 53; William D. McHugh, "Address of the President at the Second Annual Meeting, *ibid.*, p. 62.

²³Robert H. Wiebe, *The Search for Order, 1877-1920* (New York: Hill & Wang, 1967), pp. 111-113.

²⁴*Ibid.*, pp. 113-115; Richard H. Shryock, *Medical Licensing in America, 1650-1965* (Baltimore: The Johns Hopkins Press, 1967), pp. 59-60, 65.

²⁵Wiebe, *The Search for Order*, pp. 116-117; Samuel P. Hays, *The Response to Industrialism, 1885-1914* (Chicago: University of Chicago Press, 1957), pp. 48-70, 192; Alfred Z. Reed, *Training for the Public Profession of the Law* (New York: Carnegie Foundation, 1921), pp. 203-239.

²⁶E. Benjamin Andrews, "The Importance of a Patriotic and Competent Bar," *Proceedings of the Nebraska State Bar Association, 1900-1903* 1 (1903): 45, 46. (This meeting was held on 18 September 1900.)

²⁷"Report of the Committee on Legal Education," *ibid.*, pp. 48-50.

²⁸*Fifteenth Biennial Report of the Board of Regents of the University of Nebraska*, 1900, p. 26.

²⁹*Proceedings of the Nebraska State Bar Association, 1900-1903*, pp. 31, 35-36; *Laws of Nebraska, 1901*, chap. 25, p. 331; remarks of Halleck F. Rose, "Proceedings of the Nebraska State Bar Association, 1927," *Nebraska Law Bulletin* 7 (July 1928): 67; *Nebraska State Journal*, 10 April 1901.

³⁰Harold G. Reuschlein, "Roscoe Pound—The Judge," *Uni-*

versity of Pennsylvania Law Review 90 (January 1942): 292-329, argues that Pound's philosophy was much more mature at this point than I have found it.

[31]*Williams v. Miles*, 68 Nebraska 463, 470 (1903).

[32]*Bonacum v. Harrington*, 65 Nebraska 831, 837 (1902).

[33]*Leavitt v. Mercer Co.*, 64 Nebraska 31, 33, 34 (1902).

[34]Austin Wakeman Scott, *The Law of Trusts*, 4 vols., 2nd ed. (Boston: Little, Brown, 1956), 4:3300; Austin Wakeman Scott, "The Right to Follow Money Wrongfully Mingled with Other Money," *Harvard Law Review* 27 (May 1913): 125.

[35]*City of Lincoln v. Morrison*, 64 Nebraska 822, 826 (1902).

[36]*Modern Woodmen of America v. Jennie Lane*, 62 Nebraska 89, 92 (1901).

[37]*Miller v. FitzGerald Dry Goods Co.*, 62 Nebraska 270, 273 (1901).

[38]*Bonacum v. Harrington*, 65 Nebraska 831, 835 (1902).

[39]Ralph W. Breckenridge, "Law and its Administration in Nebraska," *Proceedings of the Nebraska State Bar Association, 1905* 2 (1903-1905): 90.

[40]*Batty v. City of Hastings*, 63 Nebraska 26, 33 (1901).

[41]*Cleland v. Anderson*, 66 Nebraska 252, 261, 260 (1902).

[42]*In re Anderson*, 69 Nebraska 686, 689 (1903).

[43]*Bronson v. Albion Telephone Co.*, 67 Nebraska 111, 117 (1903).

[44]*Doane v. Dunham*, 64 Nebraska 135, 136-137 (1902).

[45]*Schrandt v. Young*, 62 Nebraska 254, 266-267 (1901).

[46]*Phoenix Insurance Co. v. Zlotsky*, 66 Nebraska 584, 588-589 (1902).

[47]*Haslach v. Wolf*, 66 Nebraska 600, 602 (1902).

[48]Roscoe Pound, *Appellate Procedure in Civil Cases* (Boston: National Conference of Judicial Councils, 1941), p. 233.

[49]*Bennett v. Bennett*, 65 Nebraska 432, 434 (1902).

[50]*Hargreaves v. Tennis*, 63 Nebraska 356 (1901).

[51]Charles E. Clark, *Handbook of the Law of Code Pleading* (St. Paul: West, 1928), p. 511.

[52]*Ulrich v. McConaughey*, 63 Nebraska 10, 20 (1901).

[53]*Estate of Fitzgerald v. Union Savings Bank*, 65 Nebraska 97, 101 (1902).

[54]*Ibid.*, 102.

[55]*Murray v. Burd*, 65 Nebraska 427, 428 (1902).

[56]*German Insurance Co. v. Shader*, 68 Nebraska 1, 14 (1903).

[57]Interview with Arthur E. Sutherland, 28 December 1966.

[58]Samuel P. Davidson, "President's Address at the Third Annual Meeting," *Proceedings of the Nebraska State Bar Association, 1903* 2 (1903-1905): 35.

Chapter 5. The Law at Nebraska

[1]J. Stuart Dales to Roscoe Pound, 13 June 1903, Roscoe Pound Papers, NSHS; Emory Buckner to Roscoe Pound, 3 January 1915, Roscoe Pound Papers, HLSL.

[2]Arthur F. Mullen, *Western Democrat* (New York: W. Funk, 1940), pp. 77-78.

[3]M. B. Reese, "Report of the Dean of the College of Law," *Sixteenth Biennial Report of the Board of Regents of the University of Nebraska*, 1902, pp. 31-32.

[4]M. B. Reese, "Report of the Dean of the College of Law," *Fourteenth Biennial Report of the Board of Regents of the University of Nebraska*, 1899, p. 21.

[5]William Adams Slade, "Elisha Benjamin Andrews," in Allen Johnson and Dumas Malone (eds.), *Dictionary of American Biography*, 20 vols. (New York: Scribner's, 1928), 1:286-291; Walter C. Bronson, *The History of Brown University, 1764-1914* (Providence: Brown University Press, 1914), pp. 430-432; Alexander Meiklejohn, *Freedom and the College* (New York: The Century Co., 1923), p. 50.

[6]E. L. Hinman, "E. Benjamin Andrews," *Semi-Centennial Anniversary Book, The University of Nebraska, 1869-1919* (Lincoln: University of Nebraska Press, 1919), pp. 130-133; Edward A. Ross, *Seventy Years of It* (New York: D. Appleton-Century Co., 1936), p. 87.

[7]Roscoe Pound, "Henry Moore Bates: 1869-1949," *Michigan Law Review* 47 (June 1949): 1059.

[8]All preceding quotations, unless otherwise noted, are from

Roscoe Pound, *The Evolution of Legal Education* (Lincoln: Jacob North, 1903).

⁹Edith Abbott, *Social Welfare and Professional Education* (Chicago: University of Chicago Press, 1942), p. 62; Roscoe Pound, "Report of the Dean of the College of Law," *Seventeenth Biennial Report of the Board of Regents of the University of Nebraska*, 1905, p. 41.

¹⁰*Ibid.*, pp. 37-38; *Year Book of the College of Law of the University of Nebraska, 1906*, p. 49.

¹¹"A Word of Advice by Dean Pound," *Year Book of the College of Law of the University of Nebraska, 1904*, pp. 77-79; *Year Book, 1906*, p. 96.

¹²Pound, "Report of the Dean of the College of Law," *Seventeenth Biennial Report*, p. 39.

¹³*The Daily Nebraskan*, vol. 5, 28 September 1905.

¹⁴Roscoe Pound, "Report of the Dean of the College of Law," *Eighteenth Biennial Report of the Board of Regents of the University of Nebraska*, 1907, p. 69.

¹⁵Roscoe Pound, *Outlines of Lectures on Jurisprudence* (Lincoln: Jacob North, 1903), p. 4.

¹⁶*Ibid.*, p. 6.

¹⁷Laurence R. Veysey, *The Emergence of the American University* (Chicago: University of Chicago Press, 1965), p. 416.

¹⁸Margaret Wilson Vine, *An Introduction to Sociological Theory* (New York: David McKay Co., 1959), pp. 169-189.

¹⁹Ross, *Seventy Years of It*, p. 89.

²⁰*Ibid.*

²¹Roscoe Pound to Edward A. Ross, 2 November 1906, Edward A. Ross Papers, State Historical Society of Wisconsin; Pound to Ross, 17 May 1907, *ibid.*

²²Roscoe Pound to Edward A. Ross, 10 December 1907, *ibid.*; Edward A. Ross, *Sin and Society* (Boston: Houghton Mifflin, 1907), pp. 90, 34, 136, 41.

²³Quoted in Veysey, *Emergence of the American University*, p. 77.

²⁴L. L. Bernard, "The Social Sciences as Disciplines: United States," in E. R. A. Seligman and Alvin Johnson (eds.),

Encyclopedia of the Social Sciences, 14 vols. (New York: Macmillan, 1930), 1:344.

²⁵Roscoe Pound, "A New School of Jurists," *The University Studies of the University of Nebraska* 4 (July 1904): 261.

²⁶William Seagle, *Men of Law* (New York: Macmillan, 1947), pp. 306, 329.

²⁷Friedrich Karl von Savigny, *Of the Vocation of Our Age for Legislation and Jurisprudence*, trans. Abraham Hayward (London: Littlewood, 1831).

²⁸Max Rümelin, "Developments in Legal Theory and Teaching During My Lifetime," in M. Magdalena Schoch (ed.), *The Jurisprudence of Interests* (Cambridge: Harvard University Press, 1948), p. 4.

²⁹Munroe Smith, *A General View of European Legal History and Other Papers* (New York: Columbia University Press, 1927), pp. 172-180.

³⁰Rudolf von Jhering, *Law as a Means to an End*, trans. Issac Husik (Boston: Boston Book Co., 1913), p. lviii.

³¹Rudolf von Jhering, *The Struggle for Law*, trans. John J. Lalor (Chicago: Callaghan, 1915), p. 1.

³²Jhering, *Law as a Means to an End*, pp. liv, 27; Carl Friedrich, *The Philosophy of Law in Historical Perspective* (Chicago: University of Chicago Press, 1958), p. 158.

³³Jhering, *Law as a Means to an End*, pp. 59, 348-349; Edwin W. Patterson, *Jurisprudence: Men and Ideas of the Law* (Brooklyn: The Foundation Press, 1953), pp. 462-463.

³⁴Rudolf von Jhering, *Scherz und Ernst in der Jurisprudenz* (Leipzig: Breitkopf und Haertel, 1885), pp. 341-342; Jhering, *Law as a Means to an End*, pp. 332-333; Jhering, *The Struggle for Law*, p. 13.

³⁵Pound, "A New School of Jurists"; Roscoe Pound, "Mechanical Jurisprudence," *Columbia Law Review* 8 (December 1908): 605. In later years Pound continued to acknowledge Jhering's importance as "the first to insist upon the interests which the legal order secures rather than the legal rights by which it secures them." Roscoe Pound, *The Spirit of the Common Law* (Boston: Marshall Jones, 1921), pp. 203-204.

[36]Roscoe Pound, "Do We Need a Philosophy of Law?", *Columbia Law Review* 5 (May 1905): 343.

[37]Pound, "A New School of Jurists," p. 265.

[38]*Ibid.*, p. 257.

[39]Roscoe Pound to Omer F. Hershey, 27 January 1895, quoted in Paul Sayre, *The Life of Roscoe Pound* (Iowa City: College of Law Committee, 1948), p. 11.

[40]Pound, "A New School of Jurists," p. 266.

[41]Pound, "Do We Need a Philosophy of Law?" pp. 346, 349-350.

[42]*Ibid.*, pp. 352-353.

[43]*The Daily Nebraskan*, vol. 4, 5 January 1905. Pound returned to the deanship at the same salary. See *Eighteenth Biennial Report*, pp. 163, 173, 179, 191, for salary in 1904-1905; for the succeeding year see *ibid.*, pp. 202, 206, 212, and *Nineteenth Biennial Report of the Board of Regents of the University of Nebraska*, 1909, p. 33.

[44]*The Daily Nebraskan*, vol. 4, 23 February 1905; *Nebraska State Journal*, 2 March 1905; *The Daily Nebraskan*, vol. 4, 5 January 1905; *ibid.*, 12 January 1905; *ibid.*, 13 January 1905; *ibid.*, 9 February 1905; *ibid.*, 10 February 1905; *ibid.*, 16 February 1905.

[45]*Ibid.*, vol. 5, 21 September 1905.

[46]*Ibid.*, vol. 4, 3 March 1905.

[47]E. Benjamin Andrews to Roscoe Pound, 27 August 1906, Roscoe Pound Papers, HLSL.

[48]*The Daily Nebraskan*, vol. 4, 1 February 1905; *ibid.*, 27 October 1904.

[49]M. M. Fogg, "Roscoe Pound of Nebraska, Harvard Law School Dean," *The University* [of Nebraska] *Journal*, April 1916, p. 5.

[50]Roscoe Pound, "No Humbug at Nebraska," *The Daily Nebraskan*, vol. 4, 24 November 1904; *ibid.*, vol. 5, 19 October 1905.

[51]Alvin Johnson, *Pioneer's Progress* (New York: Viking, 1952), pp. 173-174.

[52]*Report of the American Bar Association, 1906* 29 (1906): 11.

[53]John H. Wigmore, "Roscoe Pound's St. Paul Address of 1906;

The Spark that Kindled the White Flame of Progress," *Journal of the American Judicature Society* 20 (February 1937): 176; Robert W. Millar, *Civil Procedure of the Trial Court in Historical Perspective* (New York: National Conference of Judicial Councils, 1952), p. ix.

[54]Roscoe Pound, "The Causes of Popular Dissatisfaction with the Administration of Justice," *Report of the American Bar Association, 1906*, pp. 408, 403.

[55]*Ibid.*, pp. 400, 404, 406, 408, 412, 414, 417.

[56]*Ibid.*, pp. 12-13.

[57]*Ibid.*, pp. 56, 58, 59.

[58]*Ibid.*, pp. 59-60, 63.

[59]Roscoe Pound to Edward A. Ross, 2 November 1906, Ross Papers.

[60]Pound, "The Causes of Popular Dissatisfaction with the Administration of Justice," p. 416.

[61]*Ibid.*

[62]Wigmore, "Roscoe Pound's St. Paul Address," p. 178.

[63]Judge McClain's letter, quoted in Pound to Ross, 2 November 1906, Ross Papers.

[64]*Report of the American Bar Association* 27 (1904): 129.

[65]*Report of the American Bar Association, 1906*, part 2, p. 16; Wigmore, "Roscoe Pound's St. Paul Address," pp. 177, 178.

[66]William R. Roalfe, "John Henry Wigmore—Scholar and Reformer," *Journal of Criminal Law, Criminology, and Police Science* 53 (September 1962): 285-286.

[67]Roscoe Pound to John H. Wigmore, 10 November 1906, John Henry Wigmore Papers, Northwestern University School of Law Library.

[68]Jesse Holdom to Roscoe Pound, 6 April 1907, *ibid.*

[69]Roscoe Pound to John H. Wigmore, 30 April 1907, *ibid.*

[70]Roscoe Pound to John H. Wigmore, 15 June 1907, *ibid.*

[71]Johnson, *Pioneer's Progress*, pp. 170, 182; Ross, *Seventy Years of It*, pp. 98-99; Harry Baker Humphrey, *Makers of North American Botany* (New York: Ronald, 1961), p. 52; John A. Rice, *I Came Out of the Eighteenth Century* (New York: Harper, 1942), pp. 269-294.

[72]*Nebraska State Journal*, 28 May 1907.
[73]*The Daily Nebraskan*, vol. 6, 23 May 1907; *ibid.*, 24 May 1907; *ibid.*, 25 May 1907; *Nebraska State Journal*, 28 May 1907.

Chapter 6. Chicago Years: Emergence of a Reformer

[1]John H. Wigmore to Oliver Wendell Holmes, 5 September 1907, Wigmore Papers; *Chicago Legal News* 39 (25 May 1907): 337.

[2]Albert Kocourek, "Roscoe Pound as a Former Colleague Knew Him," in Paul Sayre (ed.), *Interpretations of Modern Legal Philosophies; Essays in Honor of Roscoe Pound* (New York: Oxford University Press, 1947), p. 423; James Willard Hurst, *The Growth of American Law; The Law Makers* (Boston: Little, Brown, 1950), p. 134; James A. Rahl and Kurt Schwerin, "Northwestern University School of Law: A Short History," *Northwestern University Law Review* 55 (May-June 1960): 142, 149-150; Harold C. Havighurst, "In Memoriam: Albert Kocourek," *ibid.*, 47 (September-October 1952): 419.

[3]Rahl and Schwerin, "Northwestern University School of Law: A Short History."

[4]Robert W. Millar, "John Henry Wigmore," *Illinois Law Review* 38 (1943): 1-5; Lowell quoted in Albert Kocourek, "John Henry Wigmore," *Green Bag* 24 (January 1912): 3-8.

[5]Wigmore to Henry S. Towle, 11 June 1907, quoted in Rahl and Schwerin, "Northwestern University School of Law: A Short History," p. 150.

[6]"Pound on Wigmore," copy in my possession of remarks delivered for Pound at a meeting of the American Judicature Society, 12 August 1963, commemorating the centennial of Wigmore's birth. Professor William R. Roalfe of Northwestern called this source to my attention.

[7]Charles P. Megan, "John Henry Wigmore," *Illinois Law Review* 38 (1943): 14; William R. Roalfe, "John Henry Wigmore —Scholar and Reformer," *Journal of Criminal Law, Criminology, and Police Science* 53 (September 1962): 298.

[8]John H. Wigmore to Roscoe Pound, 21 December 1907, Roscoe Pound Papers, HLSL.

[9]*Chicago Legal News* 41 (1 May 1909): 319; "The Legal World," *Green Bag* 21 (June 1909): 369.

[10]Rahl and Schwerin, "Northwestern University School of Law: A Short History," p. 150.

[11]Charles T. Hallinan to Roscoe Pound, 11 October 1918, Roscoe Pound Papers, HLSL; quoted in *Nebraska State Journal*, 25 June 1910.

[12]George E. Hooker to Roscoe Pound, 17 October 1908, Roscoe Pound Papers, HLSL.

[13]*Chicago Legal News* 51 (1 May 1909): 319.

[14]"The Chicago Municipal Court," *The Outlook* 88 (14 March 1908): 578-579; Stanley Waterloo, "The Revolution in Chicago's Judicial System," *The American Monthly Review of Reviews* 35 (April 1907): 452-455; George W. Alger, "Swift and Cheap Justice, I," *World's Work* 26 (October 1913): 653-666; Albert Lepawsky, *The Judicial System of Metropolitan Chicago* (Chicago: University of Chicago Press, 1932), pp. 94-98; Roscoe Pound, "Some Principles of Procedural Reform," *Illinois Law Review* 4 (January 1910): 390.

[15]Roscoe Pound to Edward A. Ross, 16 November 1907, Ross Papers.

[16]Roscoe Pound to Richard T. Ely, 10 December 1907, Richard T. Ely Papers, State Historical Society of Wisconsin.

[17]Ray Ginger, *Altgeld's America; The Lincoln Ideal versus Changing Realities* (New York: Funk and Wagnalls, 1958), p. 241.

[18]Andrew R. Sheriff, "To the Editor of the Illinois Law Review," *Illinois Law Review* 4 (June 1909): 144-145; Pound, "Some Principles of Procedural Reform," p. 398.

[19]*Report of the American Bar Association* 31 (1907): 507, 509.

[20]*Ibid.*, p. 193; Edson R. Sunderland, *History of the American Bar Association and Its Work* (n.p., 1953), pp. 127-129.

[21]Roscoe Pound, "American Bar Association—The Seattle Meeting," *Illinois Law Review* 3 (October 1908): 179.

[22]Roscoe Pound, "American Bar Association—The Detroit Meeting," *ibid.*, 4 (October 1909): 198; Roscoe Pound to Edward A. Ross, 7 March 1911, Ross Papers.

[23]Edward A. Ross to Roscoe Pound, 28 March 1908, Roscoe Pound Papers, HLSL.

[24]Albion Small to Roscoe Pound, 21 December 1908, *ibid.*

[25]Richard J. Bernstein, *John Dewey* (New York: Washington Square Press, 1966), pp. 35-37; Pound's associates among social workers are discussed in Allen F. Davis, *Spearheads for Reform; The Social Settlements and the Progressive Movement, 1890-1914* (New York: Oxford University Press, 1967).

[26]Sara L. Hart, *The Pleasure is Mine* (Chicago: Valentine-Newman, 1947), p. 100.

[27]Roscoe Pound, "Introduction" to Charles Lionel Chute and Marjorie Bell, *Crime, Courts, and Probation* (New York: Macmillan, 1956), p. xiii.

[28]Roscoe Pound, "Inherent and Acquired Difficulties in the Administration of Punitive Justice," *Proceedings of the American Political Science Association, 1907* 4 (1908): 229, 230, 239.

[29]*Proceedings of the First National Conference on Criminal Law and Criminology, 1909* (Chicago: American Institute of Criminal Law and Criminology, 1910), p. 113.

[30]"The National Conference on Criminal Law and Criminology," *The Survey* 22 (26 June 1909): 449; Roscoe Pound to Richard T. Ely, 18 March 1909, Ely Papers.

[31]Hermann Mannheim (ed.), *Pioneers in Criminology* (Chicago: Quadrangle, 1960), p. ix.

[32]"The National Conference on Criminal Law and Criminology," p. 449.

[33]*Proceedings of the First National Conference on Criminal Law and Criminology*, pp. 1, 3.

[34]*Ibid.*, pp. 92-93.

[35]*Ibid.*, pp. 59-60.

[36]"The Quest for Justice," *The Outlook* 92 (17 July 1909): 619; George W. Alger, "Swift and Cheap Justice, V," *World's Work* 27 (February 1914): 428.

[37]Harry E. Smoot, "The American Institute of Criminal Law and Criminology," *The Survey* 25 (22 October 1910): 133; Rahl and Schwerin, "Northwestern University School of Law: A Short History," p. 153; Mannheim (ed.), *Pioneers in Criminology*, pp. ix-x.

[38]Albert Kocourek to Roscoe Pound, 2 October 1912, Roscoe Pound Papers, HLSL.

[39]Roscoe Pound to John H. Wigmore, 22 April 1909, Wigmore Papers; Wigmore to Pound, 26 April 1909, *ibid*.; Pound to Wigmore, 26 April 1909, *ibid*.; Kocourek, "Roscoe Pound as a Former Colleague Knew Him," p. 423.

[40]William Rainey Harper, "The President's Forty-first Quarterly Statement," *The University* [of Chicago] *Record* 6 (April 1902): 390; Richard Storr, *Harper's University: The Beginnings* (Chicago: University of Chicago Press, 1966), pp. 291-296; Charles F. Amidon to Roscoe Pound, 28 July 1909, Roscoe Pound Papers, HLSL.

[41]Roscoe Pound to Edward A. Ross, 26 March 1908, Ross Papers; Henry W. Rogers to Roscoe Pound, 30 April 1909, Roscoe Pound Papers, HLSL.

[42]A. W. Harris to Roscoe Pound, 8 February 1908, *ibid*.; John H. Wigmore to Stephen B. Pound, 12 January 1908, *ibid*.; C. C. Marlay to Roscoe Pound, 7 November 1908, *ibid*. There is a brief discussion of Nebraska's search for a chancellor in John A. Rice, *I Came Out of the Eighteenth Century* (New York: Harper, 1942), p. 272. Many distinguished scholars refused the appointment.

[43]John H. Wigmore, "Roscoe Pound's St. Paul Address of 1906; The Spark that Kindled the White Flame of Progress," *Journal of the American Judicature Society* 20 (February 1937): 176; Charles F. Amidon, "The Quest for Error and the Doing of Justice," *The Outlook* 83 (14 July 1906): 602; George Whitney Moore, "The Quest for Error and the Doing of Justice," *ibid*., 84 (8 September 1906): 75, 78.

[44]*Proceedings of the Illinois State Bar Association, 1910*, p. 173.

[45]Charles B. Letton, "Law Reform in Nebraska," *Proceedings of the Nebraska State Bar Association, 1909* 3 (1906-1909): 254.

[46]Moorfield Storey, *The Reform of Legal Procedure* (New Haven: Yale University Press, 1911), pp. 25-26.

[47]Austin Wakeman Scott, "Pound's Influence on Civil Procedure," *Harvard Law Review* 78 (June 1965): 1574.

[48]Delmar Karlen, *Primer of Procedure* (Madison: Campus Publishing Co., 1950), p. 1.

[49]"Will Society Protect Itself?", *The Outlook* 83 (14 July 1906): 593.

[50]Alpheus T. Mason, *William Howard Taft, Chief Justice* (New York: Simon and Schuster, 1965), pp. 88-120.

[51]*Proceedings of the Illinois State Bar Association, 1910*, p. 168.

[52]Everett P. Wheeler, *Sixty Years of American Life* (New York: E. P. Dutton, 1917), pp. 404-405, 409.

[53]Scott, "Pound's Influence on Civil Procedure," p. 1571.

[54]Roscoe Pound, "The Etiquette of Justice," *Proceedings of the Nebraska State Bar Association, 1908* 3 (1906-1909): 240.

[55]Roscoe Pound, "New Technicalities and Old Principles— The Appeal to 'The Wisdom of Our Ancestors,' " *Illinois Law Review* 3 (March 1909): 533.

[56]Roscoe Pound, "Some Principles of Procedural Reform," *ibid.*, 4 (February 1910): 491, 494.

[57]Lord Coleridge, "The Law in 1847 and the Law in 1889," *Contemporary Review* 57 (June 1890): 800.

[58]"Testimony of Frederick W. Lehmann," United States Congress, House of Representatives, Committee on the Judiciary, *Reforms in Legal Procedure*, Hearings, 62d Congress, 2d Session, on H.R. 16459, H.R. 16460, H.R. 16461, and H.R. 18236, 25 January 1912 (Washington: Government Printing Office, 1912), p. 13.

[59]Quoted in Francis M. Burdick, "Swiftness and Certainty of Justice in England and the United States," *North American Review* 188 (July 1908): 29.

[60]George W. Alger, "Treadmill Justice," *Atlantic Monthly* 104 (November 1909): 703, 705; Arthur T. Vanderbilt, *The Challenge of Law Reform* (Princeton: Princeton University Press, 1955), p. 53.

[61]Pound, "Some Principles of Procedural Reform," p. 505; Roscoe Pound, "Proposals of the Judges for Reform in Procedure," *Illinois Law Review* 3 (April 1909): 587.

[62]Pound, "Some Principles of Procedural Reform," p. 497.

[63]*Ibid.*, p. 395; Roscoe Pound, "Entitling Cases on Appeal or Error—Sec. 99 of Practice Act of 1907," *Illinois Law Review* 2 (December 1907): 325; Roscoe Pound, "Enforcement of Law,"

Proceedings of the Illinois State Bar Association, 1908, p. 100.

[64]*Proceedings of the Illinois State Bar Association, 1910*, p. 135.

[65]Pound, "Some Principles of Procedural Reform," p. 406.

[66]*Ibid.*, p. 394.

[67]*Chicago Legal News* 42 (25 June 1910): 370.

[68]*Proceedings of the Illinois State Bar Association, 1910*, pp. 146, 150, 155.

[69]*Ibid.*, pp. 158-161.

[70]*Ibid.*, pp. 179-180, 203.

[71]*Ibid.*, pp. 163, 167, 204-210.

[72]Edgar B. Tolman to Roscoe Pound, 17 June 1910, Roscoe Pound Papers, HLSL.

[73]George Costigan to Roscoe Pound, 23 June 1910, *ibid.*

[74]Pound, "American Bar Association—The Seattle Meeting," pp. 176.

[75]*Report of the American Bar Association* 33 (1908): 48; *ibid.*, 34 (1909): 81-82; Pound, "American Bar Association—The Detroit Meeting," p. 200.

[76]Vanderbilt, *The Challenge of Law Reform*, p. 55; Roscoe Pound, "Law and Equity in the Federal Courts—Abolishing the Distinction and Other Reforms," *Central Law Journal* 73 (22 September 1911): 204-210; Scott, "Pound's Influence on Civil Procedure," p. 1572; "Reform of Judicial Procedure," *The Nation* 89 (2 September 1909): 198-199.

[77]Roscoe Pound, "A Practical Program of Procedural Reform," *Proceedings of the Illinois State Bar Association*, 1910, p. 375.

Chapter 7. An Indictment of American Jurisprudence

[1]Roscoe Pound, "Liberty of Contract," *Yale Law Journal* 18 (May 1909): 462.

[2]Roscoe Pound, "Mechanical Jurisprudence," *Columbia Law Review* 8 (December 1908): 605.

[3]The classic formulation of the doctrine is in *Lochner v. New York*, 198 United States 45 (1905).

[4]Pound, "Liberty of Contract," p. 471.

[5]*Ritchie v. People*, 155 Illinois 99 (1895); Pound, "Liberty of Contract," p. 476.

[6]*Ibid.*, pp. 454-455.

[7]Roscoe Pound, "Do We Need a Philosophy of Law?", *Columbia Law Review* 5 (May 1905): 347.

[8]Roscoe Pound, "Press Comments on Pending Litigation," *Illinois Law Review* 3 (May 1908): 40.

[9]Roscoe Pound, book review of James C. Carter, *Law; Its Origin, Growth and Function* (1907), *Political Science Quarterly* 24 (June 1909): 317.

[10]Benjamin R. Twiss, *Lawyers and the Constitution: How Laissez-faire Came to the Supreme Court* (Princeton: Princeton University Press, 1942); Clyde Jacobs, *Law Writers and the Courts* (Berkeley: University of California Press, 1954).

[11]Pound, "Liberty of Contract," p. 465.

[12]Edwin W. Patterson, *Jurisprudence: Men and Ideas of the Law* (Brooklyn: The Foundation Press, 1953), p. 322; A. P. d'Entrèves, *Natural Law* (London: Hutchinson's University Library, 1951); Georges Gurvitch, "Natural Law," in E. R. A. Seligman and Alvin Johnson (eds.), *Encyclopaedia of the Social Sciences*, 14 vols. (New York: Macmillan, 1933), 11:284.

[13]William Seagle, *The Quest for Law* (New York: Knopf, 1941), p. 197; Pound, "Liberty of Contract," p. 457.

[14]Patterson, *Jurisprudence*, p. 84.

[15]John Austin, *Lectures on Jurisprudence*, 2 vols. (London: John Murray, 1885), 1:32. Oliver Wendell Holmes, Jr., "The Path of the Law," *Harvard Law Review* 10 (25 March 1897): 459.

[16]Thomas Hobbes, *Leviathan* (New York: E. P. Dutton, 1914), p. 83; Thomas E. Holland, *The Elements of Jurisprudence* (London: Oxford, 1895), p. 37; Holmes, "The Path of the Law," p. 461.

[17]Roscoe Pound, "Enforcement of Law," *Proceedings of the Illinois State Bar Association*, 1908, p. 88.

[18]George Alfred Miller, "James Coolidge Carter," in W. D. Lewis (ed.), *Great American Lawyers*, 8 vols. (Philadelphia: John C. Winston, 1909), 8:3-41; James C. Carter, "The Province of the Written and the Unwritten Law," *American Law Review* 24 (January-February 1890): 1-24.

[19]Pound, book review of Carter, *Law*, p. 317. Pound attributed Carter's jurisprudence to the influence of Luther S. Cushing, a student of Savigny who taught at Harvard Law School in 1849. Roscoe Pound, "Political and Economic Interpretations of Jurisprudence," *Proceedings of the American Political Science Association, 1912* 9 (1913): 99-100.

[20]James C. Carter, *Law; Its Origin, Growth and Function* (New York: G. P. Putnam's Sons, 1907), p. 173; James C. Carter, "The Ideal and the Actual in the Law," *American Law Review* 24 (September-October 1890): 769, 773-774.

[21]Carter, "The Ideal and the Actual in the Law," p. 758.

[22]*Ibid.*, pp. 759-760, 761.

[23]Pound, book review of Carter, *Law*, p. 320.

[24]*Ibid.*, p. 318. Fred V. Cahill, Jr., echoes Pound's conclusions about Carter and the unity of American legal theory at the turn of the century. See his *Judicial Legislation: A Study in American Legal Theory* (New York: Ronald, 1952), p. 17.

[25]Pound, "Do We Need a Philosophy of Law?" p. 342; Pound, "Liberty of Contract," p. 461, for the quotation from Blackstone.

[26]*Frorer v. People*, 141 Illinois 171, 186; Pound, "Liberty of Contract," p. 463.

[27]*Ibid.*, p. 460.

[28]Carter, "The Ideal and the Actual in the Law," p. 769.

[29]James Willard Hurst, *The Growth of American Law; The Law Makers* (Boston: Little, Brown, 1950), pp. 186-187; Roscoe Pound, "Common Law and Legislation," *Harvard Law Review* 21 (April 1908): 387.

[30]*Ives v. South Buffalo Railway Co.*, 201 New York 271 (1911); Pound, "Liberty of Contract," p. 467.

[31]*Schlemmer v. Buffalo, Rochester & Pittsburg Railway Co.*, 207 Pennsylvania 198, 201 (1903). On appeal to the United States Supreme Court, this decision was reversed, although only by a 5-4 decision. Justice Holmes, in the opinion of the court, held that the Pennsylvania court could not revive the discredited assumption-of-risk doctrine by merely giving it another name. *Schlemmer v. Buffalo, Rochester & Pittsburgh Railway Co.*, 205 United States 1, 14 (1906); Pound, "Liberty of Contract," p. 467.

[32]Pound, "Common Law and Legislation," p. 406.

[33]*Ibid.*

[34]Roscoe Pound to Edward A. Ross, 10 December 1907, Ross Papers.

[35]Pound, "Enforcement of Law," pp. 98-99.

[36]*Ibid.*, p. 98.

[37]William Blackstone, *Commentaries on the Laws of England*, 4 vols. (Boston: I. Thomas and E. T. Andrews, 1799), 1:70. Calvin Coolidge, *Have Faith in Massachusetts* (Boston: Houghton Mifflin, 1919), p. 4.

[38]Pound, "Enforcement of Law," p. 92.

[39]Roscoe Pound, "Spurious Interpretation," *Columbia Law Review* 7 (June 1907): 382, 383.

[40]Roscoe Pound, "The Law and the People," *University of Chicago Magazine* 3 (November 1910): 8. See also Pound, book review of Carter, *Law*, p. 357; Pound, "Mechanical Jurisprudence," p. 621.

[41]Pound, "The Law and the People," p. 15.

[42]Roscoe Pound, "Puritanism and the Common Law," *Proceedings of the Kansas State Bar Association*, 1910, pp. 50-51.

[43]*Ibid.*, pp. 53-54.

[44]*Ibid.*, p. 56.

[45]Pound, "Liberty of Contract," p. 470.

[46]Arthur E. Sutherland, Jr., *The Law At Harvard: A History of Ideas and Men, 1817-1967* (Cambridge: Harvard University Press, 1967), pp. 233, 239; A. Lawrence Lowell, "Roscoe Pound," *Harvard Law Review* 50 (December 1936): 169; A. Lawrence Lowell to John H. Wigmore, 7 February 1910, Wigmore Papers; Wigmore to Lowell, 9 February 1910, *ibid.*

[47]Pound interview conducted by Arthur Sutherland, 25 July 1962; Roscoe Pound to Edward A. Ross, 13 February 1911, Ross Papers; Emory R. Buckner to Roscoe Pound, 2 April 1910, Roscoe Pound Papers, HLSL; Omer F. Hershey to Roscoe Pound, 2 April 1910, *ibid.*

Chapter 8. Pragmatism in Legal Theory

[1]Morton White, *Social Thought in America: The Revolt Against*

Formalism (Boston: Beacon, 1957); William James, *Pragmatism: A New Name for Some Old Ways of Thinking* (New York: Longmans, Green, 1914), pp. 53-54.

[2] James, *Pragmatism*, p. 201.

[3] *Ibid.*, p. 51; William James, *Some Problems of Philosophy* (New York: Longmans, Green, 1911), p. 165n; James, *Pragmatism*, p. 57.

[4] John Dewey, *The Influence of Darwin on Philosophy* (New York: Henry Holt, 1910), p. 13; John Dewey, *The Quest for Certainty: A Study of the Relation of Knowledge and Action* (New York: Minton, Balch, 1929), p. 211; John Dewey, *Reconstruction in Philosophy* (New York: Henry Holt, 1920), pp. 123-126.

[5] Roscoe Pound, "A Practical Program of Procedural Reform," *Proceedings of the Illinois State Bar Association*, 1910, p. 375.

[6] James Harvey Robinson, *History* (New York: Columbia University Press, 1908), p. 14.

[7] Arthur F. Bentley, *The Process of Government* (Chicago: University of Chicago Press, 1908); Roscoe Pound, "The Philosophy of Law in America," *Archiv für Rechts- und Wirtschaftsphilosophie* 7 (December 1913): 213.

[8] Charles Beard, *Politics* (New York: Columbia University Press, 1908), pp. 5, 6; Thorstein Veblen, *The Place of Science in Modern Civilization* (New York: Huebsch, 1919), p. 56.

[9] Pound, "A Practical Program of Procedural Reform," p. 375; Roscoe Pound, "Mechanical Jurisprudence," *Columbia Law Review* 8 (December 1908): 609-610.

[10] Roscoe Pound, "Taught Law," *Report of the American Bar Association, 1912* 37 (1912): 977.

[11] Roscoe Pound, "Social Justice and Legal Justice," *Proceedings of the Thirtieth Annual Meeting of the Missouri Bar Association, 1912* 1913, p. 110; Pound, "Mechanical Jurisprudence," p. 621.

[12] Roscoe Pound, "The Law and the People," *University of Chicago Magazine* 3 (November 1910): 16; Roscoe Pound, "Social Problems and the Courts," *American Journal of Sociology* 18 (November 1912): 341; Roscoe Pound, "Making Law and Finding Law," *Central Law Journal* 82 (19 May 1916): 358.

[13] Roscoe Pound, "The Scope and Purpose of Sociological

Jurisprudence," *Harvard Law Review* 24 (June 1911): 598.
¹⁴Roscoe Pound, book review of Lord Halsbury et al., *The Laws of England* (1907), *Illinois Law Review* 3 (June 1908): 130.

¹⁵Roscoe Pound, "The Revival of Personal Government," *Proceedings of the Nebraska State Bar Association* 9 (1916): 122; Roscoe Pound, "Public Provision for Criminological Research," *Illinois Law Review* 3 (January 1909): 364-365; Roscoe Pound, "Anachronisms in Law," *Journal of the American Judicature Society* 3 (February 1920): 146-147; Robert H. Bremner, *From the Depths: The Discovery of Poverty in the United States* (New York: New York University Press, 1956), p. 162; Julius Stone, "The Province of Jurisprudence Redetermined," *Modern Law Review* 7 (November 1944): 184.

¹⁶Morris Cohen, "Legal Theories and Social Science," *International Journal of Ethics* 25 (July 1915): 485.

¹⁷Roscoe Pound, "Legislation as a Social Function," *American Journal of Sociology* 18 (May 1913): 762; Roscoe Pound, "Courts and Legislation," *American Political Science Review* 7 (August 1913): 367.

¹⁸Roscoe Pound, "Liberty of Contract," *Yale Law Journal* 18 (May 1909): 469, 472.

¹⁹Roscoe Pound, "The Scope and Purpose of Sociological Jurisprudence," *Harvard Law Review* 25 (April 1912): 515; Julius Stone, "A Critique of Pound's Theory of Justice," *Iowa Law Review* 20 (March 1935): 536.

²⁰ Pound, "Courts and Legislation," p. 365.

²¹Roscoe Pound, "Remarks on the death of Judge Charles E. Shattuck," 18 January 1919, manuscript in Roscoe Pound Papers, HLSL; *Proceedings of the Texas Bar Association* 37 (1918): 213-214; Roscoe Pound to Henry N. Sheldon, 18 August 1919, Roscoe Pound Papers, HLSL.

²²Roscoe Pound, "The Administration of Justice in the Modern City," *Harvard Law Review* 26 (February 1913): 315, 327.

²³Pound, "Mechanical Jurisprudence," p. 606.

²⁴Roscoe Pound, "Enforcement of Law," *Proceedings of the Illinois State Bar Association*, 1908, p. 91.

²⁵Pound, "The Law and the People," p. 14; Roscoe Pound,

"Justice According to Law," *Columbia Law Review* 13 (December 1913): 706.

[26]Pound, "The Administration of Justice in the Modern City," p. 310; Roscoe Pound, "Interests of Personality," *Harvard Law Review* 28 (February 1915): 347.

[27]Pound, "Social Justice and Legal Justice," p. 118.

[28]Pound, "The Scope and Purpose of Sociological Jurisprudence," p. 510; Roscoe Pound, "Law in Books and Law in Action," *American Law Review* 44 (January-February 1910): 35-36.

[29]Roscoe Pound, "Puritanism and the Common Law," *Proceedings of the Kansas State Bar Association*, 1910, p. 47; Pound, "Legislation as a Social Function," p. 768.

[30]*Parke-Davis & Co. v. H. K. Mulford Co.*, 189 Federal Reports 95, 115 (1911).

[31]Pound, "Courts and Legislation," p. 380; *Muller v. Oregon*, 208 United States 412 (1908).

[32]Louis Brandeis to Roscoe Pound, 6 December 1909, Roscoe Pound Papers, HLSL.

[33]A. L. Todd, *Justice on Trial: The Case of Louis D. Brandeis* (New York: McGraw-Hill, 1964), pp. 107, 258.

[34]Roscoe Pound to Olivia Pound, 9 February 1916, Olivia Pound Papers.

[35]Roscoe Pound to William E. Chilton [c. February 1916], United States Congress, Senate, Committee on the Judiciary, *Nomination of Louis D. Brandeis*, Hearings, 64th Congress, 1st Session, 2 vols. (Washington: Government Printing Office, 1916), II:251-252.

[36]"On the Way to the U.S. Supreme Court," *The Survey* 38 (8 September 1917): 507; Stephen B. Wood, *Constitutional Politics in the Progressive Era; Child Labor and the Law* (Chicago: University of Chicago Press, 1968), pp. 81-110.

[37]Roscoe Pound, "The Limits of Effective Legal Action," *International Journal of Ethics* 27 (January 1917): 159.

[38]Felix Frankfurter to Josephine Goldmarck, 25 August 1917, Edith and Grace Abbott Papers, University of Chicago Archives; Felix Adler to Julia Lathrop, 28 August 1917, *ibid.*; Florence Kelley to Julia Lathrop, 28 August 1917, *ibid.*

[39]Florence Kelley to Edith Abbott, 27 August 1917, *ibid.*

[40]Grace Abbott to Julia Lathrop, 1 September 1917, *ibid.*

[41]*Greensboro Daily Record*, 31 August 1917.

[42]Roscoe Pound to Laura B. Pound, 2 September 1917, Roscoe Pound Papers, NSHS.

[43]*Greensboro Daily Record*, 30 August 1917; *ibid.*, 31 August 1917.

[44]Julia Lathrop to Lillian Wald, 1 September 1917, Abbott Papers; Grace Abbott to Julia Lathrop, 1 September 1917, *ibid.*; *Greensboro Daily Record*, 31 August 1917; Edward S. Corwin, "Validity of the Child Labor Act," *New Republic* 12 (15 September 1917): 188.

[45]Roscoe Pound to Julia Lathrop, 17 September 1917, Abbott Papers; Pound to Lathrop, 28 September 1917, *ibid.*

[46]Lester Ward, *Dynamic Sociology*, 2 vols. (New York: D. Appleton, 1897), 2:160; Lester Ward, *Applied Sociology* (Boston: Ginn, 1906), p. 339; Robert A. Woods, "University Settlements as Laboratories in Social Science," address delivered in 1893, reprinted in Woods, *The Neighborhood in Nation-Building* (Boston: Houghton Mifflin, 1923), p. 31; Richard T. Ely, "Fundamental Beliefs in My Social Philosophy," *The Forum* 18 (October 1894): 183; Frank Parsons quoted in Arthur Mann, *Yankee Reformers in the Urban Age* (Cambridge: Harvard University Press, 1954), p. 134; Herbert Croly, *The Promise of American Life*, ed. Arthur M. Schlesinger, Jr. (Cambridge: Harvard University Press, 1965), p. 428.

[47]Roscoe Pound, "The Administrative Application of Legal Standards," *Report of the American Bar Association* 44 (1919): 463; Croly, *The Promise of American Life*, pp. 199-200; Felix Frankfurter to Morris Cohen, 3 May 1923, in Leonora Cohen Rosenfield, *Portrait of a Philosopher: Morris R. Cohen in Life & Letters* (New York: Harcourt, Brace & World, 1962), p. 253; Roscoe Pound to Ezra R. Thayer, 26 August 1915, Roscoe Pound Papers, HLSL; Roscoe Pound, "The Pioneers and the Common Law," *West Virginia Law Quarterly* 27 (November 1920): 18; Pound, "Justice According to Law," p. 701.

[48]Pound, "The Administrative Application of Legal Standards," p. 463.

[49]Roscoe Pound, "Procedure in Common Law," *Proceedings of the Seventh Annual Convention of the California Bar Association, 1916,* 1917, p. 89; Roscoe Pound, "The Place of Judge Story in the Making of American Law," *American Law Review* 48 (September-October 1914): 677; Pound, "Taught Law," p. 990.

[50]Roscoe Pound to Ezra R. Thayer, 26 August 1915, Roscoe Pound Papers, HLSL.

[51]Pound, "Taught Law," p. 980.

[52]Roscoe Pound to Laura B. Pound, 12 December 1910, Olivia Pound Papers.

[53]Zechariah Chafee, Jr., to Roscoe Pound, 23 April 1914, Roscoe Pound Papers, HLSL; Albert B. Hart to Roscoe Pound, 26 April 1918, *ibid.*; Felix Frankfurter to Learned Hand, 28 June 1913, Learned Hand Papers, Harvard Law School Library.

[54]Julian Mack to Paul Kellogg, 15 December 1913, Roscoe Pound Papers, HLSL; William Hard to Roscoe Pound, 4 April 1912, *ibid.*; Albion Small to Roscoe Pound, 30 April 1912, *ibid.*

[55]Nicholas Murray Butler, "The University President, University Teacher, and University Student," address delivered 22 February 1915, in Butler, *Scholarship and Service* (New York: Scribner's, 1921), p. 79; Edward A. Harriman to John H. Wigmore, 23 June 1909, Wigmore Papers.

[56]Robert Ludlow Fowler, "The New Philosophies of Law," *Harvard Law Review* 27 (June 1914): 724, 730.

[57]Robert Ludlow Fowler, "The Future of the Common Law," *Columbia Law Review* 13 (November 1913): 603.

[58]Roscoe Pound, "Note to Fowler, 'The New Philosophies of Law,'" *Harvard Law Review* 27 (June 1914): 735, 732; Cohen, "Legal Theories and Social Science," p. 470; Joseph H. Drake, "The Sociological Interpretation of Law," *Michigan Law Review* 16 (June 1918): 615; Albert Kocourek to Roscoe Pound, 9 June 1914, Roscoe Pound Papers, HLSL.

[59]"Opportunity of a Law School," *New Republic* 5 (13 November 1915): 33; Herbert Ehrmann, "Felix," in Wallace Mendelson

(ed.), *Felix Frankfurter: A Tribute* (New York: Reynal, 1964), p. 99; Henry M. Bates to Roscoe Pound, 25 September 1915, Roscoe Pound Papers, HLSL; Morris Cohen to Felix Frankfurter, 14 July 1933, in Rosenfield, *Portrait of a Philosopher*, p. 261; James H. Tufts to Morris Cohen, 25 March 1916, James H. Tufts Papers, University of Chicago Archives.

[60]Roscoe Pound to Laura B. Pound, 20 January 1916, Olivia Pound Papers.

[61]Roscoe Pound to Learned Hand, 5 January 1916, Learned Hand Papers.

[62]Roscoe Pound to Laura B. Pound, 20 January 1916, Olivia Pound Papers.

[63]Roscoe Pound to Olivia Pound, 9 February 1916, *ibid.*; Morris Cohen, "New Leadership in the Law," *New Republic* 6 (11 March 1916): 148; *Christian Science Monitor*, 8 March 1916.

[64]Learned Hand to Roscoe Pound, 4 January 1916, Roscoe Pound Papers, HLSL; Emory Buckner to Roscoe Pound, 7 January 1916, *ibid.*; Louis D. Brandeis, "The Living Law," *Illinois Law Review* 10 (February 1916): 461-462; O[rrin] K[ip] M[cMurray], "The Appointment of Dean Pound," *California Law Review* 4 (May 1916): 319-320.

[65]Lawrence B. Evans, "Roscoe Pound; Dean of the Harvard Law School," *Case and Comment* 23 (July 1916): 168.

Chapter 9. Organicism v. Instrumentalism: An Unresolved Dualism

[1]James C. Carter, *Law; Its Origin, Growth and Function* (New York: G. P. Putnam's Sons, 1907); *Reports of the President and the Treasurer of Harvard College, 1905-1906*, 1907, p. 53.

[2]William Howard Taft to Elihu Root, 21 December 1922, quoted in Liva Baker, *Felix Frankfurter* (New York: Coward-McCann, 1969), pp. 239-240; Henry Steele Commager, *The American Mind* (New Haven: Yale University Press, 1950), p. 378; Charles E. Wyzanski, Jr., *Whereas—A Judge's Premises* (Boston: Little, Brown, 1965), p. 191.

³William Hard, "The Law of the Killed and Wounded," *Everybody's Magazine* 19 (September 1908): 364.

⁴Roscoe Pound, "Making Law and Finding Law," *Central Law Journal* 82 (19 May 1916): 351; Roscoe Pound, "Organization of Courts," *Bulletin of the American Judicature Society* 6 (1914): 7.

⁵Roscoe Pound, "Liberty of Contract," *Yale Law Journal* 18 (May 1909): 487.

⁶Roscoe Pound, "Taught Law," *Report of the American Bar Association* 37 (1912): 989.

⁷Roscoe Pound, "Justice According to Law," *Columbia Law Review* 13 (December 1913): 708; Roscoe Pound, "Mechanical Jurisprudence," *Columbia Law Review* 8 (December 1908): 622.

⁸Roscoe Pound, "The Need of a Sociological Jurisprudence," *Report of the American Bar Association* 31 (1907): 920.

⁹Edward A. Ross, *Foundations of Sociology* (New York: Macmillan, 1915), p. 13; Richard T. Ely, *Socialism and Social Reform* (New York: Crowell, 1894), p. 3; Ross, *Foundations of Sociology*, p. 12.

¹⁰Roscoe Pound, "A Feudal Principle in Modern Law," *International Journal of Ethics* 25 (October 1914): 16, 22; Roscoe Pound, "Social Justice and Legal Justice," *Proceedings of the 30th Annual Meeting of the Missouri Bar Association, 1912*, 1913, p. 120.

¹¹Robert A. Nisbet, *The Sociological Tradition* (New York: Basic Books, 1966); Ely, *Socialism and Social Reform*, p. 4; Charles S. Peirce, "Vitally Important Topics," in Charles Hartshorne and Paul Weiss (eds.), *Collected Papers of Charles Sanders Peirce*, 8 vols. (Cambridge: Harvard University Press, 1931), 1:361; Albion Small, *General Sociology* (Chicago: University of Chicago Press, 1905), p. 74. For evidence of Peirce's influence, see R. Jackson Wilson, *In Quest of Community: Social Philosophy in the United States, 1860-1920* (New York: Wiley, 1968), pp. 35-36. Among the most useful accounts that sociologists have written on this era of American social science are Pitirim Sorokin, *Contemporary Sociological Theories* (New York: Harper, 1928), and Don Martindale, *The Nature and Types of Sociological Theory* (Boston: Houghton Mifflin, 1960). Historians have been less diligent in pursuing the organic theme in American ideas at the turn of the century, but Richard Hofstadter, *Social Darwinism in American Thought*

(Philadelphia: University of Pennsylvania Press, 1944), and Stow Persons, *American Minds* (New York: Holt, Rinehart & Winston, 1958), contain shrewd insights. Robert H. Wiebe, *The Search for Order, 1877-1920* (New York: Hill and Wang, 1967), Jean B. Quandt, *From the Small Town to the Great Community* (New Brunswick, N.J.: Rutgers University Press, 1970), and Cynthia E. Russett, *The Concept of Equilibrium in American Social Thought* (New Haven: Yale University Press, 1966), are suggestive studies, although each is marred by misleading judgments about organicism. Wiebe makes it a synonym for Hegelian idealism, Quandt regards it as an inevitable companion of communitarianism, and Russett insists that it guaranteed an open, manipulative conception of social change.

[12]Charles Horton Cooley, *Social Process* (New York: Scribner's, 1918), pp. 26, 9.

[13]Small, *General Sociology*, pp. 433-434. While serving as Brandeis' law clerk in 1919, Dean Acheson, a recent graduate of the Harvard Law School, told Holmes that Small was Pound's favorite theorist. Oliver Wendell Holmes to Harold Laski, 29 November 1919, in Mark DeWolfe Howe (ed.), *Holmes-Laski Letters; The Correspondence of Mr. Justice Holmes and Harold J. Laski, 1916-1935*, 2 vols. (Cambridge: Harvard University Press, 1953), 1:224; Roscoe Pound, "A Theory of Social Interests," *Publications of the American Sociological Society, 1920* 15 (1921): 16-18.

[14]*Ibid.*

[15]Roscoe Pound, "Interests of Personality," *Harvard Law Review* 28 (February 1915): 343, 362-363.

[16]Pound, "A Theory of Social Interests," p. 30.

[17]Alvin Boskoff, "From Social Thought to Sociological Theory," in Howard Becker and Alvin Boskoff (eds.), *Modern Sociological Theory* (New York: Dryden, 1957), p. 12.

[18]Pound, "A Theory of Social Interests," p. 33; Don Martindale, "Social Disorganization: The Conflict of Normative and Empirical Approaches," in *Modern Sociological Theory*, p. 355.

[19]Roscoe Pound, "Anachronisms in Law," *Journal of the American Judicature Society* 3 (February 1920): 142.

[20]Roscoe Pound, "Puritanism and the Common Law," *Proceedings of the Kansas State Bar Association*, 1910, p. 47.

[21]Roscoe Pound, "The End of Law as Developed in Legal Rules and Doctrines," *Harvard Law Review* 27 (January 1914): 195-234.

[22]Roscoe Pound, "The Scope and Purpose of Sociological Jurisprudence," *Harvard Law Review* 25 (April 1912): 489-516.

[23]Roscoe Pound to Edward A. Ross, 23 December 1908, Ross Papers.

[24]Roscoe Pound, "The Pioneers and the Common Law," *West Virginia Law Quarterly* 27 (November 1920): 3; Pound, "The Scope and Purpose of Sociological Jurisprudence," p. 508. In a letter to Ross, Pound proposed an address to the American Bar Association on "The Unity of Law," although he did not deliver it. Pound to Ross, 2 November 1906, Ross Papers.

[25]Roscoe Pound, book review of Giorgio del Vecchio, *Il Concetto della Natura e il Principio del Diritto* (1908), *Political Science Quarterly* 24 (June 1909): 322.

[26]Learned Hand to Zechariah Chafee, 30 March 1921, Zechariah Chafee Papers, Harvard Law School Library.

[27]Roscoe Pound, "The Revival of Personal Government," *Proceedings of the Nebraska State Bar Association, 1916* 9 (1917): 120.

[28]Pound, "A Feudal Principle in Modern Law," p. 12; Roscoe Pound, "Social Problems and the Courts," *American Journal of Sociology* 18 (November 1912): 335.

[29]Roscoe Pound, "Justice According to Law," *Columbia Law Review*, 14 (February 1914): 118; Pound, "Making Law and Finding Law," p. 356.

[30]Pound, "Justice According to Law," p. 106.

[31]Pound, "Social Problems and the Courts," p. 341; Roscoe Pound to Morris Cohen, 11 March 1914, in Leonora Cohen Rosenfield, *Portrait of a Philosopher: Morris R. Cohen in Life & Letters* (New York: Harcourt, Brace & World, 1962), p. 299.

[32]Roscoe Pound, book review of Bruce Wyman, *The Special Law Governing Public Service Corporations and All Others Engaged in Public Employment* (1911), *Harvard Law Reveiw* 25 (November 1911): 99.

[33] Roscoe Pound, "Common Law and Legislation," *Harvard Law Review* 21 (April 1908): 388.

[34] Pound, "Liberty of Contract," p. 482; Pound's remarks at the annual meeting of the Association of American Law Schools, *The American Law School Review* 3 (November 1913): 385.

[35] Pound, "Liberty of Contract," pp. 484, 486.

[36] Pound, "Social Justice and Legal Justice," p. 124; Roscoe Pound, "Judicial Organization," *Proceedings of the Texas Bar Association*, 39 (1918): 90.

[37] Pound, "Anachronisms in Law," p. 146; Roscoe Pound to Paul Kellogg, 25 July 1913, Roscoe Pound Papers, HLSL.

[38] Roscoe Pound to Morris Cohen, 11 March 1914, in Rosenfield, *Portrait of a Philosopher*, p. 300.

[39] Roscoe Pound, "Procedure in Common Law," *Proceedings of the Seventh Annual Convention of the California Bar Association, 1916*, 1917, p. 89.

[40] Pound, "The Revival of Personal Government," p. 110; Roscoe Pound, "Justice According to Law," *Columbia Law Review* 14 (January 1914): 25.

[41] Pound, "Justice According to Law," pp. 109, 21.

[42] Pound, "Social Justice and Legal Justice," p. 123; Roscoe Pound, "The Administrative Application of Legal Standards," *Report of the American Bar Association* 44 (1919): 448-449.

[43] Roscoe Pound to Laura B. Pound, 3 November 1889, Olivia Pound Papers; Roscoe Pound to Stephen B. Pound, 21 March 1911, *ibid*.

[44] Roscoe Pound, "Democracy and the Common Law," *Case and Comment* 18 (January 1912): 451; Roscoe Pound, "The Law and the People," *University of Chicago Magazine* 3 (November 1910): 4-5.

[45] Pound, "Democracy and the Common Law," p. 450; Roscoe Pound, "The Judicial Office in the United States," *Proceedings of the Iowa State Bar Association* 20 (1914): 97.

[46] Roscoe Pound, "Reform in Court Organization," *Proceedings of the Texas Bar Association* 37 (1916): 211.

[47] Roscoe Pound to Sophonisba P. Breckinridge, 22 November 1915, Abbott Papers; Roscoe Pound to Thomas Reed Powell

[1917], Thomas Reed Powell Papers, Harvard Law School Library.

[48] Roscoe Pound, "The Law School," *Reports of the President and the Treasurer of Harvard College, 1915-1916*, 1917, pp. 140-153.

[49] Memorandum from Roscoe Pound to Learned Hand, undated, Hand Papers.

[50] Erwin N. Griswold, "Intellect and Spirit," *Harvard Law Review* 81 (December 1967): 295.

[51] Pound, "The Law School," *Reports, 1915-1916*, p. 140.

[52] Howard S. Becker, "The Nature of a Profession," *Education for the Professions [Yearbook of the National Society for the Study of Education, 61 (1962)]*: 37-38, discusses the critical role of the idea of service in the professional mystique.

[53] Roscoe Pound, "The Philosophy of Law in America," *Archiv für Rechts- und Wirtschaftsphilosophie* 7 (March 1914): 389.

[54] Roscoe Pound, "The Lay Tradition as to the Lawyer," *Michigan Law Review* 12 (June 1914): 636-638.

[55] Gertrude Seymour, "The One Who Went Free," *The Survey* 30 (14 June 1913): 372.

[56] Roscoe Pound to Julian Mack, undated, quoted in Mack to Paul Kellogg, 24 February 1914, Roscoe Pound Papers, HLSL.

[57] Roscoe Pound to Edward T. Devine, 18 June 1913, *ibid.*

[58] Roscoe Pound to Paul Kellogg, 23 July 1913, *ibid.*

[59] Julian Mack to Paul Kellogg, 15 December 1913, *ibid.*; Mack to Kellogg, 24 February 1914, *ibid.*; Roscoe Pound to Kellogg, 26 November 1919, The Survey Papers, Social Welfare History Archives Center, University of Minnesota; Pound to Kellogg, 18 November 1922, *ibid.*

[60] Roscoe Pound, book review of Mary Richmond, *Social Diagnosis* (1917), *The Survey* 39 (1 December 1917): 254.

[61] Mary Richmond, *Social Diagnosis* (New York: Free Press, 1965), pp. 365-367.

[62] Mary Richmond to Roscoe Pound, 3 December 1917, Roscoe Pound Papers, HLSL. For the growth of a professional spirit in social work, see Roy Lubove, *The Professional Altruist: The Emergence of Social Work as a Career* (Cambridge: Harvard University Press, 1965).

[63]Pound's remarks at a meeting of the Missouri Bar Association, *Proceedings of the Thirtieth Annual Meeting of the Missouri Bar Association, 1912*, 1913, p. 19.

[64]Roscoe Pound, "Juristic Problems of National Progress," *American Journal of Sociology* 22 (May 1917): 721.

[65]Pound, "Taught Law," pp. 976, 995; Pound, "Juristic Problems of National Progress," p. 726. Everett C. Hughes, *Men and Their Work* (Glencoe: Free Press, 1958), p. 79, describes the tendency of professionals to claim social leadership in everything that touches their specialties.

[66]Roscoe Pound, "Society and the Individual," *Proceedings of the National Conference of Social Work, 1919*, 1920, p. 104.

[67]Roscoe Pound, "Regulation of Judicial Procedure by Rules of Court," *Illinois Law Review* 10 (October 1915): 167.

[68]Roscoe Pound, "Cardinal Principles to be Observed in Reforming Procedure," *Central Law Journal* 75 (23 August 1912): 150.

[69]Pound, "Reform in Court Organization," p. 205.

[70]Pound, "Taught Law," p. 995.

[71]Pound, "Anachronisms in Law," p. 144.

[72]Roscoe Pound, "The Administration of Justice in the Modern City," *Harvard Law Review* 26 (February 1913): 328.

[73]Harold Laski to Oliver Wendell Holmes, 13 January 1918, *Holmes-Laski Letters*, I:127.

[74]Morton Keller, *The Life Insurance Enterprise, 1885-1910* (Cambridge: Harvard University Press, 1963), pp. 235-242, 263.

[75]Brief of Plaintiff in Error, *New York Life Insurance Company v. Deer Lodge County*, 231 United States 495 (1913). The court ruled that insurance was not interstate commerce.

[76]Pound, "Society and the Individual," pp. 105-106.

[77]Pound, "The Lay Tradition as to the Lawyer," p. 638.

[78]Pound, "Society and the Individual," p. 106.

[79]Pound, "The Administrative Application of Legal Standards," p. 450.

[80]Pound, "The Lay Tradition as to the Lawyer," pp. 629-630.

[81]Pound, "The Law and the People," p. 13.

⁸²Pound, "The Limits of Effective Legal Action," *International Journal of Ethics* 27 (January 1917): 151.

⁸³Roscoe Pound, "The Philosophy of Law in America," *Archiv für Rechts- und Wirtschaftsphilosophie* 7 (December 1913): 218; Pound, "Taught Law," pp. 983-987; Roscoe Pound, "Codification," in Andrew C. McLaughlin and Albert B. Hart (eds.), *Cyclopedia of American Government*, 3 vols. (New York: D. Appleton, 1914), 1:305; Pound's remarks at the annual meeting of the Association of American Law Schools, *Report of the American Bar Association* 37 (1912): 933.

⁸⁴Karl Llewellyn, "A Realistic Jurisprudence—The Next Step," *Columbia Law Review* 30 (April 1930): 435.

⁸⁵Pound, "The Judicial Office in the United States," p. 104.

Chapter 10. Variations on Familiar Themes

¹Benjamin Cardozo to Roscoe Pound, 31 July 1920, Roscoe Pound Papers, HLSL.

²Roscoe Pound, *The Spirit of the Common Law* (Boston: Marshall Jones, 1921); Roscoe Pound, *Interpretations of Legal History* (London: Cambridge University Press, 1923); Roscoe Pound, *An Introduction to the Philosophy of Law* (New Haven: Yale University Press, 1922); Roscoe Pound, *Law and Morals* (Chapel Hill: University of North Carolina Press, 1924).

³Arthur E. Sutherland, Jr., *The Law at Harvard; A History of Ideas and Men, 1817-1967* (Cambridge: Harvard University Press, 1967), pp. 244-246.

⁴Roscoe Pound to Louise Pound, 1 February 1917, Roscoe Pound Papers, HLSL; Roscoe Pound to Oliver Wendell Holmes, 24 July 1919, *ibid.*; Roscoe Pound to James Harvey Robinson, 28 March 1919, *ibid.*

⁵Roscoe Pound to Laura B. Pound, 27 April 1918, Olivia Pound Papers; Roscoe Pound to George R. Nutter, 29 October 1919, Roscoe Pound Papers, HLSL; Louis Brandeis to Roscoe Pound,

28 May 1919, *ibid.*; Albion Small to Roscoe Pound, 7 March 1919, *ibid.*

[6] *To The American People: Report upon the Illegal Practices of the United States Department of Justice* (Washington: National Popular Government League, 1920); Lucille Milner, *Education of an American Liberal* (New York: Horizon, 1954), pp. 135-136.

[7] "Testimony of Zechariah Chafee," United States Congress, Senate, Subcommittee of the Committee on the Judiciary, *Charges of Illegal Practices of the Department of Justice*, Hearings, 66th Congress, 3d Session, 19 January-3 March 1921 (Washington: Government Printing Office, 1921), p. 199; Roscoe Pound to Harlan Fiske Stone, 3 February 1921, Roscoe Pound Papers, HLSL; Roscoe Pound to Senator Thomas Sterling, 2 March 1921, *ibid.* Charles Nagel praised Pound for trying to excite an indifferent bar. Nagel, *Speeches and Writings, 1900-1928*, 2 vols. (New York: G. P. Putnam's Sons, 1931), 1:99.

[8] Oliver Wendell Holmes to A. Lawrence Lowell, 2 June 1919, in Mark DeWolfe Howe (ed.), *Holmes-Laski Letters; The Correspondence of Mr. Justice Holmes and Harold J. Laski, 1916-1935*, 2 vols. (Cambridge: Harvard University Press, 1953), 1:211.

[9] Jerold S. Auerbach, "The Patrician As Libertarian: Zechariah Chafee, Jr. and Freedom of Speech," *New England Quarterly* 42 (December 1969): 526-528; Jerold S. Auerbach, "Enmity and Amity: Law Teachers and Practitioners, 1900-1922," in Donald Fleming and Bernard Bailyn (eds.), *Law in American History* (Boston: Little, Brown, 1971), pp. 551-601.

[10] Roscoe Pound to Henry M. Bates, 25 May 1921, Roscoe Pound Papers, HLSL; Harlan B. Phillips (ed.), *Felix Frankfurter Reminisces* (New York: Reynal, 1960), pp. 176-177; Henry Aaron Yeomans, *Abbott Lawrence Lowell* (Cambridge: Harvard University Press, 1948), pp. 318-327.

[11] Zechariah Chafee to Learned Hand, 1 June 1921, Chafee Papers; Roscoe Pound to Bruce Bliven, 7 May 1923, Roscoe Pound Papers, HLSL; William Howard Taft to Roscoe Pound, 2 May 1923, *ibid.*; Roscoe Pound to Roger Baldwin, 8 September 1923, *ibid.*; Charles B. Letton to Roscoe Pound, 13 May 1922, *ibid.*; Roscoe Pound to Norman Hapgood, 8 May 1925, *ibid.*;

Elizabeth McCausland, *The Blue Menace* (Springfield: Springfield Republican, 1928), p. 19.

[12]Edward A. Ross to Roscoe Pound, 18 April 1923, Roscoe Pound Papers, HLSL; Pound to Ross, 24 April 1923, *ibid.*; *Capital Times*, 13 January 1925; *The Daily Missoulian*, 2 February 1925.

[13]Petition in Wilson M. Powell to Roscoe Pound, 28 January 1925, Olivia Pound Papers; Petition to Roscoe Pound, 23 January 1925, Roscoe Pound Papers, HLSL; Benjamin Cardozo to Roscoe Pound, 25 January 1925, *ibid.*; Calvert Magruder to Roscoe Pound, 23 January 1925, Olivia Pound Papers.

[14]Julia Lathrop to Grace Abbott, 12 February 1925, Abbott Papers; Roscoe Pound to *Milwaukee Journal*, 2 February 1925, Olivia Pound Papers; Roscoe Pound to John Callahan, 28 January 1925, *ibid.*; Roscoe Pound to Theodore Kronshage, 29 January 1925, *ibid.*

[15]Roscoe Pound to Henry M. Bates, 3 February 1925, Roscoe Pound Papers, HLSL; Roscoe Pound to Laura B. Pound, 6 February 1925, *ibid.*; Lawrence H. Larsen, *The President Wore Spats: A Biography of Glenn Frank* (Madison: State Historical Society of Wisconsin, 1965), pp. 50-51; August W. Derleth, *Still Small Voice: The Biography of Zona Gale* (New York: D. Appleton-Century, 1940), pp. 166-168; Belle and Fola LaFollette, *Robert M. LaFollette*, 2 vols. (New York: Macmillan, 1953), 2:1153-1155.

[16]Roscoe Pound to John Callahan, 27 January 1925, Olivia Pound Papers; M. G. Glaeser to Roscoe Pound, 29 January 1925, Roscoe Pound Papers, HLSL.

[17]Roscoe Pound, "The Future of the Criminal Law," *Columbia Law Review* 21 (January 1921): 7, 15.

[18]Raymond Moley, *Our Criminal Courts* (New York: Minton, Balch, 1930), p. 220; Raymond Moley, *Politics and Criminal Prosecution* (New York: Minton, Balch, 1929), pp. 16-23.

[19]Raymond Moley to Roscoe Pound, 22 December 1920, Roscoe Pound Papers, HLSL; Roscoe Pound, "Felix Frankfurter at Harvard," in Wallace Mendelson (ed.), *Felix Frankfurter; A Tribute* (New York: Reynal, 1964), p. 138; Raymond Moley, "The History of the Survey," in Roscoe Pound and Felix Frankfurter (eds.), *Criminal Justice in Cleveland* (Cleveland: Cleveland Foundation,

1922), pp. 655-662; Learned Hand to Felix Frankfurter, 27 July 1921, Hand Papers.

²⁰The survey contributors were Raymond B. Fosdick, Alfred Bettman, Reginald Heber Smith, Herbert B. Ehrmann, Burdette G. Lewis, Herman M. Adler, Albert Kales, and M. K. Wisehart; Florence Ellinwood Allen, *To Do Justly* (Cleveland: Western Reserve University Press, 1965), p. 48; Roscoe Pound to Raymond Moley, 4 June 1921, Roscoe Pound Papers, HLSL.

²¹Felix Frankfurter to Roscoe Pound, 8 July 1921, *ibid.*; C. H. Carmer, *Newton D. Baker, A Biography* (Cleveland: World Publishing Co., 1961), p. 185; *The Press*, 7 January 1921.

²²Roscoe Pound to Samuel Doerfler, 10 January 1921, Roscoe Pound Papers, HLSL; Pound, "Felix Frankfurter at Harvard," p. 138; Herbert B. Ehrmann, "Felix," in Mendelson (ed.), *Felix Frankfurter*, pp. 103-104.

²³Roscoe Pound to W. F. Coleman, 17 February 1921, Roscoe Pound Papers, HLSL; Roscoe Pound, "Criminal Justice in the American City—A Summary," in Pound and Frankfurter (eds.), *Criminal Justice in Cleveland*, pp. 580, 588.

²⁴Sheldon Glueck, *Roscoe Pound and Criminal Justice* (Dobbs Ferry, New York: Oceana, 1965), pp. 19-20, 52.

²⁵Pound, "Criminal Justice in the American City," p. 588.

²⁶Pound, *Interpretations of Legal History*, pp. 134-135.

²⁷Pound, "Criminal Justice in the American City," pp. 651, 652. For a different view, see Louis H. Masotti and Michael A. Weinstein, "Theory and Application of Roscoe Pound's Sociological Jurisprudence: Crime Prevention or Control?", *Prospectus: A Journal of Law Reform* 2 (April 1969): 431-449. They argue that Pound, torn between "pragmatic idealism" and "pragmatic realism," wanted to emphasize preventive justice, but his fear that public opinion would not sustain a larger crusade forced him to suggest narrow reforms. I locate the source of restraints in his common law conscience rather than the force of public opinion, which seemed to welcome a general housecleaning.

²⁸*The Press*, 14 September 1921; *The Cleveland News*, 14 September 1921.

²⁹"Criminal Justice in Cleveland," *New Republic* 28 (19 October

1921): 205-206; Jerome Michael and Mortimer J. Adler, *Crime, Law and Social Science* (New York: Harcourt, Brace, 1933), pp. 267-268; Walter James Shepard, "Political Science," in Harry Elmer Barnes (ed.), *The History and Prospects of the Social Sciences* (New York: Knopf, 1925), p. 441; Felix Frankfurter, "Surveys of Criminal Justice," *Proceedings of the National Conference of Social Work*, 1930, p. 63. The survey had an immediate effect on Cleveland; it led to a new and more efficient prosecutor's office, a unified court system, a probation department, and a continuous survey commission. Within five years the length of time from arrest to conviction had been cut in half. Raymond Moley, "The Cleveland Surveys—Net," *The Survey* 50 (15 May 1923): 230-231; Oscar Hallam, "Movements for Better Law Enforcement to Date," *Report of the American Bar Association* 51 (1926): 687.

[30]"Report of the Twenty-Fourth Annual Meeting of the Association of American Law Schools," *The American Law School Review* 6 (March 1927): 89; Roscoe Pound to Herbert S. Hadley, 26 December 1925, Roscoe Pound Papers, HLSL.

[31]Roscoe Pound, "What Can Law Schools Do For Criminal Justice?"*Iowa Law Review* 12 (February 1927): 112; Glueck,*Roscoe Pound and Criminal Justice*, p. 8; Francis B. Sayre, *Glad Adventure* (New York: Macmillan, 1957), p. 140; Roscoe Pound to Albert M. Chandler, 23 March 1926, Roscoe Pound Papers, HLSL; Sutherland, *The Law at Harvard*, pp. 278-281.

[32]Roscoe Pound to Jerome Frank, 25 April 1931, Roscoe Pound Papers, HLSL.

[33]Roscoe Pound to Paul Sayre, 16 November 1945, Olivia Pound Papers.

[34]Zechariah Chafee to Roscoe Pound, 15 January 1930, Roscoe Pound Papers, HLSL; Pound's remarks in *Enforcement of the Prohibition Laws: Official Records of the National Commission on Law Observance and Enforcement*, 5 vols. (Washington: Government Printing Office, 1931), 3:141; "Statement by Roscoe Pound," *National Commission on Law Observance and Enforcement: Report on the Enforcement of the Prohibition Laws* (Washington: Government Printing Office, 1931), pp. 159-160; Frankfurter, "Surveys of Criminal Justice," p. 69.

[35]Erwin N. Griswold, "Roscoe Pound, 1870-1964," *American Bar Association Journal* 50 (August 1964): 736; W. Barton Leach, "The Law At Harvard: A Quasi-Review with Personalia,"*Harvard Law School Bulletin* 19 (March 1968): 6; James B. Conant, *My Several Lives: Memoirs of a Social Inventor* (New York: Harper Row, 1970), pp. 109-110; Zechariah Chafee to Roscoe Pound, 25 June 1928, Roscoe Pound Papers, HLSL; Roscoe Pound to Julian Mack, 26 June 1928, *ibid.*

[36]Roscoe Pound to Edwin S. Lines, 29 April 1927,*ibid.*; Roscoe Pound to Walter Lippmann, 26 January 1927, *ibid.*; Roscoe Pound to Eustace Seligman, 23 May 1927, *ibid.*

[37]Roscoe Pound to James Westfall Thompson, 13 October 1921,*ibid.*; Roscoe Pound to Frank Boesel, 5 December 1924,*ibid.*

[38]Samuel Williston, *Life and Law: An Autobiography* (Boston: Little, Brown, 1941), p. 193; Leach, "The Law At Harvard," p. 6.

[39]*Boston Transcript*, 17 September 1934; Charles Beard, "Germany Up to Her Old Tricks," *New Republic* 80 (24 October 1934): 299; "Dean Pound and the Nazis," *ibid.*, 81 (12 December 1934): 130; Julian Mack to Roscoe Pound, 18 September 1934, Roscoe Pound Papers, HLSL; Felix Frankfurter, "Memorandum," 14 September 1934, Felix Frankfurter Papers, Library of Congress.

[40]Felix Frankfurter, "Diary," December 1927-March 1928, January 1930-March 1930, *ibid.*; James M. Landis, "Diary, 1928-1931," James M. Landis Papers, Library of Congress.

[41]Brainerd Currie, "The Materials of Law Study," *Journal of Legal Education* 3 (Spring 1951): 332-334; Julius Goebel et al., *A History of the School of Law, Columbia University* (New York: Columbia University Press, 1955), pp. 311-313; *The Institute for the Study of Law. The Johns Hopkins University. An Immediate Program* (Baltimore: n.p., 1929), pp. 37, 40; Charles E. Clark, "The Educational and Scientific Objectives of the Yale School of Law," *The Annals* 167 (May 1933): 168, 169; Justin Miller, "New Developments in Law Schools," *ibid.*, 145 (September 1929): 115, 117, 119.

[42]Roscoe Pound, "The Law School," *Reports of the President and the Treasurer of Harvard College, 1927-1928*, p. 202; Roscoe Pound, "Preventive Justice and Social Work," *Proceedings of the National Conference of Social Work*, 1923, p. 161.

[43]Roscoe Pound to Henry M. Bates, 30 March 1925, Roscoe Pound Papers, HLSL; Roscoe Pound, "Present Tendencies in Legal Education," *Nebraska Law Bulletin* 15 (November 1936): 210.

[44]Roscoe Pound to Henry M. Bates, 16 April 1928, Roscoe Pound Papers, HLSL; Pound to Bates, 2 July 1928, *ibid.*

[45]Roscoe Pound, "The Future of the Common Law," *University of Cincinnati Law Review* 7 (November 1933): 360.

[46]Pound, "Present Tendencies in Legal Education," p. 216; Sidney Post Simpson, "The New Curriculum of the Harvard Law School," *Harvard Law Review* 51 (April 1938): 965-987; Sutherland, *The Law at Harvard*, pp. 282-286.

[47]Roscoe Pound to Robert P. Patterson, 9 October 1935, Robert P. Patterson Papers, Library of Congress; Roscoe Pound, "The Work of the American Law School," *West Virginia Law Quarterly* 30 (November 1923): 6.

Chapter 11. A Restless Retirement

[1]Benjamin Cardozo, "Jurisprudence," *Selected Writings of Benjamin Nathan Cardozo*, ed. Margaret E. Hall (New York: Fallon, 1947), p. 10; Edward A. Purcell, Jr., "American Jurisprudence between the Wars: Legal Realism and the Crisis of Democratic Theory," *American Historical Review* 75 (December 1969): 424-446, is the best recent sketch of the realists.

[2]Underhill Moore, "Rational Basis of Legal Institutions," *Columbia Law Review* 23 (November 1923): 612; Jerome Frank, *Law and the Modern Mind* (New York: Brentano's, 1930), p. 260; Karl Llewellyn, "A Realistic Jurisprudence—The Next Step," *Columbia Law Review* 30 (April 1930): 450, 453.

[3]Karl Llewellyn, "Some Realism About Realism—Responding to Dean Pound," *Harvard Law Review*, 44 (June 1931): 1237; Felix Cohen, "Transcendental Nonsense and the Functional Approach," *Columbia Law Review* 35 (June 1935), p. 812.

[4]Herman Oliphant, "A Return to Stare Decisis," *American Bar Association Journal* 14 (February 1928): 73; Karl Llewellyn, *The*

Bramble Bush (New York: Oceana, 1960), pp. 66-68; Leon Green, *Judge and Jury* (Kansas City: Vernon Law Book Co., 1930), pp. 162-163, 174.

[5]Frank, *Law and the Modern Mind*, p. 7; Felix Cohen, book review of Frank, *Law and the Modern Mind*, *American Bar Association Journal* 17 (February 1931): 112.

[6]Llewellyn, "Some Realism About Realism," p. 1236; Joseph C. Hutcheson, "The Judgment Intuitive: The Function of the Hunch in Judicial Decision," *Cornell Law Quarterly* 14 (April 1929): 285.

[7]Walter Wheeler Cook, "Scientific Method and the Law," *American Bar Association Journal* 13 (June 1927): 303; Llewellyn, "Some Realism About Realism," p. 1236.

[8]Oliver Wendell Holmes, Jr., "The Path of the Law," *Harvard Law Review* 10 (March 1897): 460-461; Underhill Moore and Gilbert Sussman, "Legal and Institutional Methods Applied to the Debiting of Direct Discounts—II. Institutional Method," *Yale Law Journal* 40 (February 1931): 561. Wilfrid E. Rumble, Jr., analyzes the connection between legal realism and the behavioral studies of contemporary political scientists in his *American Legal Realism; Skepticism, Reform, and the Judicial Process* (Ithaca: Cornell University Press, 1968).

[9]Jerome Frank *Courts on Trial* (Princeton: Princeton University Press, 1949), p. 250.

[10]Roscoe Pound, "Fifty Years of Jurisprudence," *Harvard Law Review* 51 (March 1938): 791; Felix Cohen, "The Problems of a Functional Jurisprudence," *Modern Law Review* 1 (June 1937): 8-9; Llewellyn, "A Realistic Jurisprudence—The Next Step," p. 435; Herman Oliphant, "Parallels in the Development of Legal and Medical Education," *The Annals* 167 (May 1933): 162.

[11]Rumble, *American Legal Realism*, pp. 76-77, lists several realists who served the New Deal.

[12]Roscoe Pound, book review of Walter Wheeler Cook, *Cases and Other Authorities on Equity* (1923), *Harvard Law Review* 37 (January 1924): 397; Roscoe Pound, *Contemporary Juristic Theory* (Claremont: Ward Ritchie, 1940), p. 36.

[13]Pound's remarks in *Report of the American Bar Association* 55 (1930): 178; Roscoe Pound, "Hierarchy of Sources and Forms in Different Systems of Law," *Tulane Law Review* 7 (June 1933): 481; Roscoe Pound, "Enforcement of Law," *Proceedings of the Illinois State Bar Association*, 1908, p. 94; Roscoe Pound, "The Call for a Realist Jurisprudence," *Harvard Law Review* 44 (March 1931): 706. Pound's argument for zones of certainty drew heavily on the work on Albion Small. Compare Pound's demand for certainty in commercial law with the language of Small's argument that civilized society required "*assured constancy of the conditions involved in association* [original italics]." Small, *General Sociology* (Chicago: University of Chicago Press, 1905), p. 608.

[14]Roscoe Pound to Karl Llewellyn, 21 March 1931, Roscoe Pound Papers, HLSL; Pound, "The Call for a Realist Jurisprudence."

[15]Morris Cohen to Roscoe Pound, 9 July 1938, in Leonora C. Rosenfield, *Portrait of a Philosopher: Morris R. Cohen in Life & Letters* (New York: Harcourt, Brace & World, 1962), p. 307; Cohen to Pound, 25 September 1938, *ibid.*, p. 310; Roscoe Pound, "American Jurisitic Thinking in the Twentieth Century," *A Century of Social Thought* (Durham: Duke University Press, 1939), pp. 157, 162; Roscoe Pound, "Modern Administrative Law," *Reports of the Virginia State Bar Association* 51 (1939): 385; Roscoe Pound, "The American Idea of Government," *American Bar Association Journal* 30 (September 1944): 497-503.

[16]Karl Llewellyn, "Through Title to Contract and A Bit Beyond," *New York University Law Quarterly Review* 15 (January 1938): 162; Jerome Frank, *Save America First* (New York: Harper, 1938).

[17]Thurman Arnold, "Judicial Councils," *West Virginia Law Quarterly* 35 (April 1929): 193-238; Roscoe Pound, "The Function and Prospects of Judicial Councils," *Journal of the American Judicature Society* 23 (August 1939): 56; Pound's remarks in *Proceedings of the American Law Institute* 2 (1924): 384.

[18]Roscoe Pound to Henry M. Bates, 31 January 1939, Roscoe Pound Papers, HLSL; Jerome Frank, "Why Not A Clinical

Lawyer-School?" *University of Pennsylvania Law Review* 81 (June 1933): 911; Roscoe Pound, "Present Tendencies in Legal Education," *Nebraska Law Bulletin* 15 (November 1936): 208-209.

[19]Cohen, "Transcendental Nonsense and the Functional Approach," p. 834.

[20]Roscoe Pound, "The Future of the Common Law," *University of Cincinnati Law Review* 7 (November 1933): 357-358; Roscoe Pound, "The Judicial Office Today," *American Bar Association Journal* 25 (September 1939): 736.

[21]Dean Acheson, *Morning and Noon* (Boston: Houghton Mifflin, 1965), pp. 107-108.

[22]"Report of the Special Committee on Administrative Law," *Report of the American Bar Association* 63 (1938): 339, 346-351, 337-338.

[23]"Testimony of Roscoe Pound," United States Congress, Senate, Committee on the Judiciary, *United States Court of Appeals for Administration*, Hearings on S. 3676, part 4, 12 and 14 May 1938 (Washington: Government Printing Office, 1938), pp. 178, 181-182.

[24]Louis L. Jaffe, "Invective and Investigation in Administrative Law," *Harvard Law Review* 52 (June 1939): 1232, 1236; James M. Landis, "Crucial Issues in Administrative Law—The Walter-Logan Bill," *ibid.*, 53 (May 1940): 1091; Jerome Frank, *If Men Were Angels* (New York: Harper, 1942), pp. 33-36, 41, 51; Harlan F. Stone, "The Common Law in the United States," *Harvard Law Review* 50 (November 1936): 17.

[25]Roscoe Pound to O. R. McGuire, 10 November 1939, Roscoe Pound Papers, HLSL; "Report of the Special Committee on Administrative Law," p. 336; Jerome Frank, "Experimental Jurisprudence and the New Deal," *Congressional Record*, 73d Congress, 2d Session, 18 June 1934, 78:12413; Roscoe Pound, "Administrative Law and the Courts," *Boston University Law Review* 24 (November 1944): 208; James M. Landis, *The Administrative Process* (New Haven: Yale University Press, 1938), p. 39; Kenneth Culp Davis, "Dean Pound and Administrative Law," *Columbia Law Review* 42 (January 1942): 101.

[26]Roscoe Pound to Walter F. Dodd, 18 April 1938, Roscoe

Pound Papers, HLSL; Pound, *Contemporary Juristic Theory*, pp. 21-22; Roscoe Pound, "The Recrudescence of Absolutism," *Sewanee Review* 47 (January-March 1939): 28.

[27]Roscoe Pound, "The Future of Law," *Yale Law Journal* 47 (November 1937): 11; Roscoe Pound, "Some Implications of Recent Legislation," *West Virginia Law Quarterly* 45 (April 1939): 212.

[28]Roscoe Pound, "Visitatorial Jurisdiction over Corporations in Equity," *Harvard Law Review* 49 (January 1936): 392; Roscoe Pound, *The Task of Law* (Lancaster: Franklin and Marshall College, 1944), p. 52; Roscoe Pound to Henry M. Bates, 22 December 1942, Roscoe Pound Papers, HLSL.

[29]The *Report of the Attorney-General's Committee on Administrative Procedure* (Washington: Government Printing Office, 1941) demonstrated that the New Deal agencies were more just and efficient than their earlier counterparts.

[30]Roscoe Pound to Melvin M. Johnson, 16 March 1921, Roscoe Pound Papers, HLSL; Roscoe Pound, "The Law of Property and Recent Juristic Thought," *American Bar Association Journal* 25 (December 1939): 997.

[31]Roscoe Pound, "The Future of the Criminal Law," *Columbia Law Review* 21 (January 1921): 11; Roscoe Pound, "Individualization of Justice," *Fordham Law Review* 7 (May 1938): 158.

[32]Roscoe Pound, "Public Law and Private Law," *Cornell Law Quarterly* 24 (June 1939): 480; Pound, *Contemporary Juristic Theory*, p. 5.

[33]Roscoe Pound, "Why Absolute Government Fails," *Nation's Business* 27 (July 1939): 11, 60; Pound, "Some Implications of Recent Legislation," pp. 219, 217; Roscoe Pound, "The Constitution: Its Development, Adaptability, and Future," *American Bar Association Journal* 23 (October 1937): 744; "Message from the President," 76th Congress, 3d Session, *House Documents*, 18 December 1940 (Washington: Government Printing Office, 1940), p. 23; Roscoe Pound, "The Place of the Judiciary in a Democratic Polity," *American Bar Association Journal* 27 (March 1941): 133, 139.

[34]Roscoe Pound, *Social Control Through Law* (New Haven: Yale

University Press, 1942), pp. 28-29; Roscoe Pound, *The Formative Era of American Law* (Boston: Little, Brown, 1938), pp. 69-70, originally delivered as lectures in 1936; Roscoe Pound, "The Political and Social Factor in Legal Interpretation: An Introduction," *Michigan Law Review* 45 (March 1947): 603.

[35]Pound, *The Task of Law*, pp. 73, 89; Roscoe Pound, "The Humanities in an Absolutist World," *American Association of University Professors Bulletin* 30 (Summer 1944): 214.

[36]Roscoe Pound, book review of Sheldon Glueck (ed.), *The Problem of Delinquency* (1959), *Harvard Law Review* 73 (May 1960): 1428; Roscoe Pound to R. C. Cornuelle, 6 February 1956, Roscoe Pound Papers, HLSL.

[37]Roscoe Pound to Henry M. Bates, 28 August 1941, *ibid.*; Roscoe Pound, "Law and Federal Government," *Federalism as a Democratic Process* (New Brunswick: Rutgers University Press, 1942), p. 30; Roscoe Pound, "The Judicial Process Today," *Michigan State Bar Journal* 26 (May 1947): 13.

[38]Roscoe Pound to John Rothschild, 26 February 1921, Roscoe Pound Papers, HLSL; Roscoe Pound, "The Scope and Purpose of Sociological Jurisprudence," *Harvard Law Review* 25 (December 1911): 160; Roscoe Pound, "The Revival of Natural Law," *Notre Dame Lawyer* 17 (June 1942): 313.

[39]Edmund Cahn, "Jurisprudence," *Annual Survey of American Law, 1944* (New York: New York University School of Law, 1946), p. 1160; interview with James H. Chadbourn, 16 July 1968; Pound interview conducted by Arthur Sutherland, 25 July 1962.

[40]*Portland Press Herald*, 19 July 1947; Roscoe Pound, "Reconstruction in China" [c. 1948], unpublished manuscript in Roscoe Pound Papers, HLSL; Roscoe Pound, "Other News of China," *American Affairs* 10 (July 1948): 176-178; Roscoe Pound to H. H. K'ung, 14 March 1949, Roscoe Pound Papers, HLSL; Roscoe Pound to Pierre F. Goodrich, 12 April 1949, *ibid.*; Roscoe Pound to P. H. Chang, 6 June 1947, *ibid.*; "Roscoe Pound's Analysis of Chinese-American Affairs—Hits United States Aims for Compromise, Misconception of Red Role," *Congressional Record*, 81st

Congress, 1st Session 15 (2 April 1949): 3765-3767.

[41]Roscoe Pound, "Law and Courts in China: Progress in the Administration of Justice," *American Bar Association Journal* 34 (April 1948): 275-276; Walter P. Armstrong, "Thomas Babington, Lord Macaulay: Historian of England and Law Reformer in India," *American Bar Association Journal* 34 (November 1948): 994-995; Roscoe Pound, "Development of a Chinese Constitutional Law," *New York University Law Quarterly Review* 23 (July 1948): 392; Roscoe Pound, Introduction to Chen Li-Fu, *Philosophy of Life* (New York: Philosophical Library, 1948).

[42]Roscoe Pound to Louise Pound, 14 November 1946, Roscoe Pound Papers, NSHS; interview with James H. Chadbourn, 16 July 1968; Roscoe Pound to Louis Wyman, 11 September 1957, Roscoe Pound Papers, HLSL; Roscoe Pound to A. G. McDowell, 12 May 1958, *ibid.*; *Washington Daily News*, 19 January 1959.

[43]Roscoe Pound, "Law in the Service State," *American Bar Association Journal* 36 (December 1950): 977; Roscoe Pound to Olivia Pound, 7 April 1952, Roscoe Pound Papers, NSHS; Pound, "Law in the Service State," pp. 978-979; Roscoe Pound, "Philosophy of Law and Comparative Law," *University of Pennsylvania Law Review* 100 (October 1951): 4-10; Roscoe Pound, "Administrative Absolutism and Civil Liberties in England: The *Liversidge, Greene,* and *Duncan* Cases," *Harvard Law Review* 56 (March 1943): 814.

[44]Roscoe Pound, "The Idea of a Universal Law," *UCLA Law Review* 1 (December 1953): 10-11; Roscoe Pound, "Annual Survey of Law: Decisions of Courts Show Some Dangerous Trends," *American Bar Association Journal* 33 (November 1947): 1094-1095; Pound, "The Judicial Process Today," pp. 7-8; Roscoe Pound to Price Daniel, 5 September 1951, Roscoe Pound Papers, HLSL; Sam Yorty to Roscoe Pound, 7 May 1953, *ibid.*; Pound, "Philosophy of Law and Comparative Law," p. 15.

[45]Roscoe Pound, *Jurisprudence* (St. Paul: West, 1959).

[46]Roscoe Pound, "The Case for Law," *Valparaiso University Law Review* 1 (Spring 1967): 201.

Coda

¹Samuel Williston, book review of J. H. Landman, *The Case Method of Studying Law* (1930), *Harvard Law Review* 43 (April 1930): 972; Karl Llewellyn, "A Realistic Jurisprudence—The Next Step," *Columbia Law Review* 30 (April 1930): 435.

²For a rare exception to this theme, see Judith Shklar's perceptive caveat in her *Legalism* (Cambridge: Harvard University Press, 1964), p. 236.

³Harold Laski to Oliver Wendell Holmes, 26 January 1920, in Mark DeWolfe Howe (ed.), *Holmes-Laski Letters; The Correspondence of Mr. Justice Holmes and Harold J. Laski, 1916-1935*, 2 vols. (Cambridge: Harvard University Press, 1953), 1:236; Felix Frankfurter to Learned Hand, 10 May 1916, Hand Papers; Holmes to Laski, 16 August 1924, *Holmes-Laski Letters*, 1:645; Laski to Holmes, 17 April 1932. *Holmes-Laski Letters*, 2:1377.

⁴Roscoe Pound, "Juristic Problems of National Progress," *American Journal of Sociology* 22 (May 1917): 721.

A Note on Sources

There are two principal collections of Pound manuscripts: the Roscoe Pound Papers at the Harvard Law School Library, and the Roscoe Pound Papers at the Nebraska State Historical Society. The Harvard collection, vast and disappointing, consists largely of Pound's drafts of lectures, articles, speeches, and books. Most of the correspondence prior to 1920 is limited to incoming letters alone. Pound's replies, carefully preserved in letter books, were destroyed in a flood during the late 1920s, along with diaries, newspaper clippings, and other valuable materials. The collection has a separate file of correspondence with Oliver Wendell Holmes, copied from the Holmes Papers.

The Roscoe Pound collection at the Nebraska State Historical Society is smaller but richer. It is supplemented by the Laura Biddlecome Pound Papers and the Olivia Pound Papers. There is an interesting file in the Olivia Pound collection that includes letters from Roscoe, while he was a student at Harvard; he and Olivia maintained a long but sporadic correspondence in later years. In the mid-1940s, at the request of Paul Sayre, she prepared four valuable essays—"Stephen Bosworth Pound," "Roscoe Pound," "Home Life of the Pound Family," all in the Roscoe Pound Papers, and "Laura Biddlecome Pound," included in the Laura Biddlecome Pound Papers. There is a copy of the Sayre biography with corrections in Olivia's hand at the Nebraska State Historical Society. Other collections there include the Louise Pound Papers, of little value for this study; the Samuel M. Chapman Papers; and the A. H. Kidd Papers. Chapman and Kidd,

345

both lawyers, had professional connections with Pound, and his letters to them reveal the nature of his practice.

The John Henry Wigmore Papers at the Northwestern University School of Law Library and the Edward A. Ross Papers at the Wisconsin State Historical Society contain many valuable letters. They are especially strong for the years between 1906 and 1915. The Richard T. Ely Papers, also at Wisconsin, contain fewer Pound items of value. The Grace and Edith Abbott Papers at the University of Chicago Archives are strong on Pound's role in the Child Labor Case. The James H. Tufts Papers, also at Chicago, contain insights about Pound from sensitive outsiders. I found the Zechariah Chafee Papers, the Thomas Reed Powell Papers, and the Learned Hand Papers, all at the Harvard Law School Library, useful for understanding Pound's career at Harvard. The Felix Frankfurter Papers, which Harvard and the Library of Congress share, and the James M. Landis Papers, Library of Congress, contain useful information about developments at Harvard. There is a poignant letter in the Robert P. Patterson Papers, Library of Congress, in which Pound decries events at Harvard during his last years. *The Survey* Papers at the Social Welfare History Archives, University of Minnesota, demonstrate Pound's relationship to advanced social-justice Progressives. The Pound letters in the Louis D. Brandeis Papers at the University of Louisville School of Law merely duplicate items in the Pound Papers at Harvard. The E. J. Palmer Papers, State Historical Society of Missouri, contain Henry A. Gleason's judgment on Pound's role in the development of ecology.

Index

347